SEX,
DRUGS,
RATT
& ROLL

SEX, DRUGS, RATT & ROLL

MY LIFE IN ROCK

STEPHEN PEARCY
WITH SAM BENJAMIN

G

GALLERY BOOKS

NEW YORK LONDON TORONTO SYDNEY NEW DELHI

G

Gallery Books
A Division of Simon & Schuster, Inc.
1230 Avenue of the Americas
New York, NY 10020

First Gallery Books trade paperback edition April 2014

GALLERY BOOKS and colophon are registered trademarks of Simon & Schuster, Inc.

For information about special discounts for bulk purchases, please contact Simon & Schuster Special Sales at 1-866-506-1949 or business@simonandschuster.com.

The Simon & Schuster Speakers Bureau can bring authors to your live event. For more information or to book an event contact the Simon & Schuster Speakers Bureau at 1-866-248-3049 or visit our website at www.simonspeakers.com.

Designed by Jaime Putorti

Manufactured in the United States of America

10 9 8 7 6 5 4 3 2 1

Library of Congress Cataloging-in-Publication Data

Pearcy, Stephen, 1959–
Sex, drugs, Ratt & roll : my life in rock / Stephen Pearcy with Sam Benjamin.
pages cm
1. Pearcy, Stephen, 1959– 2. Rock musicians—United States—Biography. 3. Ratt (Musical group) I. Benjamin, Sam. II. Title.
ML420.P369A3 2013
782.42166092--dc23
[B]
2012045962

ISBN 978-1-4516-9456-7
ISBN 978-1-4516-9458-1 (pbk)
ISBN 978-1-4516-9457-4 (ebook)

I dedicate this book to my loving mother, Joanne (RIP):
you're now dancin' with the angels, walkin' on the clouds.
Robbin "King" Crosby (RIP), brother: gone but never forgotten.
And to all my dear friends lost since the party began,
you're forever in my heart.
And to all the hard-core Ratt 'n' Rollers out there
for making my trip so far a dream come true.

SEX, DRUGS, RATT & ROLL

INTRO

NO HUMAN SHOULD HAVE to remember fumbling drunkenly over his newborn baby daughter in Beverly Hills Hospital in Los Angeles, California, trying and failing to cut her umbilical cord with surgical scissors, *pushing* the scissors back and forth, booze and pills playing hell in his stomach. Wanting to do this worse than anything he's ever wanted to do before, yet unable to get a good enough grip on the steel handles to do the job.

"Go ahead, Mr. Pearcy," the doctor urged.

I tried again, gaping in total wonder. My daughter squalled, her face bright red, her body covered in goo. I stifled a mouthful of acid reflux.

"These are surgical, right?" I mumbled. I sawed the blades back and forth, the umbilical cord twisting slippery and red, bulbous and veiny. The enormity of the event was causing my nerves to go haywire.

I made my thumb and forefinger like rods. *I am the greatest cord cutter in the world,* I promised myself. *I can do this.*

I sliced through my daughter's umbilical cord. She cried especially loud for a moment, and it was the most beautiful sound I have ever heard in my entire life. Beautiful enough to make you cry, want to get clean, become pure again, surf. She was the most beautiful jewel, angel I have ever seen. Changed my life forever after that.

My brain should have been a smoking ruin, hole eighteen at the 1945 Hiroshima Golf Classic. I was on hydrocodone and weed and heroin and Budweiser and strange trim for most of the major events of the last five decades. But somehow, glimmering moments of my rock-and-roll journey splash out at me like fireworks in my cerebral cortex, at times when I least expect it.

I may be taking my dog, Puppy, to the veterinarian. We sit together in a leather-chair-filled office in Van Nuys, both of us quiet and docile. I'm leaning over the counter to take a look at the papers, and then suddenly it's 1983, and I'm driving a Datsun B-210 north on Hollywood Boulevard, listening to KLOS, swerving from lane to lane, licking barbecue sauce off my fingers. Then, with no warning at all, Ratt's first single comes on the air. I'm so fucking stunned and elated, I almost drive into oncoming traffic.

Then the memory is gone. It's just me and Puppy again. I'm staring into his black eyes, and he's staring right back. One of us has a skin condition; the other smokes too much.

For such a long time, I tried not to remember any of this. Threw a blanket over everything, courtesy of booze, dope, pills, rage. But the past didn't go anywhere. It sat there, stubborn and pissed off, waiting for me to come home.

YOU'RE TALKIN' TO ME

IN 2009, I PACKED myself off to rehab in Pasadena, California, in an attempt to wean myself from that nagging booze/pills/grass/heroin habit I'd picked up over the last several decades. There was an initial period of hell, better known as withdrawal, followed by a long stretch of a much more annoying kind of torture: therapy.

It's the price of getting clean, I guess. They help you ditch the drugs, make it so your bandmates no longer have to stick mirrors underneath your nostrils to see if you're still alive when you go into one of your increasingly frequent nods in the recording studio—and then you have to sort of humor them when they say, *What* else *about you can we clean up?*

I was assigned a decent, flabby therapist named Dr. Harold Roberts, who had the nerve to imply that I might have a few *other* addictions to my name, too.

"What I'd like to ask you, Stephen, is, have you ever considered yourself a *sex* addict?"

I laughed. "How would I even know?"

"A sex addict might, for instance, spend the majority of his waking hours trying to procure sex."

"I'm a rock singer," I said. "If you have to try to get laid, then there's definitely something wrong."

"Did you ever have a period of your life when you went from partner to partner, without due regard for their personalities?"

"Yes. The 1980s."

"Okay." Dr. Roberts laughed. "All right. Humor can be a defense mechanism. How many partners might you have had?" He said it casually, but I could see his interest was growing.

"You know that guy John Paul?" I said. "Lives in Italy?"

"The Pope?" Dr. Roberts asked.

"More than him."

"Again with the humor," said Dr. Roberts.

"My stamina in the mid-'80s was unparalleled," I began. "I was tearing down three chicks a day when we were on the road, under ideal conditions."

"Three? But I don't even see how that's possible."

"It's possible when you're organized. It's possible when you have a *team*."

They were well-trained and faithful soldiers—Phil, Joe, and Road Dog—each one ready to scout the hottest trim around and slap passes in those girls' hands. They'd continue throughout our show, scanning the audience, knowing my type perfectly. After the encore, there would be twenty-five giggling blondes lined up, all incredible tits, flat stomachs, and golden asses. I just had to pick.

"But of course you're exaggerating," Dr. Roberts said.

"Now," I continued, "if you want to throw down on tour, you have to learn how to do it right. You space out the trim—one before the show in your dressing room, one midshow, during the drum solo, and then obviously, one at the hotel that night."

A momentary silence filled the room.

"Or on the bus."

The doctor was writing something down in his notebook.

"But you must stay organized. For instance, always make sure to take a Polaroid of each of your girls. Write her phone number on the back with a Sharpie. Then hand that off to your security guy to stick in his Rolodex, so that you have it for next time you come through Jacksonville or Corpus Christi."

"Mr. Pearcy, this is compulsive behavior, don't you agree?"

"No, it's *smart* behavior. I grew up with this, man. I was at Van Halen shows for a long time before my band broke, and I knew the best bands had their systems down. I always told my guys when we got big, we'd do it right."

The doctor and I stared at each other for a while. It was nice and quiet in that office. You pay through the nose if you go to rehab, at least if you go to some of the posher places. The one I went to, embarrassingly, is the place where Dr. Drew filmed his celebrity rehab show. I liked the cleanliness and general high production value of the whole place, though.

"Back in the day, I used my itineraries to keep track of every single chick I ever met or put myself into. I kept them my whole adult life. Had stacks and stacks and stacks of them. They got burned by my super-pissed girlfriends. I'd just write the girl's name, her phone number, the city I met her in, and a rating. You know, seven, eight, maybe a nine. Once in a while, a true ten. And if we had sex, I'd mark it with three x's. And if we did something else, I'd write that. Then I'd try to add some sort of signature description, like 'see again.' Or 'fly out.' Or 'kinda funky.'"

"Do you have anything else that you want to tell me, Stephen?" Dr. Roberts said. "Anything that you'd like to get off your chest?"

Where do I start?

THE YOUNG AND THE DAMNED

I WAS BORN SCREAMING in Long Beach, California, on July 3, 1956, a slick, black-haired ball of muscle, part German, part Irish, part who knows what. Pure mutt.

I'm a twin: I came out first.

My most distinct memories of childhood are of unrelenting California sunshine and the moist smell of crabgrass in our small, ragged backyard. Our family never had much money, and I never had real pets. My older brother and I became ghetto zookeepers, collecting beady-eyed possums, raccoons, and squirrels. I would put on electrical gloves and try to hug the animals to my chest.

"He's going to bite you," my brother warned me. "He probably has rabies."

My brother and I pooled our allowances and purchased rats from the pet store, storing them in cheap wire cages. One night, a renegade rat with steely whiskers escaped his cage and went to town on our pet turtle. In seconds, he had begun to suck the turtle's body out from underneath the shell.

"Will, watch this!" I cried, fascinated.

"It ain't nothing."

"But he's . . . he's *killing* him."

Our turtle died a terrifying, slow death that night, right before our eyes. The rat looked wholly unrepentant, teeth dripping with blood, eyes bright and alien.

"We better off him, too," said my brother. "Go get me my knife."

"But why?" I cried.

"Dammit, Stephen, don't start crybabying over a goddamn *rat*. That thing's a menace. You saw it yourself. He's a common murderer. We're going to have to put him down."

My brother clutched the rat's stomach in his left hand and as it struggled, he used his free hand to slash its throat with a knife. Rat blood flowed onto his hands and the toes of his sneakers. Together we buried the disemboweled body in the backyard.

"That was fucking very uncool of you," I choked.

"You sound weird when you say *fuck*," my brother mused.

■ ■ ■

MUSIC WOULDN'T PIERCE ME WITH ITS terrible talons for a very long time. Which is not to say I didn't *feel* it when I heard it; more like, I was utterly clueless when it came to its finer points. Some would argue I stayed that way throughout my career.

When I was about fourteen, my older sister had a "cool" boyfriend, with a mop of thick black hair and big forearm muscles. He dressed like a greaser, an outdated look by the early '70s, but his rebel vibe came through, and that was what mattered. He smoked filterless Camels, the official cigarette of the who-gives-a-fuck set.

"Listen to this, man." He handed me a pair of large '70s headphones that led from my sister's eight-track player. "This is *real* music."

I fitted the phones over my ears and bopped my head appreciatively. "She's *awesome*," I remarked politely.

"*Who's* awesome?" he sneered.

"Janis," I said. "Janis Joplin? Right?"

"Oh, *man*," my sister said, embarrassed. "My little brother thinks *Led Zeppelin* is Janis *Joplin*?"

I stammered, "I was just kidding."

Pretty funny that I had absolutely no clue who Led Zeppelin was, considering how infatuated I'd become with the band in later teenage years, pestering record store clerks all across Southern California for the latest bootlegs until finally one shouted at me, "I'll LET YOU *KNOW*, Pearcy! Okay?"

A similar event transpired at the home of my friend Victor Mamanna. On his bedroom wall, Victor had a large poster of an ugly, scary-looking chick. She was pale-faced, crow-eyed, with long black hair dripping from her skull. I studied the poster carefully, repulsed by the imagery.

"That is one *freaky*-looking chick," I said.

Victor cracked up laughing. "Stephen. That's Alice Cooper!"

"She's a dog," I said.

Victor roared. "Cooper's a *guy*! And a *genius*."

I shrugged. How was I supposed to know?

Music was a groove, sure, but my first love, even as early as the age of ten, was the girls. They just did it for me—all of them. At my Catholic school, St. Gerard's, I didn't mess with kickball, or marbles, or any of that basic Boy Scout crap; no, I spent all my recesses trying to charm the babes in my class into the boys' restroom.

"I'm not going to go in *there*," giggled most girls who I tried to get into the bathroom.

"Come on," I coaxed. "It'll be fun. We'll be all alone."

Somehow, I managed to tempt many of them inside. We tried to French kiss, I tried to cop a feel. Childish graffiti decorated the walls around us.

While the plaid skirts were world-class, Catholic school wasn't perfect. I was a fairly appalling student. I had a talent for art, and I wasn't bad at English, but after that, my aptitude and attention span dropped off a ten-foot riser. Classroom time was better spent spitballing my friend Andy Holgwen's hair without him feeling the weight of it, or fucking with the school savant, a huge Japanese kid, Louis Watanabe. That kind of immature shit often earned me personal time with our head nun, a frightening woman known as Sister Barbara.

"Put out your hand, Stephen."

"Oh, no, I ain't." I smirked. "I know what that's all about."

"Put our your *hand*," Sister Barbara hissed.

"So you can smack it with your ruler?" I laughed, smashing each hand firmly underneath the opposite bicep. "Not a chance."

Sister Barbara stared me down, her face hard and bleak.

"Do as I say, Stephen, or I won't be responsible for the consequences."

"Sister," I warned her, "if you smack me with that ruler, I'm gonna smack you right back."

Wrong thing to say. The nun colored instantly, a hot crimson flush spreading from neck to forehead, her face becoming all twisted lips and knitted eyebrows.

"We'll see what your mother has to say about that," she said, her voice dangerously quiet.

I kept my arms crossed defiantly.

My mother arrived half an hour later. The nun explained our situation succinctly. "Your *son* informed *me* that I am in *danger* of being *struck* by him."

With no hesitation, my mom reached out and smacked me hard across the back of my head. *Whip-crack!* "Like this?"

Man, you just didn't want to cross my mom. She was nothing like my older sister, who threw brooms and irons at us when mom was at work. Most of it was just frustration, and love was behind it all. My mother had a tough row to hoe. My dad was rarely around, and when he did show up, he was either drunk, dragging on dope, or ominously silent. Only when I would fill those shoes later would I understand the nature of his addictions.

My father, Bill Pearcy, seemed to believe I was weak, and as a veteran of the Korean War, he wasn't particularly happy about that. He did his best to toughen me up, though if you watched it from afar, you might liken it to the way other men tenderize meat. He bounced my head off plenty of walls. For some reason, instead of developing the stiff upper lip he wanted for me, I continued to just cry like a baby.

"I'm sending you boys to karate lessons," he decided one day.

We studied karate in a dingy strip mall, and I surprised myself by learning the punches and kicks. Soon I could fight. My reflexes were sharp, but still he wasn't satisfied. When I spilled my milk at the table, I got a smack on the jaw. When I yelled at my sister, I took one on the chin.

"Things will get better," my mother promised me. "Things will *change.*"

But they never did. I got pummeled, again and again. I seemed to be the only kid in the family he liked to smack; that kinda confused me. *Wouldn't it be kind of fun to smack your* other *kids around a little bit?* I thought. *Do you find me to have, like, an especially punchable face?*

One time he beat the shit out of me with surprising enthusiasm, jabbing my face with the force and intensity of a boxer. The next morning, my brother shook me awake.

"Hey, Stephen?"

"What?" I croaked. My eyes were swollen; my throat felt stiff and awful.

My brother softened. "Want to go catch a pet?"

That afternoon, my brother and I found a wild rabbit in the fields near the house. I was in love at first sight. It was the softest, warmest creature I had ever held against my skin. I cradled it in my arms, feeling the heartbeat of something gentle and good.

With no warning at all, the little monster tore its tiny white teeth into my forearm and wouldn't let go. I had to punch his crazy fucking body off my arm, bashing it against our picnic table, again and again, until finally, stunned, it relaxed its death grip and hopped away.

DRIVE ME CRAZY

RATT WAS BORN FROM the ruins of Mickey Ratt, in Southern California, in 1982. The dysfunctional band and our sleazy brand of musical passion were a direct product of my ragged upbringing, but we're also *such* a 1980s creation. Ratt could only have been born in that weird decade. We are a consequence of the bizarre tastes of the time.

Weirdness abounded in the 1980s, spreading like a virus. It was the golden era of MTV and the dawn of image rock, where Aqua Net hair spray stood in as a secret fifth member of rock bands and vast piles of potent cocaine decorated the oak desktops of many an aging, open-shirted Hollywood record executive. Sam Kinison, a shrieking, maniacal ex-preacher from Tulsa, Oklahoma, slowly became a fixture on the metal scene in the latter half of the decade, as recognizable and respected as any member of Mötley Crüe, Cinderella, or Twisted Sister. He loved the screams of guitars and the caresses of rock sluts, and I was proud to be part of his entourage.

In 1987, Kinison recorded a version of the Troggs hit "Wild Thing" and began to climb the charts himself. For his music video, he hired Praise the Lord scandal alumna Jessica Hahn and her crudely sculpted, giant-size boob job, and put her into a wrestling ring. Kinison and Hahn fought it out, then smooched weirdly. Steven Adler, Steven Tyler, Joe Perry, Tommy Lee, Richie Sambora, Sebastian Bach, Billy Idol, and I were all there, making cameos, standing by awkwardly. At a certain point, Tommy and the Guns N' Roses guys began throwing beers and spitting on Jessica, who looked surprised, then aroused, then demented. Sam kept screaming louder and louder.

None of it made sense unless you were coked to the gills, which, of course, everyone was, except me—as everyone knows, I only had a vial of krell around for the girls who needed a wake-up call. There were giant bowls of blow everywhere you looked in those days. My jaw tightens just thinking about it.

The '80s was my decade, but I refuse to take responsibility for all that went on. Scott Baio produced an album of soft-rock songs, Jason Bateman guest-starred on *Win, Lose or Draw*. Gary Busey burst out of bathrooms at parties in Beverly Hills, eyes bulging and his jaw tighter than a running back's. Michael J. Fox boinked Sarah Jessica Parker, Sarah Jessica Parker dated Nicolas Cage, Nicolas Cage got down with Uma Thurman, Uma Thurman ran into the arms of Don Johnson, Don Johnson dived into Barbra Streisand. Nikki Sixx dated Vanity, Prince's creation. She was a light-skinned diva with hair like a glam rocker and a freebase habit that would have alarmed Richard Pryor. Millions of eyeballs watched both

Nikki and Vanity on television, creating a power couple comparable to Sean Penn and Madonna, or Slash and Traci Lords. Robbin Crosby dated Apollonia.

Cocaine was never my drug, but I might have been the only one who felt that way. (I dabbled here and there. It made me sleep more than hyped me up.) George Clinton, on the other hand, did so much blow in the '80s that he spoke in tongues. Rick James burnt a chick with a crack pipe—or so we hear. Stevie Nicks had a hole in her nose the size of an eyeball. The only sober musician for miles around may have been young Tiffany, whose ballad "I Think We're Alone Now" topped the pop charts for months in 1987. The song played constantly. You couldn't get away from it.

We were recording artists of the Reagan era, crafting power chords, *American* music, earning platinum albums and untold millions of dollars. We were flailing around like Godzillas, whipping our immense tails, destroying everything in our path. We shoveled painkillers down the hatch, chased them with domestic beer, and flipped over our cassette tapes. It was the '80s, and the smell of money was in the air.

■   ■   ■

BY THE TIME I WAS ELEVEN, I was a teenager, smoking, drinking, getting kicked out of Catholic school for the minor offense of groping some girl behind the gym on a perfect L.A. night in 1968. You might say I was an Instant Teenager. And I stayed that way forever: also, Constant Teenager.

After being expelled from Catholic school, the only possible solution was Orville Wright Junior High School, located in Westchester, near the airport, LAX. Andy Holgwen came with me. We added to our posse Victor Mamanna (of the Alice Cooper poster), Mike Hartigan, and Dennis O'Neill, a good-natured blond surf kid who would slowly evolve, over the next few years, into the kind of bell-bottom-wearing, bong-smoking, tapestry-digging hippie pothead upon which the foundation of the stonerrific 1970s were built.

We were a tight gang of hooligans, young punks obsessed with Schwinn Stingray bikes and the idea of copping trim—or, more realistically, at least an ass squeeze here and there. We lived for speed and joy and escape, and the maximum amount of freedom a twelve-year-old could grab. We raced to school, to the beach after school. We pushed and cursed relentlessly, pretending to be older than we were.

"Watch out, man, move to the side. You go too slow, fag!"

"How am I a fag? Your hair goes down to your ass!"

Cars existed only for us to fuck with. We weaved recklessly through traffic on our bikes, dodging buses, flipping off pedestrians, ignoring the furious honks of the cars around us. At lunch, we'd sneak off campus, haul ass over to the mall, and engage in shoplifting.

Backyard parties were the cool thing to do on weekends. The five of us congregated at every gala, wearing Levi's and tennis shoes, smoking shitty joints and eating crossroads, a type of amphetamine popular at the time, referring to the scored cross mark on the tablet. California was a polluted hell at the time, but in Playa del Rey or in Venice, at some rich kid's place, with Deep Purple or Cream warbling over the stereo system, soft breezes blowing on the back of your neck, the pleasure of being alive was undeniable.

My dad was out of the picture. Tired of the constant fighting and abusive behavior, my mom had eventually mustered up enough nerve to leave him. He lived out of a seedy motel near the airport, laboring at killing himself in one never-ending, horribly painstaking, perfect smack binge. My sister and I visited him there in his bunker a few times, celebrated a grim birthday in his room, complete with cake and soda pop.

"Blow out the candles, Stephen," my dad instructed me. His face was swollen and miserable. The cake was frosted elaborately.

I took in an enormous breath. My cheeks swelled as I prepared to huff the flames into oblivion.

"Stop playing around and just do it already," he muttered.

Deflated, I just let the breath wheeze out of my mouth.

We didn't linger for long. My mother yanked us out soon after the cake was cut. My dad gave me a weak hug right before I left, and that was basically it—forever. He overdosed a couple of months later. My mom lied about it, told us it was a heart attack. I'd be an adult before I would find out how he really died—and what he went through; and the predilections I would eventually inherit.

Sometimes she asked me if I missed him. I would always answer yes, and once in a while, I even meant it. But for the most part, what the hell was there to miss? The guy's main contribution to my life was tearing the skin off my face with his enormous knuckles. Ask my brother and sisters if they missed him. Although maybe not my sister Debbie, because I still have a memory of her holding up a serrated steak knife at him the last time he laid into my mom, sobbing her eyes out, screaming, *Get the FUCK away from her or I'll gut you!*"

Without our father, we were on our own, but it didn't feel bad. I've always been good at being alone. My mother, however, wanted a partner, and after mourning the loss of my father, she started dating a guy named Jim, a good-looking dude her own age, kind of a playboy type. He was a man's man who hunted elk and had a thick brown mustache.

When I was fourteen, I became obsessed with drag racing. Everywhere we moved, through my early teens, it seemed there was always a dragster or funny car parked nearby. Through a set of strange coincidences, I managed to insinuate myself onto a pit crew for one of the best racers in Southern California, Walt Rhoades, a kind man who owned a ragged dog that ate lit cigarettes.

"Stephen," Walt instructed me, "check this out."

Walt dropped his smoke on the pavement. His dog attacked the butt, extinguished it with his muzzle, then slobbered the cigarette into his mouth. He sucked furiously, swallowed the tobacco, and finally coughed out the filter. The whole operation took no more than five seconds in total.

"Amazing," I said.

"Perfect animal, right?" Walt agreed, nodding.

Racing had it all: danger, noise, speed, and style. Each day I dreamed of nitromethane and methanol, and of becoming the nation's youngest Top Fuel drag racer. I was obsessed with every detail: the hammering sound, the shrieking metal, the blasting tailpipes, the parachutes on the cars. Walt took me to every racetrack in Southern California. It was before the days of semis, plush coaches, and the multimillion dollar race deals we see today.

"Here comes Pearcy staging his Top Fuel car!" I'd whisper to myself, at night, in bed, entertaining myself by creating intricate fantasy races.

My mother met Walt and approved of him sufficiently, allowing him to take me to Indianapolis with him when he raced at the nationals—the biggest, most important race on the circuit. The Super Bowl of drag racing. The morning we were set to take off, my mother walked me out to the curb.

"Make sure to eat, Stephen. And don't let those damn cars trap you and roll on top of you."

"Mom," I said, embarrassed, "I know my way around a race-track."

"Watch out for him, Walter."

"Of course, Mrs. Pearcy." Walt tossed his half-smoked cigarette on the ground and his dog fell on it with relish.

"What is that . . . dog doing?" my mother asked, horrified.

"Breakfast," said Walt.

I recall the races perfectly: the earsplitting sound, and the pure deafening adrenaline created by the churning and gunning that went on for an eternity before the starting green, our pit crew so alert with nervous excitement we were higher than any man could get on amphetamines, swarming Walt in his space-suit helmet and goggles, inspecting every inch of the anteater-snouted dragster, moving in perfect synch, reading one another's body language with total clarity. I was the guy who poured the bleach for the burnout; I was the guy who poured the used oil against the fence. And I was loving every minute of it.

When I came back that summer, my mother moved us down to San Diego, where Jim had a house. I wasn't anxious to go with her: I had my racing dream to follow—to become one of the youngest drivers on the circuit. I loved L.A. But I had no choice in the matter.

On my very first day of school at Clairemont High—which, a decade later, would serve as the model for Cameron Crowe's *Fast*

Times at Ridgemont High—I arrived in the parking lot early, nervous, a meek, lonely, new-kid sensation inhabiting my body like a flu bug.

"HEY!" came a voice. "You want a *beer,* man?"

A dude with a thin blond mustache and a waterfall of dirty hair offered me a translucent plastic cup full of amber liquid. At his hip stood a small pony keg.

I stared at him, confused. "Thanks, not right now?" It was seven thirty in the morning.

Before I moved to San Diego, I thought I was a pretty competent pothead. But these Clairemont kids just blew me out of the water. There was no roach too small to smoke, no pill too speedy to pop, no vodka too cheap to guzzle at Clairemont High. At lunch, around the flagpole, blossoming concentric circles of stoners passed an endless procession of joints around and around. Pretty, braless girls in faded bell-bottom jeans pulled enormous bongloads in broad daylight, coughing up a storm, awash in the pungent scent of marijuana. There were ten-dollar bags of weed, four fingers deep, for sale. Uppers, downers, acid—anything went. Even keg parties in front of the school before class.

For a good long time, I wasn't sure what the fuck was going on.

I was fine with going to school with a bunch of deviant partiers; given enough time, I would probably come to enjoy it, if not surpass them in their habits. But on those first few mornings, I felt like a fish out of water. How to describe it? I guess it boiled down to that I was still a full-blooded Angeleno at heart. Dirty, scraggly, greasy— all about the cement and the industry. These kids were patchouli, feathers, peace signs, pendants, too clueless or too buzzed to realize the '60s were over, and that the hippies had lost.

Mostly, I was just new. I didn't know anybody. That was the long and short of it. Not to mention I had a new "cool" stepdad at home to deal with—my mom's new man, Jim. The man with the well-trimmed porno 'stache. I gave him a little speech, right out of the gate.

"You had better be good to her," I said. I was a little shrimp of fifteen, but my voice was dead serious.

"Hey, Steve!" he laughed. "I like your style!"

"I'm not kidding," I said, unblinking.

I don't know where that came from—maybe from some part of me that was trying to grow up into a man. It didn't really matter. Jim was going to do what Jim was going to do. He was *hip,* man, kept a stash of marijuana in the trash compactor, which me and my brother discovered in about ten days and set upon like industrious little mice.

"Don't take too much, Stephen," my brother warned me.

"This stuff smells like *garbage,*" I said, sniffing the buds.

"Well . . . how could it not?"

Jim's liquor cabinet wasn't safe, either. Vodka could be gulped straight, then refilled with water. I figured it was the price of doing business with our family. And hey, I had to fit in with the kids at Clairemont—right?

"I go to the weirdest school ever," I confessed to Andy, the first weekend I made it up to Los Angeles. "There are kids dropping acid in the cafeteria! Just eating tabs right out in the open, and the teachers don't say a word."

"Those San Diego dudes wouldn't know good acid if it hit them," said Andy.

"What do you mean?"

"We got *Pyramid* acid up here now, Stephen. Everyone's talking about it." Andy reached across me to dig around in his desk drawer. "Wanna eat some?"

Andy and I dropped doses on our tongues. Within an hour, we were watching the walls melt.

Round-trip flights up to Los Angeles were just twenty dollars. If I played the lonely-guy card just right, I could convince my mom to pop for one. Around lunchtime on Fridays, I'd chow down on a hit of Pyramid blotter. By the time my mother arrived to take me to the airport, all the hairs on my arms and legs would be standing on end. By the time I was in the air, soaring over stretches of clouds and mountains, those magnificent vistas seemed to really mean something.

But in the end, the high always petered out, and I always had to come home. Jim's house in San Diego wasn't too bad. It stood atop a large hill that overlooked the bay and SeaWorld. Our hill was steep and attractively treacherous, and if I cruised down on my bike without touching the brakes once, I could attain speeds of nearly forty miles an hour, long hair flying behind me, teeth rattling as the bike jagged down the blacktop. Top Fuel racing it wasn't, but it was all I had.

One day, pulling my fastest-man-on-a-Schwinn routine, I came to the end of a road in our neighborhood, looked down, and there was a deep, diving canyon, a vast expanse of secret, dusty mountain terrain. Straining my ears, I heard the out-of-tune plunkings of an acoustic guitar.

"Hey!" I yelled, after a minute. "Hey! Who's down there?"

There was nothing for a moment. Then a voice: "Come on down and find out!"

I abandoned my bike by the side of the road and scrambled down the hill, sliding around, then finding my footing beneath me. When I reached stable ground, I was greeted by the sight of a scraggly-bearded teenage boy and his peaceful blond female counterpart. She was wearing a white peasant blouse. He was shirtless, strumming the guitar I'd heard, and an unlit joint was gummed to his lips. They grinned at me like friendly aliens.

"Who are you?" I said, slightly spooked.

"We're Canyon People," they explained.

"Do you . . . live here?" They looked so at home in their kooky surroundings. I had a sudden vision of them eating bark to survive.

"No," laughed the girl. "We come here to hang out, play music. Get high. What's your name?"

"Stephen," I said.

"Well? Wanna jam with us?"

"I don't jam," I admitted. I looked pointedly at their joint. "But I smoke."

So the Canyon People, for lack of any other company, became my first San Diego friends. They were unrelentingly nice, to an occasionally nauseating degree, grease-toughened dragster that I was—but how could you argue with a pack of twenty to thirty largely interchangeable hippie moppets who basically lived to swallow reds, smoke Thai stick, and throw nighttime sing-along parties complete with acoustic guitar, tambos, and kegs? (Yes, occasionally they managed to pass hundred-pound kegs of beer down into the canyon.) Most importantly, I'd found a clique, a way to fit in, and I intended to stick with it.

School became bearable once I had friends. San Diego was a playground, possibly the most lush and beautiful place I'd ever been. Canyon parties led to beach parties. I learned how to surf. My buddies from Los Angeles would come down to see me on weekends. The sun tanned my skin a golden-brown. One evening on the beach, a cute little black-haired chick and I lost our innocence to each other, sand swirling around us, and it was every bit the experience I had imagined it to be.

Everything was going real smooth, in fact, until the afternoon I took off biking after getting high at the house of a couple of People's Park members in our neighborhood. I was gaining speed, pumping hard, that voice going in my head, *Here he is, ladies and gentlemen, witness the youngest Top Fuel drag driver in the world! Steve Pearcy, off to a smashing start, folks,* just barreling down a hill, hauling ass.

I whipped around a corner, and unfortunately, a woman in a station wagon at the approaching intersection was hauling ass of her own, not to mention a trailer, and she didn't see me until it was way too late. She hit me squarely, and I flew off the bike, going upward in that perfect blue San Diego sky, swimming freakily with my arms, my bike long gone on its own trip and it seemed like the seconds stretched into perfect long minutes and then into hours and then days.

Then I hit the pavement with a brutal crunch of leg bone and cartilage, so hard that my *teeth* and my *hair* still remember it.

The pain was instant and intense: eye-opening.

Adrenaline coursed through my veins and I kept trying to rise up off the ground. Both of my legs had instantly swollen with blood. My legs, already the size of an elephant's, inflated my jeans like a life preserver.

"Don't move!" the woman who'd hit me yelled, running toward me. "Stop it! Stay down!"

"GET THE FUCK AWAY FROM ME!"

"Stop it!" cried the woman. "Stop moving, dammit!" After some time, off in the distance, I heard the faint wail of sirens.

Soon, a fire engine screeched to a stop next to us. Men jumped from the cab of the truck and surrounded me. Strong hands lifted me. I was placed on a hard board, fixed to it by nylon straps. I was weirdly coherent and saw what was going on around me. They loaded me into the ambulance and I watched the horrified faces of the crowd that had begun to gather around me. I tried not to scream, but the pain was like a whole other universe. I believe my mom and my brother and sisters were there, having heard the sirens not too far from the house.

The ambulance flew through San Diego traffic, headed to the ER. I was unloaded, wheels down, whipped through the hallways. As I was admitted, an orderly gave me the quick once-over.

"This one'll never walk again," he said, quietly.

That was the last thing I heard before I disappeared into shock.

ALL TIED UP

FOR TWO WEEKS, I was down for the count. No speaking, no thinking. I just lay motionless on my back, drinking in the blurry haze of hospital beeps and smells and fuzzy overhead lighting. If it hadn't been for the dull, throbbing pain that seemed to pump from my core, I might have thought I was dead.

Then: movement. An unfamiliar sound. And the strong whiff of bad breath.

I cracked open an eyelid, grimacing at the effort, and found myself looking directly into the pupils of a weird-looking doctor.

"The boy *lives*," the doctor cackled. I shifted my gaze down to his name tag. It read DR. HANDLER.

"Hey man," I groaned.

"Stephen Pearcy," Dr. Handler said patiently, "do you know where you are right now?"

"In a hospital?"

"Correct. You're at Doctors Hospital. You are a *very. Lucky. Young. Man.* Did you know that?"

"Lucky?" I mumbled. An immense throb of pain ripped through me like a hot wave.

"Oh, yes. Absolutely. Not everyone comes out of an accident like yours with their spinal cord intact. But you did, and that means we can fix you."

"What happened to me?"

"You were hit by a car. Both of your legs were shattered. It'll take a serious operation to get you walking again. But we'll get you there."

"How long will it take?" I looked down at my legs. Both of them were all tied up in ropes, strapped into traction. They hung there, huge and useless.

He gave me an encouraging pat on my arm. "Try not to make any immediate plans. I think we've got you here for a while."

You find out real quick who's your true-blue friend when your legs are fucking bundles of firewood and you're stuck in room 342B for months on end. My L.A. buddies, Andy, Victor, Dennis, and Mike got it together quickly to pile into a car and drive down to give me shit:

"Pearcy, I *told* you to learn how to ride your bike. . . ."

"What does this button do? Raise your . . . Oh! Sorry! . . . are you okay??"

"Stephen, I gotta be honest with you, man, you look *terrible*. But truthfully, you looked terrible before the accident. . . ."

The novelty of cheering me up wore off pretty quickly for them, though, and those guys soon disappeared from sight. I couldn't really blame them—it was several hours down to San Diego, and it was summer. I would rather have been going surfing, too. Walt Rhoades popped in to see me once or twice, but then he went over the guardrail at some racetrack in his Top Fuel dragster and ended up in a hospital himself. Mostly it was just my mom who was there for me, sitting beside me, slipping her hand into mine, encouraging me to stay focused and positive, to pray.

My surgery involved a bone graft from my hip, and a tangle of wires and metal rods had to be inserted in and around my shattered femurs. The whole thing took more than eight hours. Today, the procedure would be a lot more streamlined, but it was the early 1970s, and techniques varied greatly from hospital to hospital. Success depended largely upon the skills of the supervising surgeon.

"He'll be just fine," Dr. Handler assured my mother when I came swimming out of the anesthesia. "Some amount of pain for the next few weeks, of course. But nothing Stephen can't handle."

Nothing I couldn't *handle*? The postoperative pain felt like a mass of swarming poison ants had been unleashed into my lower body. It made the original car accident seem like a gentle swat in comparison. Plain and simple, it was torture. And that's where the IVs of morphine drip started. I can still remember the setup: the tall metallic pole, the plastic tubing that ran the liquid opiate into me, the tiny catheter that was inserted into one of many veins, even the clear surgical tape that bound the apparatus to my arm and hand. If I sound a little nostalgic as I recall the paraphernalia of my very first addiction, forgive me; I'm having a little junkie moment.

My days fell into a steady pattern: boredom, then pain, then morphine. Then a rush of joy, followed by a calmness. Then sleep. If I was lucky, when I woke from my doze, there would be some semblance of an appetite; but more likely, I'd just feel kind of blah, as the morphine rush dulled and faded. Then pain would enter the scene, black and sharp. So I'd wait for the next infusion. The time did pass by.

I guess those nuns didn't quite beat all the faith out of me, because at night, when the ward got deathly quiet except for the breedle of some oldster's heart machine and the soft squeak of the nurses' shoes, I actually did find myself taking my mom's advice and praying. *Let me walk again, please.*

My legs showed no immediate signs of healing, though, and that was kind of distressing. If the man upstairs was listening, he was dragging his feet. John Dudrow, a surfer friend of mine from the Canyon People, whose arm hair had been bleached white by the San Diego sun, offered more immediate assistance.

"Brought you a hit pipe and a little baggie," Dudrow whispered to me.

Dudrow and I puffed away in a workmanlike fashion, stuffing the one-hitter again and again, exhaling each hit directly into my shitty little hospital pillow to mask the smell. Stir-crazy the way only a teenage boy trapped in a hospital in the middle of summer could be, with the aid of weed I could feel temporarily satisfied with staying right where I was. When I was fucked-up enough, I truly didn't mind being laid up in a hospital bed.

And when I was surging on a fresh dose of morphine? Forget about it. I became a master of self-medication, vibing out the moment when the newly connected IV drip was at its most powerful, then taking an enormous hit of Dudrow's weed and holding it in for what seemed like ages. *Fuck regular walking,* I thought, choking on smoke. *I'll spirit-walk. . . .*

It was almost enough to make a guy feel happy. But I had teenage hormones to do battle with, too, and in my present condition, certain needs just weren't being met.

"Dude, bring me a *Playboy*," I begged Dudrow the next time he came in for a visit.

"I'll swing you something," he said. "What's your preference, man? Blonde? Brunette? Black chicks?"

"I just need to see some tits."

Dudrow didn't let me down. One week later, he handed over a skin magazine, its cover still warm from having been smuggled into the hospital under his shirt. It was *Playboy*'s July issue.

"It's my dad's," Dudrow warned. "Don't mess it up." And that's how the world's soon-to-be most frequently utilized porno magazine took up residence underneath my mattress.

Watching life happen from a hospital bed put things in a whole new perspective for me. New patients were accepted to the ward; under my watch, they got well and were released. One day, the doctors began to wean me off the IV drip. Pain pills were administered instead. They packed a weaker punch and were generally a lot less fun. Depression peeked its little head out at me.

"Dude, you gotta wheel me out into the sun," I begged Dudrow on his next visit. "I need a change of scenery."

"I'm not sure they'll let me do that."

"They certainly fucking will," I said, my voice cranky. "I live here now."

Dudrow used his best bullshitter tone on the nurses, and somehow, within an hour's time, he had me out in the courtyard. The warm sun felt incredible on my skin, the best medicine that had ever existed on the planet.

But of course, an hour later, I was right back inside. There was simply no way around it. I was a *bedridden invalid:* even a goddamn *wheelchair* was out of my reach. Searching for a way to exert some control over my own life, I grew mildly obsessed with my own cleanliness. I shat into a bedpan: Lose a point. But I received daily sponge baths from nurses and interns, which included my asshole and balls. Gain a point. As my healing progressed, dead blood began to accumulate in my legs. It raised the skin along the line of the suture, forming plump mesas along my pale white thighs.

"Let me clean them out myself," I said. "Just give me the cloths. What do you say?"

"I don't see why not," Dr. Handler agreed. "Just be thorough."

Each evening, I'd squeeze my leg from knee to hip, pinching the incision gently until dark purplish, jellylike blood oozed forth from underneath the stitches. I mopped and cleaned myself, eventually gaining a precision and sure-handedness that would have impressed an obsessive-compulsive.

In other words, I had too much time on my hands. I was beginning to lose my shit. Stricken by serious cabin fever and on-again, off-again depressive cycles, I was dogged by weird, morbid notions, like *Why don't they put that IV drip back in my fucking arm, except this time, an overdose, so I don't ever have to wake up. . . .* Fortunately, at this critical juncture, they changed my sponge-bath nurse, and I began to be visited each day by a sexy little redhead, dressed all in white, from cap to toe.

I'm not sure if she was sent by God or by central casting, but I definitely had included shit like this in my prayers, so maybe it was divine intervention after all.

"Are you Stephen?" She carried a basin and a purple sponge. Warm water slopped against the basin walls. "I'm here for your bath."

My breath rose unsteadily.

"Yeah. So, you're, like, a nurse?"

"I'm *studying* to be a nurse," she said. "I'm an intern."

"Is that right?" I said, feigning interest, as I gazed longingly at her tits. She gave the sponge a squeeze, soapy water extruding from all of its holes.

"You have the *coolest* hair," she confessed. "All the girls who work here say so."

"I guess it's the only part of my body that's not broken."

She touched my body softly. "What happened to you?"

"I got into an accident," I said.

Gently, with incredible sympathy and concern, she began to run the sponge across my chest and arms. Warm water ran across my tired muscles, massaging me, unlocking all the tension in my body.

"Soap my leg area, okay?" I said. "It's kind of dirty."

"Your *leg* area?" she said, smiling. "Like, around your knee?"

"Draw these curtains," I suggested, "and I'll show you exactly where."

It took some gentle coaxing. But soon the thin green cloth curtains were drawn around us, and we were encapsulated in a snug little rectangle of hospital privacy.

"You're cute," I whispered. "Jump up here."

"But you're not healed." She giggled. "I might break you."

"At this point," I said, "I'll take that chance."

She hesitated, then pulled up her nurse's skirt around her waist. Her upper thighs were palest white. I hooked my index finger into the waist of her little white drawers and rolled them down her thighs. Seventies bush: an excellent vintage. She climbed aboard carefully.

"I'm worried," she whispered, her eyes shining.

"Just don't bounce," I said. "Or my femur may snap," I added seductively.

I discovered a crucial law that afternoon: Women adore broken men. They cannot resist the urge to fuck you back to health. I would use this secret off and on for the rest of my life.

From that moment on, from candy stripers to senior nurses, my game was constantly on. No attendant was too homely, no caretaker too misshapen: They all received a dose of bedridden teenage come-ons, and when I turned on the twin beams of charm and sympathy, most of them could be persuaded into at least a little kiss. Some of them laughed at me, but it was well worth it. I had something to live for again.

Time moved onward. Some days slid by quickly, but others dragged out with brain-crushing slowness. No matter how many visitors I had, no matter how many candy stripers I managed to swindle into showing me their tits, I was still mostly a mess. My biggest ambition in life had been to become a drag racer, but despite my legs having begun their slow mending process, the truth had long since become clear: I wasn't going to be racing any cars.

So, what then? Why should I even bother to take the next breath? It's probably not the smartest thing to start thinking on an existential plane when you're all of fifteen years old, but being strapped to a polyurethane mattress for a hundred and eighty days or so will force a few peeks into the gaping maw.

What the hell do I care about? I asked myself. *What am I even good at?*

I stared up at the ceiling, hoping for some response. None came. Then an acquaintance of a stoner friend of mine entered my room one afternoon during the second half of visiting hours, strumming on an acoustic guitar.

He plunked a few awkward chords, then handed me the guitar by its neck.

"You know anything about these?"

"Not really," I said, accepting the guitar. I had never held one before, but I instantly liked the way it felt in my grasp. Lighter than I had imagined.

"My sister was dating this guy, and I think he cheated on her or something," he said. "She doesn't want to give it back. I said maybe you'd want it."

"I can't play," I said. I strummed a few strings to prove my point. The guitar made a discordant sound.

"Well, learn," he suggested. "You got something else you need to do?"

I looked at him for a second. "Nah." I gripped the guitar the same way he did, by the neck, and offered it back to him. "Thanks."

He shook his head quietly. "I'm not taking that guitar back. You want to throw it away, be my guest," he said, shrugging. "But my sister will be pissed if I bring it back home."

He rose and left, closing the door after him.

I waited until he was probably halfway down the hall. Then, carefully, I gave the guitar a tentative strum. Muddy. Meaningless.

"This is crap," I muttered. But inside, something was moving.

■　■　■

ON THE DAY I WAS FINALLY ready to leave the hospital, Dr. Handler said, "Stephen, we're really going to miss you around here."

My stay had been the second longest of any patient's in the history of Doctors Hospital. "I can't wait to leave," I confessed. "Sorry." I left the hospital in a wheelchair, with the entire staff cheering me on. Everyone was pretty proud that I hadn't withered up and died in there, I guess.

Life turned out to be anything but normal. I returned home and then to Clairemont High School, but while everyone else was pushing and screaming and shouting, I crutched meekly around the hallways, feeling excluded from the conversations going on around me.

It was hard to relate. Teenagers are just trying to get by in the first place—hormones are raging through them, taking their brains captive. They don't know how to be nice to a dude on crutches with two mending legs. I remember this wacky-looking girl with stringy hair and freckles, who stared a hole in me as I struggled with my locker combination.

"What *happened* to you?" she asked.

"I was born this way."

She stared at me for a long time, then said, "My brother is deaf."

"Maybe he and I should hang out." I slammed my locker door shut and crutched off.

I didn't just feel like a loser out in the halls. The sentiment extended to the classroom, too. I'd missed a significant amount of class while my bones were knitting, and hadn't spent much time in the hospital hitting the books. From math to English to history, I was miles behind everyone else.

I felt like an outcast among the happy, loud, constantly stoned teenagers who roamed the halls of Clairemont High School. Lunchtime drinking sessions in the gravel parking lot weren't really an option in my current state: I couldn't navigate the rocks. Dances were obviously out. What I really feared more than anything else, though, was that some big kid, drunk off his ass in the cafeteria, would accidentally stumble on top of me and send me back to the hospital with freshly reshattered legs.

"I really don't want to go there anymore," I told my mom at dinner. "It's not safe," I said, knowing that would get to her. "Plus I'm so far behind, on account of being in the hospital for so long. I can move at my own pace if I get a GED."

My mom examined me for a long moment. "Would you mind telling me," she said finally, "why I always seem to let you do whatever you want?"

"Mom! Are you *seriously* going to let him stay home from school?" my twin sister, Stephanie, cried. "That's so unfair!"

"Hey, I want to get my GED, too!" my brother said, outraged.

My mother shot them the look of death. "Everyone be *quiet*. Stephen has a health situation here, so the rules are a little different for him. All right?"

It was all I could do not to throw up my hands and celebrate. Hell *yeah*! I was on my own schedule now. Immediately, I took full advantage, rising late, preparing delicious English muffin breakfasts for myself, catching up on my '70s daytime TV. Life got even better when my pain pill prescription came in from Dr. Handler. A double handful of hydrocodones brought back memories from the good old morphine-drip days. Chase 'em back with a shot of vodka, followed by a slim little joint, courtesy of stepdad Jim's trash-compacted buds, and I was in heaven.

I could definitely get used to this, I thought to myself, buzzing gently, as I rolled my wheelchair slowly back and forth on the patio that overlooked the San Diego Harbor. *Crippled or not, this is the good life.*

My legs grew stronger. Before long, I was testing the limits of those crutches to get around the house. At first, I was so damn pleased with myself. Then the pain in my underarms started. I'd always been skinny to begin with, but my pectoral muscles had done a disappearing act while I was in the hospital. The hard, unforgiving plastic of the crutch pads crushed the ridges of my chest. But I kept on making journeys across the living room, my arms and wrists burning like hell, then into the bathroom, and then, goddammit, all the way to the front door, where I leaned up against the wood, exhausted, and tried to catch my breath.

"Fuck me," I whispered to myself. "I think I'm walking."

That acoustic guitar wasn't getting a bad workout, either. Utilizing my own self-taught technique, I would throw a needle on a Jimi Hendrix record, turn the volume up full blast, then try to riff my way along with him.

My sister was dating a musical kind of dude, a long-haired Bay Park hippie named Pat Tamasky, and one day he started showing up after school to show me his guitar tricks. "Holy shit, dude, you can *play*," I told him. He was really exceptional. It was like being next to Duane Allman.

"Oh, it's not all that complicated," said Pat modestly. "See? You just put your fingers here. Then you grip the strings real tight with the pads of your fingers—like this, right?"

I watched him, attempting to memorize his quick, dexterous moves. Pressing my fingertips painfully hard into the strings, I gave a pluck. A heartrending twang emanated from my instrument.

"You'll get there, man," Pat said. "Stick with it."

I kept up the twanging. I loved the feel of the guitar in my arms and held it on my lap all the time, like a pet. Eventually, the sounds that came out of my guitar became a little easier to listen to. I didn't suck so completely.

"How are those legs doing, man?" Pat asked, the next time he showed up.

"I'm getting stronger," I said, flexing my left knee. "See?"

"Cool." He pointed to my guitar. "You getting any good at that thing yet?"

I shrugged. "I'm all right. I don't sound like you, that's for sure."

Pat grinned. "So what's the deal? You housebound, man? Or do you want to come around and play music with me? Me and a couple of other guys, we want to do some ZZ Top and Allman Brothers tunes."

I took a moment to think it over. "It would probably do me good to get out of the house once in a while."

"Great!" said Pat. He hooked his arm casually around my sister's waist. "None of us can sing. What about you, man. Do you sing?"

My sister laughed. "Stephen does *not* sing."

Pat smiled. "Well, I know you're in love with that guitar right there," he said. "But if you ever get the notion to shout some tunes, you should join us. You kind of *look* like a singer."

With that seal of approval, I found myself a part of my first-ever band: Firedome. With Pat and his buddies taking care of bass, percussion, and guitar, I was free to function as head crooner. We belted out half-faithful covers of "In Memory of Elizabeth Reed," "La Grange," and "Gotta Get to Know You," making the scene at a few memorable beach parties, dominating a kegger or two, and totally rocking the shit out of a handful of birthday parties. It was surprisingly fun. I'd never really wanted to get up in front of people in that way before, but with a crutch lodged underneath one arm, the other hand holding tight to the microphone stand, I felt weirdly content.

Three weeks later, on a warm Saturday evening, my mom dropped me off by myself in the parking lot of the San Diego Sports Arena. In various pockets, I'd stuffed a three-dollar general admission ticket to see Led Zeppelin, two hits of LSD, a big bag of good weed, and a pack of rolling papers. When she drove off, I took a deep breath, gobbled the acid, then made my way inside.

I found a place to stand by myself in the back, where I began rolling joints like a machine, the atmosphere so incredibly electric and tense the hairs on my forearms were standing straight up, stiff.

"I'm ready," I announced to no one, lighting up my first joint. But Zeppelin didn't come on for *hours*. There was no opening band, no seats on the floor: Our sole form of entertainment was a ten-foot balloon with ZEPPELIN WORLD TOUR scrawled across it that all the idiots around me kept punching and kicking, pushing it back up into the air, again and again . . .

The LSD began to turn my legs into a dangerously jellylike substance, and my mouth went cotton-dry. But then the thunder started. Lights flashed. The mighty Zeppelin stormed the stage, and all hell broke loose. Page! *Plant!* I watched them, shocked, thinking absurd thoughts with my mouth hanging open. *Does that guitar have two necks, or am I tripping?* Yes and yes. And hey: *Is the San Diego Sports Arena beginning to* levitate?

It was madness, absolute madness. When "Stairway" started, all the chicks in the audience went into heat and stripped off their underwear and tossed it onstage. Bonham beat the living shit out of his skins, smashing his way through a forty-minute drum solo for "Moby Dick." The crowd fell into full frenzy mode, pushing and clinging, mixing and whirling in a sea of bodies. I didn't panic. Instead, I felt exhilarated and took two steps forward, as if experiencing a faith healing. Warm flesh pressed up against me from all sides, and I let the bodies take me with them. Like tides, we slowly moved forward, then back, all of our eyes glued to the primordial *force* up onstage, knowing we were part of it, that we'd created this vibe and moment and night together.

I was changed. I cannot describe it any better than that.

After the show ended, they put the lights on, and I looked around, noticing a brown-haired girl with a gorgeous smile.

"Wasn't that the greatest thing you've ever seen?"

She giggled. "It was amazing. Have a good night."

"Hey, hold on a second," I said. "Don't go. Let me get your number. Let's hang out sometime."

She looked like she wanted to be convinced. That's when I hit her with the big guns.

"You know," I said casually, "I'm in a band."

The girl just laughed. "You're very cute, but we just saw a *real* band. You're not in a real band."

She gave me a wave, and I watched her fine little ass as she flounced away.

Someday, I thought to myself. *Someday.*

LAY IT DOWN

WHEN RATT WAS FIRST getting huge—when the label had begun milking its finest glam cow for all it was worth, squeezing until the udders were nearly dry and we could only pass glitter; when we were doing runs that would start in Lubbock, Texas, and wouldn't end until Ames, Iowa, seventy-five shows in the span of ninety days, bringing rock to rednecks, jamming hard in Norman, Oklahoma, headbanging from Wichita, Kansas, to Dothan, Alabama, slogging our way through the most relentless, bus-driven, sludge-infested tours you ever heard of, with no true days to rest in between, just metal, metal, metal, and a Red Lion Inn at the end of every rainbow, if you were lucky—I always managed to figure out a way, each day, to steal some time to myself.

This story reminds me why.

It was Valentine's Day 1987, and Ratt was in Kansas City, out on tour to promote the new album, *Dancing Undercover.* Backstage after the show was bedlam as usual: Our carpenter was screaming at the pyrotechnics guy, while our tour manager pounded his fist on a trash can lid. I was completely exhausted, but in that clean, honest way, from having howled my heart out for two and a half hours.

I was drinking a cold beer and I'd begun rolling the first joint of many when I was introduced to a cocktail waitress in her early forties with wrinkles on her forehead, dirty hair, big boobs, and the good-natured disposition native to women across Middle America.

"Oh my God! It's finally you!" she cried. "*Stephen Pearcy!* I get to meet my favorite singer!"

"Hi there, what's your name?"

She hugged herself to my chest. "Oh, man!!"

Laughing, returning her hug, I attempted to untangle myself from her. Very reluctantly, she released me. "I'm so sorry." She giggled, "My name is June. I'm just excited to finally meet you. Every year, when you guys play Municipal Auditorium, I'm *here*, you can believe it! I love Ratt. And I just adore you."

Clutched in June's mitts was a backstage laminate, adorned with a pair of lips. That should have been my first warning sign, as lips passes denoted the unfortunate fact that the bearer might have had to, well, earn her way backstage.

"Well," June said, "I got someone with me, who I want you to meet."

"Who?"

"Cinnamon!" she snapped. "Cinnamon, get over here!"

A gorgeous young blond thing appeared out of nowhere and sidled up next to June, wearing the teeniest jean shorts I'd ever seen. Thighs so toned and buttery they looked like food. She wore a black

Ratt T-shirt, '86 spring tour, all sliced and diced, offering plenty of ventilation.

"This is Cinnamon," June said. "My *daughter*."

My mind reeled.

"Hey," said Cinnamon.

"Let me run something by you, Stephen," said June, shouldering me a few feet to the side, so we could speak more privately. "If it's not too strange," she said calmly, "I would like you to have a relationship with my daughter."

"What . . . are you talking about?" I asked as pleasantly as I could.

"I would like Cinnamon and you to be together," she said, her tone reasoned and gentle. "I'm not saying marriage, necessarily. Unless that happened to develop in a natural way. I just think the two of you would get along very well."

Fifteen feet away, young Cinnamon watched the discussion. I waved weakly. Cinnamon waved back. "I don't quite know what to say to that," I said.

"Well, how about this," suggested June. "How about I just let you two young folks alone for an hour or so? You could take Cinnamon into your dressing room. Get to know her for a little bit. Who knows? You just may end up liking her."

What possible universe could this exist in? Hmm, the Metal Universe, a privileged one for its inhabitants, apparently. And I admit, my resolve was quickly weakening: Cinnamon was so golden, so perfectly formed . . . and I was so trashed from the road. Not to mention, I hadn't had sex all day. Now, assuming she was even of age—how, I wondered, might I fuck this little treasure without hating myself in the morning?

"Yes," continued June, "I'll just sit out here and have a few beers with the Ratt gang. Meanwhile . . . Cinnamon? CINNAMON!" she snapped. Her daughter flew to attention. "Honey, Stephen would just *love* to get to know you." She whispered in her daughter's ear, gave her a few meaningful jabs, then she pushed her into my arms.

"Hold on," I said, pushing Cinnamon back toward her mother. She looked confused. "I need to talk to you." We walked into my dressing room and closed the door behind us.

"What's up, Stephen?" June said pleasantly.

"First of all, is she even eighteen?" I demanded.

"Of *course* she is!" she laughed. "Gosh!"

"And what's her deal? She looks super innocent."

"She is innocent," said June proudly. "She's a virgin."

"And you want to give her to *me*?" I yelled. "Are you crazy, lady?"

"Oh, I'm *crazy* now?" said June, her own voice rising dangerously. "I'm offering you my freaking daughter's *virginity,* and all of a sudden, *I'm crazy*?"

"Just tell me one thing, okay?" I said. "When Mötley came through here last month, did you bring your daughter?"

She stared at me hatefully for a moment; then she spoke. "*We couldn't get backstage.*"

■ ■ ■

NOT TOO LONG AFTER THE EARTH-SHATTERING Zeppelin experience, Firedome broke up, and I fell into a funk. I'd been sure we'd been destined to go multiplat. But I rebounded quickly: There were other bands out there.

Exciting things were happening, anyway. I was beginning to walk again. One of my favorite destinations for practice was the boardwalk down by Pacific Beach: I'd hitch a ride down there, and then, without a single crutch in sight, I'd start my pacing. I'd shuffle, old-man style, past chicks tanning themselves, and finally find myself trolling though Licorice Pizza, the best record store in town. I was taking one of these tentative strolls through Pizza's rock section one afternoon when Tommy Asakawa, a cool Japanese dude, approached me.

"Yo, bro," he said. "Haven't I seen you singing around town?"

"Possibly."

"Well, you sound pretty good! Me and my buddy Chris, we're trying to get a band together. How about you come try out for us?"

"I don't know," I said. I took another tentative step, holding on to the edge of a record bin, and pushed past Tommy. "I'm actually more interested in playing guitar these days."

"We got the guitars covered. Trust me. Just come on down and belt out a tune or two for us," Tommy insisted. "We really need a guy with pipes."

I had nothing better to do, so the next day, I hitched a ride over to Tommy's garage and sang a couple of tunes for the guys.

"Dude, what did I tell you?" Tommy said to his friend. "He can sing, right?"

"I guess so," said Chris Hager. He looked like a cross between Buck Dharma and Michael Schenker. "You're not bad, dude."

"Seriously," I repeated. "I want to focus on guitar."

By this point, I'd gotten good enough at my instrument that I'd begun to sort of enjoy how I sounded. I couldn't throw down any crazy solos, but at least it didn't sound like a kitten was being butchered every time I plucked a string.

"No," said Chris, rather kindly.

"See, we're actually *good* at playing the guitar," Tommy explained.

I took the hint. I would sing. But I decided that if I was going to do these guys the favor of being their vocalist, I should also be the one to name the band. My suggestion was to call ourselves Crystal Pystal.

"Crystal *Pystal*?" Chris said. "What the fuck does that even mean?"

"Who cares? It's got a classy, decadent feel to it," I said. "Kind of rocking, too, don't you think?"

"Sure, Stephen," said Chris.

Chris and Tommy laughed at me, but I got my way, and we started rocking, right off the bat. The new band was a significant step up from Firedome, even though we played a similar brand of gigs: clambakes, church parties, three-keggers. I was stoked about us, I really was—I enjoyed singing, and I was pulling chicks from these parties as good as or better than the pretty girl who'd snubbed me at the Zep show. Man, it wasn't hard at all. You just got out there onstage, sang a couple of tunes, and soon they were ripping the clothes right off your body. I couldn't believe it had taken me this long to figure it out. I was seventeen years old, and life was starting to feel golden.

One of the biggest benefits of being in the new band was the friendship that formed between me and Chris. And before I put any more words in his mouth, I'll let you hear what he first thought of me, in his own words.

CHRIS HAGER, GUITARIST, CRYSTAL PYSTAL, AND MICKEY RATT:

There were definitely better singers.

It took Stephen a while to develop his voice. But he had this mystique and this aura about him. He was always kind of a compelling guy. When he tried out for us, we started playing, and Stephen's sort of back in the corner. You could hardly even hear what he was saying, but he looked cool. Afterward, he asked me for a ride home. On the way back, I'll never forget this, he said, "We could MAKE it!" Like, in the music industry. I remember him saying, "It could be DONE!" I was like, What is this guy talking about?

He was kind of a trippy guy. He was very excited. And sort of vehement about, it could be DONE! I'm thinking, God, I've hardly even heard you sing.

He had this long hair, halfway down his back. He was sort of introverted in a way, but he and I hit it off. He was really into bootleg Led Zeppelin albums. He had all this cool stuff I'd never even heard of. He had stuff coming out of L.A., new stuff that he knew about. He was sort of hip from the beginning.

The songs we wrote, when I listen to them now—they were okay. They weren't great songs or anything. But we had this look, and this different thing going on. People wanted to see us. Eventually we developed a pretty good following down here in San Diego.

I remember we used to talk about "making it big." And we would talk about putting cocaine in our cereal, for sugar. That was one of Stephen's favorites. "You watch, man. We'll be putting that shit in our cereal, just like fucking sugar." It was our running joke.

I figured Pystal was destined for greatness, for sure. But after a few months, Tommy decided he wanted to go out on his own.

"No offense, man," he said, politely. "I'm looking for a different kind of sound."

Chris and I immediately met back at my house to talk strategy.

"What the hell are we going to *do*?" Chris said, worried. "Tommy was the backbone of the group."

"We form our own band," I said. "Now that we know the ropes."

"But who'll play rhythm guitar?"

"Me," I said.

"Be serious."

"I *was* being serious," I said, annoyed.

"Okay, fine," said Chris, putting up his hands. "You'll play rhythm, I'll play lead. We'll find a bass player and a drummer. But what'll we call ourselves? That Crystal Pystal business can't happen again."

"Been thinking about names all day," I said casually. "See, there's this comic book rat I've been reading about, all right? He's *rude*. He's constantly drunk, always talking shit, and basically acts hilarious. Like, a total asshole. Basically, he just fights and fucks a lot."

"Go on."

"His name is Mickey," I continued. "Mickey Rat. He doesn't take shit from anybody. He just—"

"Fights and fucks a lot?"

"So? What do you think?"

Chris considered. "If I'm hearing you correctly, you're suggesting that we name our new band after an X-rated comic book rodent?"

"But we'll spell it R-a-t-t. That way, once we hit the big time, we'll never get sued."

Chris shrugged. "It's not quite as bad as Crystal Pystal," he said, finally.

None of us really gave too much of a shit about what we were called. We just wanted to play loud music, and hopefully get laid and high as we did it. Within a couple of weeks, we found a bass player, Tim Garcia, and a drummer, Bob Eisenberg. Mickey Ratt was born, and San Diego had a new favorite son.

CHRIS HAGER:

When we were playing in San Diego, it was before any-body had ever heard of AIDS, so it was a time of really free sex. The twin girls that lived down the street, Stephen and I used to date them. They were barely legal, and we started hanging out and dating them and fucking them. They were hot. We weren't talking about ugly chicks here.

They would come over, have sex with him, and then split! And then they'd come back! He just had this power, this mystique. He was laid-back, but he was super cool. Some-how, when he would make his move, he was undeniable.

I had a bit of money from the accident, which I figured I had coming to me after having been a human pincushion for a year, so I immediately set about squandering it—a talent of mine, which, even as the years pass, never seems to fade.

"Like the action on this custom Les Paul?" I asked Chris, grin-ning. "I'm telling you, watch your back, man, or your rhythm guitar-ist is gonna take over lead."

I bought a custom-made Explorer, too, because I was in love with it, and both of the guitars were loaded with Bill Lawrence pick-ups, which were insane. You can't get them anymore. I miss them dearly. Throw in a couple of Marshall amps, and Mickey Ratt sud-denly had a little power to it.

CHRIS HAGER:

His mom worked at a doctor's office, and we used to go pick up bottles of Valium and bottles of Dalmane, and other sedatives. And when I say bottles, I mean a bottle of 120. He'd get these prescriptions from his surgery, and we'd pop two or three or four of these things, and we'd literally bounce off the walls. Take a few Valiums, smoke a joint, and drink a Mickey's Big Mouth. We were just fucked up. This was probably a good half of the time. At least.

Our first drummer, Bob Eisenberg, was a full-blown rocker jock: he ran marathons and always pulled chicks. He had a good sense of rhythm and a solid connection to high-quality Colombian cocaine. A few months into the band's tenure, he got busted. I thought it would be prudent to give him the ax.

"Of course, you're right," Chris said. Then he added, looking sheepish, "Although, we also *could* give him another chance."

Mickey Ratt was always practicing. Late afternoon, we would set up in my living room and run through our set, much to the chagrin of the people who actually lived there, like my stepdad, Jim.

Thrift shops supplied the necessary costumes, producing an eclectic, haphazard look that, if you wore it with pride, looked mildly innovative and somehow hip. Vests covered with pins and buttons, worn without a shirt, could always get you in the door, but on wilder, drunker occasions, bathrobes and open-necked karate uniforms were good choices. Always, T-shirts with the necks ripped out, cock-hugging bell-bottom jeans, and silk shirts with collars that stretched to the tips of your shoulders. Leather pants had not yet entered our lexicon. Once they did, they would change everything.

Mickey Ratt took every opportunity to play, including battles of the bands. At one such occasion, I met a tall, handsome, blond Viking of a guy named Robbin Crosby. He was there with his group, Phenomenon.

"You guys are great," he said. "I really like your sound."

"Well, hey, thanks," I said. You could never tell if other musicians were going to dig your band, or just throw you a bunch of crap because they were too competitive. "You want to smoke a joint?"

"Yeah, sure. I'm Robbin. Seriously, dude, it was a lot of fun, you guys are tight."

"Well, Phenomenon isn't half bad either," I admitted, sparking up a little number. "Hey, man, have you seen the chicks here tonight? I'm impressed."

Robbin flashed me the most brilliant smile I'd probably ever seen in my life to that point. "Don't I know it," he said.

"See anyone you like?"

"No, man. I got a chick and I'm pretty deep in love with her. Her name's Tawny. Tawny Kitaen. Have you met her?"

"Nope," I said. "Nice to have a girlfriend though, right?"

"It's actually kind of terrible. Can't hang with any of these," he said, motioning to the cuties who were just starting to congregate around us.

"That *is* too bad," I agreed, my gaze falling on the perfect, corduroy-striped ass of a blond-haired girl who looked like the younger sister of a San Diego cheerleader.

"Yeah, love's the absolute worst," said Robbin, grinning.

I would see Robbin around from time to time after that, him and Tawny. They were living in an apartment down on Ingram Street, just around the corner from my grandmother Betty. Many Sundays, when I came to take my grandmother shopping, he'd be around, hanging out on the street.

"Stephen Pearcy," said Robbin, by way of greeting. "Of the great and legendary Mickey Ratt."

"I want you to meet my grandmother Betty."

"So nice to meet you, Betty," he said. "Are you two having a nice morning?"

"Yes. Stephen gave me some marijuana," Betty informed him. "For my glaucoma."

"That's very sweet of him," Robbin said gallantly. "Your grandson is a very nice boy. Stephen, can I talk to you real quick? Privately?"

We ducked into a corner.

"Someone was telling me you go up to Los Angeles a lot still."

"Yeah, I do," I said.

"And that you sometimes get good acid when you do."

"That's true."

"I'm tired of this windowpane shit."

"Bunkest acid in the world."

"So?" said Robbin. "Can you help us out?"

"Sure," I said. "I'm going up next week. And when I come back down, I'll bring you the strongest Pyramid acid you've ever had in your life."

"*Awesome*," he said, a smile spreading across his face.

"Consider it done," I said.

"You're the best, man," he said. Then to my grandmother, "Betty, it was a pleasure."

"Yes, dear," said my grandmother, giving him a little wave. "Have a beautiful day. What a nice boy!"

Slowly I began to get more and more serious about the music thing. First of all, I realized that I wasn't musically literate enough. I hadn't experienced enough sounds. The San Diego Sports Arena was this fantastic resource for me—like a library, almost. Every weekend they had another monster act: Ted Nugent, Blue Öyster Cult, Deep Purple. I tried to make the scene as often as I could. At one concert—it could have been an Aerosmith or Peter Frampton show—I was walking around during intermission and I spied a stunning brunette.

"Hi there," I said, swooping in for the kill. "I'm Stephen Pearcy."

"Oh, I'm Tina."

"What do you think of the music?" I said.

"Amazing," she said.

"You know," I said, trying to sound casual, *"I'm* in a band."

She hesitated for a second. Then she smiled.

Sparks flew between me and Tina. She was much younger than me, and so fucking beautiful I thought my eyes would pop if I looked at her for too long. Seriously: She had one of those faces that was so perfectly formed, it actually hurt to look at her. She was super smart, but her dream was to be a model.

"Do you think that's shallow?" she asked, embarrassed.

Shallow? Was she kidding? The fact that she was even bashful about choosing a line of work based on her appearance was enough to show me that she was about ten times as deep as I was. Our love bloomed; and love, as Robbin pointed out, is the absolute worst. But it was also the best, because with Tina, I relaxed. With Tina, I was in the moment.

Tina was a virgin and she wanted to stay that way. I was so in love that I didn't even try to change her mind. Her dad didn't really like me: I was the rocker boyfriend, not the jock he'd imagined for his daughter, a few years older than his kid, leading her down the path of darkness. I understood his position. After all, I was tasting the fruits of Babylon for hours on end in her bedroom, knocking the bed into walls in everything-but-sex teenage passion, then waltzing downstairs, completely straight-faced, as if nothing had even occurred.

"Will you take me up to Los Angeles sometime?" she asked. "I want to see where you grew up."

"Oh, sure," I answered. "Sometime soon."

But not right away. I had business up there, best done alone. I had sheets of acid to score. My connection was this kid Mike, who I'd met through my brother.

L.A. was 150 miles away, but it might as well have been a million, if you didn't own a car. My mom wasn't popping for any plane tickets anymore. So hitching was my solution, a perfect exercise in basic survival if I've ever seen one. But it was all worth it to get to see my friends up in L.A. They were still the closest guys in my life. Victor and Andy and Mike and Dennis—they hadn't changed much.

"So you graduated from . . . hey, what was it you graduated from again, Pearcy?"

"I got my GED," I said to Andy. "Asshole."

Those guys were in no hurry to get out into the real world of jobs and responsibility. Victor and Mike were into music, and they spent most Saturday afternoons jamming out in the fresh air of Culver City public parks.

"Dude," Victor told me, "there's a band out here that you really have to take a look at."

"Oh, yeah?" I said. "Who's that?"

"Van Halen," he said.

"Never heard of them."

"Take my word for it," said Victor. "They *cook*."

I assured him that I'd make sure to visit the Strip the next time they had a gig. Then I attended to my other business. I found my brother's friend and scored a couple of sheets.

"Twenty bucks, brother. And that's a friend price." He grinned. "I only wish that I could watch you lose your mind on this."

"You should come down south and hang out sometime," I said.

"San Diego?" he laughed. "Nah. I'm afraid I'd turn into a hippie. Smog suits me."

I shrugged. His loss. I walked down to the freeway on-ramp, my thumb out.

"Now listen, Robbin," I said, when I'd arrived home safely, "this is *strong stuff*. I don't recommend doing more than one hit of it."

He nodded.

"In fact," I continued, "my friends and I sometimes take a pair of scissors and cut a hit in half. Eat one half, then wait an hour or so, see how you feel. You might not even need the other half, you know?"

Robbin nodded again. "Cool. I'll take two."

"Two hits?"

"Yes." He looked at me gravely. "Is ten bucks cool?"

"That's plenty," I said, confused. "But, who's the other one for?"

"Two for me," Robbin said.

"But I just *said*—"

"I know what you said."

"Suit yourself," I said, laughing. You had to dig Robbin's style. Two hits of Pyramid acid would turn the most psychologically stable human being on the face of the planet into a gibbering wreck for sixteen hours at minimum. But no one was going to tell that to Robbin Crosby.

As for me and Chris, we dropped one hit of Pyramid apiece, in order to get juiced up for a Boston show. Then we got in his car to drive the mile and a half to the Sports Arena, gunned the engine, and promptly forgot we were even driving.

"Chris?" I said. My voice sounded funny in my head. "Hey, Chris."

"Yep," said Chris.

He continued to drive along in silence, going about ten miles an hour.

"Hey," I mumbled, "would you say I have weird hands?"

"Where are we going?" said Chris suddenly. His Peugeot bounced off the divider in the middle of the road and bounced us back into our lane. We both jolted upright.

"Shit, man!" I exclaimed, laughing. "We're frying. Pull over, you idiot!"

"No, I can make it, I can make it," he insisted, his voice hoarse. "The arena is only a mile away."

Against all odds, Chris managed to guide us into the parking lot of the Sports Arena. But once we'd parked, the LSD truly launched into attack mode, exploding all the unused pockets in my brain. Everywhere I looked, fractals were forming and melting, tiny kaleidoscopes in motion. Around us, night quickly began to fall, and with it came a sense of weird foreboding and evil. In my mind's eye, I could sense thousands of rowdy fans, clustered in every recess of the parking lot, guzzling beer and smoking cheap pot, gulping down quaaludes, wanting to fuck and kill. I slunk down deep into my bucket seat.

"Chris," I whispered hoarsely. "I actually might not make it *inside* for the show. Is that cool?"

"I'm not moving," he mumbled back, "from this car."

Some days later, Robbin would tell us how he had gobbled down his two hits and then, an hour later, the dude went surfing.

"Best day of my life," he confessed. "Thank you so much, man."

Robbin had an enormous appetite, whether you were talking drugs, food, women, or music that shredded. Out of all the aspiring musicians in San Diego, he was the one who was most heavily into metal. Judas Priest was one of his favorite bands. I listened to my first Priest album ever over at him and Tawny's place.

"Listen to *this*, man," he demanded. "Both of you."

"We're listening, calm down."

Robbin cocked his head and motioned for us to be silent. As if on cue, Priest churned out a chorus of heavy, gorgeous riffs. Robbin's massive six-foot-four frame shook with excitement.

"You just got your fucking head blown off there, didn't you?" he said, with utter reverence. "Seriously, wasn't that fucking *disgusting*?"

"You're right, man." I laughed.

Robbin just understood what rock was all about, and embodied the best parts of it without even having to try.

"Did you know Robbin got offered a contract by a minor-league baseball team?" Tawny asked me once.

"Huh? I didn't know he even played."

"He was a huge star in high school," she said, matter-of-factly.

"Well?" I said. "Is he going to take it?"

"Are you kidding?" she laughed. "He goes, 'I'm not a jock anymore. They can suck this dick. I like *metal*.'"

■ ■ ■

THE NEXT TIME I CAME UP to L.A., Victor was on my ass about Van
Halen again. But things got busy down in San Diego. Tina and I got
tangled up in some tongue acrobatics, slowing me down. I hit the
freeway too late to grab a good ride and I never made it to the show.
Victor was looking quite smug the next time I saw him.

"I'm not sure I've ever seen a crowd get so thoroughly slayed."
He sighed. "You missed a classic for the ages, Pearcy."

"Look," I said. "When do these guys play next?"

"Two weeks from now. Whisky a Go Go. Be there."

I said I'd be there for sure this time. In the meantime, I started
to do some research on the band. This was in 1977 or so. I don't
think Van Halen had even been signed yet. They might have been
doing some demos, but they definitely didn't have a record in any of
the stores that I checked into. Only one clerk even knew who I was
talking about, though he was quick to assure me, just like Victor, that
Van Halen's show was not to be missed. As the date came nearer,
one thought kind of came to my mind over and over again.

*If these guys are so cool, I don't want to just see them. I want to
meet them.*

I took off for Los Angeles at exactly one o'clock in the afternoon,
intent on getting to the Whisky in time for the sound check. I'd
always paid attention at the San Diego Sports Arena when I went to
shows, and I'd noticed one thing: The bands came early. I'd milled
around outside many an Aerosmith or Ted Nugent or ZZ Top concert hours before the doors opened, chatting with hot groupies who
promised me that they'd try to get me in with them. It had never
happened yet; I blamed it on my lack of tits.

But this band was small. There wouldn't be groupies or a crowd at sound check.

I sped up Highway 5 and made the switch to the 101 just outside of downtown L.A. I crawled north through the midafternoon traffic, cursing the sluggish progress. *Come on, come on . . .* Finally, the Sunset exit showed, and I dropped down onto surface streets. I pushed my car west, notching steady progress, until finally, I was just in front of the Whisky.

The timing of my arrival couldn't have been more perfect. Just as I hooked a right onto Clark Street and pulled into an open space, David Lee Roth was walking up the stairs on the outside of the building, about to pull open the Whisky's side door.

It was now or never.

"Yo, Dave!" I yelled. "Want to smoke a joint?"

It sounds unbelievable—that I'd be dumb enough to ask, or that he'd be dumb enough to say yes. But then again, if I was a partying kind of guy, on my way to sound check on some perfect California afternoon, and some long-haired kid offered to get me high, I'd probably say "Sure."

"Sure," Roth laughed. "Come on, man. Hurry up."

Unable to believe my luck, I parked and followed him in. In my palm, held on to for dear life, was the clumsily rolled joint that I'd packed special from San Diego.

"This is really good shit," I promised him as we walked up the steps to the backstage area.

"That's what they all say."

He and I soon got down to puffing. Members of Van Halen were tripping around the dressing room, and there I was with them: *Stephen Pearcy, rock-and-roll infiltrator!*

"So what's your story, kid?" Dave asked.

"I'm in a band," I said. "Down in San Diego."

"Hey, imagine that!" He took a solid hit and then coughed. "What do you call yourselves?"

"Mickey Ratt," I said.

He nodded, appearing to consider it for a second. "That's kind of fucking weird," he decided, finally. "We were going to call our band Rat Salad."

We smoked until the joint was almost gone, and then Dave kind of nicely blew me off.

"Thanks for the toke, bro. I gotta get ready to sing. . . ."

"Absolutely," I said. "It was cool to meet you."

I could have left right there, but then I saw a dude fiddling with a really cool-looking guitar.

"Hey, man," I said, "that's a sweet instrument you've got there."

He looked up at me, his eyes bright. "Thanks. I built it myself. . . ."

As it turned out, Eddie Van Halen was friendly and completely easy to talk to, as long as you knew something about guitars, because that was the only thing that guy thought was worth talking about.

"I'm way into Vox amps these days. . . ."

"You like Vox 30s?" I asked.

"Vox 30s are the best. I got two swivel-beetle Vox cabs," Eddie said, a touch of longing in his voice, "but only one Vox head. It's *killing* me."

"Hey," I said, excited, "I have an extra Vox head! I could loan it to you!"

"Say what?" he cried. "Let me buy that thing off you!"

We were speaking the same language, and it was beautiful. Ed and I hung together for almost an hour, and when it was time to part ways and let him get ready for the show, we exchanged phone numbers.

"Give me a call anytime, man," Ed said. "And you better stick around to watch the show."

I'm in, I thought. *I'm fucking in.*

I was on goddamn cloud nine. Couldn't get any happier. Or at least that's what I thought, until the show started. There was no opening act, and the crowd was surprisingly tiny—there couldn't have been more than thirty people in the whole place, the band included. But I shit you not, these guys played like they were at the Forum. I had been to many, many rock concerts in my life by this point, maybe upward of a hundred. But I had absolutely never witnessed a group generate so much raw energy, so instantaneously, and without the support of a large audience.

"LADIES AND GENTLEMEN," Dave screamed, "WE'RE VAN . . . HALEN!"

Dave was strutting around like the biggest cock on the walk. Ed was slamming his body against the cabinets, shredding that hand-made guitar to fucking bits. They were badass, in a word, and as I watched them there, my jaw literally dropped open. I had to admit to myself that, as good as I felt Mickey Ratt was starting to be, *we got a long way to go.*

But these guys sure made the journey look like a hell of a lot of fun.

MONKEY ON OUR BACKS

ONE STRANGE THING ABOUT remembering the good old days is that if I think about them long enough, it makes me want to do some drugs.

Getting clean is a trip. No doubt about it. I love being able to get up in the morning and not feel like I have to get right to work on demolishing a twelve-pack. Not that I'm totally squeaky or anything like that, mind you. In fact, Chris Hager's mad at me right now. He volunteered to be my AA dude—my sponsor, if you will—because he's been sober for fifteen years, or something insane like that, and wants me to get there, too.

"You don't want to start backsliding." That's his mantra. "I know you don't want *that*."

Hmm, I don't know: A little backsliding sounds kinda good. When rock dudes get sober, watch out—they're always on the hunt for *you* to get sober, too. Sometimes it feels kind of ironic. Especially when you stop to consider all the TVs you hurled off balconies together. All the liquor you poured on each other's hair.

I mean, I'm not talking about buying a fucking balloon of *heroin* here. Just, you know, a joint or something. Maybe a five-dollar watermelon-flavored medicinal-marijuana lollipop, to help me soak up the basic stupid enjoyment of life. There's no rule against that, is there? Or maybe there is. AA is full of them. I've been to my share of joyless, washed-out AA meetings in the past couple of years. Jesus, I don't want to sound ungrateful or anything, but there's really no worse way to kill a morning than smoking half a pack of cigarettes, drinking eighteen cups of coffee, and listening to some dudes with fading tattoos talk about how they learned to walk the straight and narrow.

Rehab was more my speed. More private. The truth is, I'd go back to rehab in a heartbeat if I didn't have to pay so damn much for it. I slept like a *baby* in rehab. And therapy tickled the hell out of me. I kept getting this weird confessional high.

My therapist, Dr. Roberts, was an absolute master at getting me to spill my guts.

"What shall we talk about today, Stephen?"

I grinned. "Ah, you can't fool me," I said. "You just want to hear about trim. Am I right?"

"With all due respect, Stephen, I think you're way off base there. . . ."

"Well, I'll give you something, just to tide you over. Once I had this adventure with Ron Jeremy. Do you know who that is? The porn dude? His nickname is the Hedgehog?"

Dr. Roberts gave me a too-casual shrug.

"Ha! You *do* know who I'm talking about! You just won't admit it because you don't want me to laugh at you for whacking off. Listen, I won't laugh at you, man, for whacking off every night. You're cool. You're my therapist."

"Just go on, Stephen," sighed my therapist.

"Well, Ron was always around the rock scene in the late '80s and early '90s. It made sense: Porn chicks loved rock dudes, and rock dudes loved the porn chicks right back. Savannah and I dated for a while—remember her? But it was a weird time. We both loved getting high so much that after a while, all we would do was get so blasted neither of us would remember to fuck the other one. Our romance went nowhere. My buddy Joe Anthony and I used to spend days locked up in her hotel room with her and her buddies doing everything, but forgetting to get to the point."

Dr. Roberts scribbled something in his notebook.

"Now, one thing about Ron Jeremy, he always loved to be the life of the party. He was always fun to be around, just didn't give a shit about anything. I'm like that myself.

"So anyway, Ron and I got to be friends. One night, we saw each other out at a club. He had three chicks on his arm. 'Pearcy,' he said, 'let's blow this scene. Let's get a motel room with my chicks.' And I was kind of like a wind-up doll in those days when it came to trim: You just put it in front of me, and I followed. So Phil Schwartz, my concierge, drove—whether in a limo or one of my Porsches, Phil was at the wheel. We followed Ron to his destination, Pornification."

"Right," said Dr. Roberts.

"Now, I had been hitting the bottle pretty hard, but I had also been eating some pain pills, because I had a toothache that was really acting up. Nothing a few OxyContins couldn't fix. Like usual when I indulged too hard on the opiates, I sort of felt like

I was floating on air, and at the same time, like I might puke up a lung."

"Mmm," said my therapist.

"It's not a real good state to fuck in," I said. "That's the only reason that I bring it up. By the time Ron and I made it back to his hotel room in the Valley, I'd pretty much decided I'd rather just watch."

"You were too inebriated to take part?"

"Yeah. But also, by the late '80s, man, I'd had so much sex, I just wasn't that greedy for it anymore," I said. "When you get to a certain point, it all sort of starts to blend together, if you can dig that."

The look on my therapist's face told me he had no idea what I was talking about.

"You find yourself wanting something else," I explained. "You want to fall in love. You want to be with one chick. And a couple of years later, wouldn't you know it, that's precisely what happened to me. That's when I met the mother of my kid. But I'll save that story for another time. . . ."

"Let's talk about that now," Dr. Roberts said.

"No," I said. "I want to finish telling you about Ron and this hotel room. Ron started plowing one of the babes while I just sat on the other bed and watched. 'Hope you don't mind,' he said. I'm all, 'Dude, are you kidding? This is like watching a live porno. Go for it.' He was all sweaty and hairy, and his chick had these tits that were so fake it looked like if you grabbed them you could feel the plastic wrinkling under her skin. It was awesome."

"Why did you want to watch?"

"Because it was cool. Because it was weird, and really gross. I'm into that kind of thing. After about ten minutes, one of the other girls goes, 'I'm bored. I'm going to go take a bath,' and she got up to go to the bathroom. Ron took one look at me and said, 'Pearcy, what do you need, a written invitation?' So I followed her in."

"I thought you didn't feel like having sex," my therapist pointed out.

"I didn't," I said. "But I went in there, and this chick was already in the bath. The whole room was all warm and humid, which made me feel even sicker. The light was yellow and bright, and my head started to pound, so I closed the toilet lid and sat on top of it. This chick was soaping herself all over with that little bar of free soap. She was kind of hot, but like most porn chicks, she had some major flaws."

You could hear birds chirp outside Dr. Roberts's window.

"That's when I *really* started to feel sick. I don't know what I'd eaten that night, probably a hamburger, or half a fried chicken. My gut was churning. This chick gave me this weird look and said, 'You're in a band, right?'

"'Sure am,' I said. 'Ever hear of the Stones?'

"She looked confused. 'Which one are you?'

"'Ringo,' I said. 'Why are you taking a bath?'

"She thought about it, then said, 'I wanted to get clean.'

"Then she invited me to get in the water with her, but I was feeling so sick right then I wouldn't have been able to get into a spa pool, much less a tiny bathtub in some hotel room in the Valley. But I stumbled to my feet, unhooked my belt, and asked for some head."

"And she agreed?" asked Dr. Roberts.

"You just don't get it, do you, man?" I said. "In the '80s, if you were in a rock band, when you asked for a hummer, you got a hummer."

Dr. Roberts nodded and wrote something down on his pad. Maybe it was *motherfucker.*

"So I had my pants unbuckled, and I was standing there, getting serviced, trying not to catch a head rush. Then my legs started trembling. There wasn't much muscle control left there. But this chick was talented at what she did, and she worked me to the point of no return. I pulled out of her mouth and did my duty all over her chest.

"'YOU DIRTY SON OF A BITCH,' she yelled. 'WHY IN THE HELL DID YOU JUST SPLATTER ME?'

"I was like, Huh?

"'But I thought you did porn . . . ' I mumbled.

"'I WAS TAKING A BATH!' she screeched furiously. 'I WAS TRYING TO GET *CLEAN*!!'

"'Clean from fucking *what*??'" I yelled. It was the craziest thing I'd ever heard. Suddenly I felt faint, staggered backward. I told Ron, 'See ya. We're gone!' Who knows why we drove out there in the first place?"

Dr. Roberts stared at me for a long time. "Then what happened?"

"That's about it," I said. "It was one of my more normal nights."

■　■　■

SOMEWHERE AROUND MID-1978, MICKEY RATT BEGAN to really catch on down in San Diego. We graduated from the backyard birthday parties and the keggers and started playing real clubs, like El Cajon's Straight Ahead Sound, using first-class equipment and playing songs that rippled with our own raw, vital energy. Sometimes Robbin's band, Phenomenon, split a bill with us; other times we played alongside a group called Teaser, featuring a talented local guitarist named Jake E. Lee. No matter who we played with, we slayed. We were on a serious roll, riding the crest of local-star popularity. And I was *digging* it.

"I just get the feeling that Mickey Ratt is starting to outgrow this town, man," I said to Chris one day.

"What are you talking about?" he asked. "We haven't even played the fairgrounds."

"But we *will*," I said. "And once we do, where will we go then?"

"The Civic," said Chris. "And then the Roxy. Dude, how many chicks do you think we'll pull if we do the *Roxy*?"

"I don't know, Chris," I said. "But I'll be honest with you: I'm starting to believe that getting laid is just not enough anymore."

"What are you trying to say here? You don't appreciate our groupies anymore? You don't *like* the idea of playing the fairgrounds?"

"Look, I want to play the fairgrounds, okay? But we sound *great*. I'd put us up against *anybody*." My voice was rising in excitement. "Given the right break, we could rule a lot more than San Diego. We could dominate the *world*, man!"

"All right," Chris said. "All right, man. Calm down. I believe you. Let's do it."

But calming down was not an option for me. When an idea hatched in my head, it ruled me. An excited little voice that came from inside my brain stubbornly refused to shut up. *You guys can MAKE it*, it said. *You have something special.* Before I went to sleep every night, I dreamed about the road to the top, in full color and meticulous detail. I was seeing us as Led Zeppelin, Blue Öyster Cult, Aerosmith, Alice Cooper. I wasn't conceited, I was convinced. And sure, I might have been a tad delusional: Mickey Ratt was still basically a good garage band at this point. But without that irrational belief in myself and our mission, I'd probably still be down in the Canyon, strumming on an acoustic. It was go big or go home.

Tina, in order to satisfactorily fulfill her responsibilities as girlfriend of up-and-coming rock dude, was forced to listen to a few superstar monologues too.

"I don't know *how* I'm going to make it happen, exactly," I told her, caressing her perfect little body, "but you better believe it, I will make it happen."

"I believe in you, baby," she said. "You'll do it. I know you will."

"You love me, huh?" I asked, grinning.

"Yes, I do, a little," she admitted.

"So when are we going to *do* it?" I asked.

"Do what?"

"You *know* what," I said, tapping her on the thigh playfully.

Sex when you're young, and completely in love, it's like this whole other animal, a completely different enterprise. I remember watching Tina's eyes light up when we moved up and down together for the first time, joining, holding hands, kissing lightly. It was enough to make you believe in some kind of order to the universe—that you had been somehow *destined* to meet this beautiful girl at the intermission at some show, stoned out of your mind, ears still humming from the guitarist's riffs. It was enough to make you believe that now you were together, there'd be no need for anyone else.

Just as I was sure that Tina and I were the perfect couple, I was similarly convinced that Mickey Ratt was destined to "make it." And though I still didn't have a very precise understanding of what had to be done in order to make that dream a reality, I made sure to keep calling the only guy I knew who was clearly on the path: Eddie Van Halen.

"Hey, man, I don't know if you remember me—I'm Stephen Pearcy. We met backstage at the Whisky a while ago?"

"Sure, dude. You were the one with that Vox head, right?"

"Right, yeah! Are you still interested in checking it out?"

"Definitely. Come on up to my house in Pasadena. We'll hang out."

We made plans, and he gave me his address. Later that week, I ran into Robbin in a record store down by the boardwalk.

"What's going on, Stephen?"

"Not much, dude," I said casually, picking my way through the latest in Zeppelin bootlegs. "Just, you know, heading over to Eddie Van Halen's house tomorrow."

"What the hell are you talking about?"

"Just going up there to Eddie's to hang out," I repeated, smiling. "You want to come along?"

"Uh, *yes*?"

We tooled up to Pasadena together in Robbin's van.

"So are you going to tell me how the hell you met Eddie Van Halen?" Robbin asked, eyeing me as he drove.

I told Robbin the story of how I'd met him.

The drive seemed to take forever. I kept turning around in my seat to make sure my Vox amp was still in the back of the van.

"Dude, I wonder what an up-and-coming rock star's house looks like," I said. "It's probably pretty fucking wild."

When we arrived at the Pasadena address, all we found was a small, modest house, clean and tastefully decorated. Inside was Eddie, sitting on a small cot in a tiny bedroom about the size of a washroom. An unplugged electric guitar was strapped over his shoulder, and he played it constantly as he talked.

"What up, guys?"

"Do you . . . live with your parents?"

"Totally," Eddie said. "Me and Alex like the rent here."

I relaxed. Maybe I didn't have that far to go, after all.

Robbin and Eddie got along instantly, which was no surprise, as there wasn't a man alive who Robbin couldn't befriend in a heartbeat. The three of us just sat around talking about gear for hours on end. The floor of Eddie's tiny bedroom was absolutely strewn with guitar parts.

"So, are you building these guitars yourself?" Robbin said.

"Sure. I get guitar parts at Charvel. They throw a lot of parts away, so they give them to me cheap."

Ed loved the amp I'd brought him, but that was nothing compared to Robbin, whose eyes absolutely started goggling when he saw the Flying V guitar that Ed had been working on.

"You gotta let me buy that off you," Robbin said. "*Please.*"

"Sure," Ed said, shrugging. "That one needs a little work, but if you're serious about buying it, I could fix it up for you soon."

It was just the coolest afternoon. We hung out for a few hours, then Robbin and I decided to split.

"Totally good guy, huh?" I said, as we were driving back.

"Absolutely," Robbin agreed. "I wish he lived down in San Diego, so we could jam together."

"Or we lived up there," I said, pointedly.

San Diego was fun. It was probably the most beautiful place on earth. But I was starting to get really itchy. When I had needed a place to heal, my mom and Jim had given me a space to do it in. Finally, though, I was fully recovered, and I wanted more.

"I'm thinking of taking the plunge," I told Chris. "Making the move up north."

"Why, man?" he asked.

"Why do you think? For the good of the band, man," I said. "How the hell are we going to get signed down here?"

He looked confused. "Are we even in *position* to get signed?"

"Dude, we have to be thinking constantly about the next step. Do you think Van *Halen* would let themselves live down here, and potentially be missed by the music industry?"

Chris shook his head and sighed. "No," he said, finally. "That mighty band would never do that."

Mickey Ratt pressed onward. Our first drummer was gone; with his new replacement, our beat seemed steadier. I wrote constantly, using my own anxiety and desire for fame and recognition as the best kind of songwriting inspiration. Slowly, we began to get booked at larger venues: the Plaza Hall, Bing Crosby Hall, and then, finally, the Del Mar Fairgrounds.

"Fuck, this is amazing!" Chris cried. "Half a year ago, we were playing to fifty people! I think there must have been *fifteen hundred* there tonight!"

"Cool," I said. "But we're still small-time."

"Stephen," Chris said, "you're starting to worry me. Be happy with what you have. We're one of the biggest bands in the whole town."

I knew I should be more grateful. I should have felt lucky to even be walking, after my accident. But it was tough. As the months went by, the small city felt more and more confining. Through my accident settlement, I was able to buy my first car, a green Datsun B-210, and I used it to venture up to Los Angeles almost every weekend that we didn't have a gig.

"Are you *cheating* on me?" Tina asked one day.

"No," I said, surprised. "Why?"

"Because you're always gone. You're always *up there*. . . ."

But it wasn't another girl who had stolen my heart: it was the Strip itself, and my vision of us as a part of it. As 1978 turned into 1979, I found myself constantly standing outside the Troubadour, or Gazzarri's, or the Whisky a Go Go, thinking to myself, *I should be playing* here, *not the goddamn fairgrounds.* San Diego was close enough to L.A. to nearly be a suburb of it, and we had a hell of a lot of good musicians down there. But as far as the record industry was concerned, we might as well have been in Oklahoma.

"Nothing's going to happen for any of us here," I insisted to Robbin. "The guys in your band know that, right?"

Robbin shrugged. "I love it down here. So does Tawny."

"So you're just gonna play music, go to the beach, and fuck your brains out for your whole life?"

"Hmm," said Robbin, thinking for a moment. "That sounds about right."

It was absolutely staggering to me: Nobody seemed to get what I was talking about. *Open your eyes,* they all said to me. *We got a sweet deal here. We live in paradise, and we're pulling the best chicks in town. Dude, we just played to* fifteen hundred *people!*

I began to have trouble sleeping. My hair, always my pride and joy, began to frizz from the anxiety. I stood in front of the mirror one afternoon despondently, holding a pair of my mom's kitchen scissors. *Shit,* I thought. *If I look cool in a crew cut, maybe I'll enlist.*

One afternoon, I got a phone call from Eddie.

"Hey, dude, I need a favor! We're playing the San Diego Sports Arena tonight. Listen, it's a much bigger place than we normally play, and we're low on equipment. Can you help us round up some cabs?"

"*Hell* yeah, man," I said, snapping to immediate attention. "We'll be right there!"

I got on the phone like a man possessed. "Robbin!" I yelled. "Ed's playing the Sports Arena. He needs some cabinets. Get a stack from your boys!"

"I'm on it!"

"Tommy—remember that band I told you about, Van Halen? Well, they're playing the Sports Arena tonight. They need cabinets."

"Right on, Pearcy, sure thing, as long as they get me backstage after the show. . . ."

I organized an obscenely huge pile of equipment for the band. All day long, we trucked it back and forth, using Robbin's van and my Datsun for the mission, even enlisting the services of Chris's tiny Peugeot. That night, Van Halen played on *our* Marshalls, using *our* Vox heads, in front of a crowd of thousands, including the entirety of the San Diego hard rock music community.

And they just *blasted* us.

"I *told* you. I told you!" I yelled, over and over. "Man! *Now* do you guys understand?"

"Wow," Chris said, utterly amazed. "Yes. I understand."

Van Halen was electrifying, explosive. They were as fun as Aerosmith, but more musically complicated, maybe more adventurous. They were as charismatic as Zeppelin, but less mystical and more grounded in a California party vibe. Really, they were their own beast, with their own unique sound. But one thing was abundantly clear: They were big rock.

I drove home that night from the arena feeling more content and more convinced regarding my own destiny than I had in months. Being part of the show, even just as a glorified roadie, was tremendous fun. I was so puffed up on adrenaline, I almost felt like I'd played the arena myself. But it was more than that: The band that I'd been bragging about for months and months really *was* something special. They were going to be huge—everyone who'd seen them that evening knew it. And I'd called it.

"I guess you do have pretty good taste," Chris admitted the next afternoon, when we met over at my mom's house for practice.

"That band's going somewhere, man. Meanwhile, we're stuck right here, going through the motions."

"San Diego's not that bad . . ." Chris began.

"I'm in my twenties, Chris," I said. "I live with my mom."

"Yeah, and?"

"Things have to change. And they have to change soon," I said. "We're about to be in the *nineteen eighties*."

"So?" Chris laughed. "What does that even mean?"

"Things change when decades change. *Tastes* change. The seventies gave us soft rock and disco. I think that's all about to be over."

"What kind of music do you think is about to hit?" he asked.

"Fucking *metal*," I whispered. "The hard shit."

Chris began pacing the floor of my mom's living room. "So what does that mean for us?"

"It means we're going to play on stages in front of *thousands* of people," I said. "We're going to make a ton of money, drive sports cars, and buy our mothers swimming pools. I want Mickey Ratt on the cover of every rock magazine, right next to Ozzy and Priest! But to really go for it," I said, "we gotta leave."

"Okay. When?"

"January first," I said. "Nineteen eighty. We're gone."

"But where will we go?"

"There's only one place to go," I said. "The Sunset Strip."

OUT OF THE CELLAR

IN A NEW CITY, you can feel reborn. New smells fill the air—such as the faint aroma of industrial garbage. New sights dot the horizon—such as homeless men in shit-encrusted jeans, punching one another in the face. New sounds caress the ear—such as the honking of desperate idiots trapped on side streets, hell-bent on their missions to nowhere.

"I'm glad to be back," I sighed, satisfied.

Chris and our drummer, John Turner, moved with me into the two-car garage at my old friend Dennis O'Neill's house, in Culver City, across from the DMV. Dennis was out on his own by this time, secure in his own apartment, but his mother remembered me from the old days. She said we were welcome to stay for as long as we wanted.

"The only other people who've lived in here before have been cars," she said, simply.

We moved our gear into the small space and set up the three beds in a triangular formation. We were almost sleeping on top of our amps. I knew it was crucial that we treat our move as an opportunity to gather momentum and focus, and get down to business immediately. I dictated an ambitious practice schedule.

"Nine o'clock a.m.: wake-up time," I read from my notebook. "Nine thirty: a healthy breakfast. Ten o'clock: band practice begins."

"Can you book me time to take a shit?" Chris asked. "Mornings are good for me."

I hadn't had to share a room since I was a kid, so there was a bit of an adjustment period. Chris accused us of having poor hygiene habits. And none of us could turn a blind eye to the fact that John was a tireless fart machine.

My mother reacted to the move with her typical generosity, never failing to shower me with enthusiasm and support. But when I really listened to her voice, I could tell she was missing me. So in those first weeks, I tried to call as often as I could, transporting fistfuls of nickels to the pay phone down the street, so as not to abuse my house privileges with Mrs. O'Neill.

"Oh, I miss you, honey," my mom said when she heard my voice. "See you soon, right?"

"I'm going to be up here for a while," I said. "This is the city I know best."

"But . . ." she said jokingly, "what if you break your legs again?"

I laughed. "I'm not going to be drag racing, Mom. I'm going to be singing. I'm probably safe."

Little did I know our first gig in Los Angeles would get a hostile reaction from my own band members that made me fear for my life. It was to take place at an ice rink in Culver City.

"Ladies and gentlemen, WE'RE . . . MICKEY . . . *RATT!*"

Twenty or so fifteen-year-olds with earmuffs stared back at us blankly.

"What the fuck is this, Stephen?" Chris whispered.

"I'm sorry," I said. "But we had to play our first show somewhere."

I tried to be more selective after that, though I firmly believed that it was better to be playing at a venue that you hated than to sit at home and complain about the way that the booking gods had treated you.

"Every gig we get, we get better and better," I insisted. "Plus, there's the money to think about."

"The ice rink only paid a hundred bucks," John said.

"Yeah?" I said. "Well, I didn't see you giving away your share."

We had some serious problems in those early days, one being lack of a steady bass player. Tim Garcia, our main guy down in San Diego, had a baby on the way, and he had decided not to make the trek up. Once in a while he would show up to fill in. Tim was always the guy who remembered every song, every key, every nuance of our set. We relied on him to assist us in the things we couldn't remember.

One evening, we had a show scheduled and he couldn't make it.

"Fuck it," I announced. "*I'll* play bass. We'll go out as a three-piece." I borrowed a Travis Bean bass from a friend of Victor Mamanna's, Victor Stolpey. I was in. I was playing bass.

"Stephen," Chris cautioned, "you can't just pick up the bass and expect to know how to play it."

"Are you kidding me?" I sneered. "How complicated could the bass be? There're only four strings."

To me, the main thing was getting out there to be seen and

heard, not playing perfectly. I was like Steve Martin's Jerk, who sees his name in the phone book and rejoices. *Finally: I'm somebody now!* I just wanted my name in the damn phone book.

"Gig tonight, dudes," I announced, coming home to Mrs. O'Neill's, after a long day of trekking back and forth from café to café, club to club, in my B-210.

"Oh, thank God," said Chris, relieved, as he lay back on his cot. "We need to make some cash—I haven't eaten all day."

"I *told* you guys I'd get us playing before you knew it," I said, shaking my head. "No one ever listens to me. Now, shit, we gotta get our set list ready: We're doing the Bla Bla Café at nine p.m. sharp— and those guys are going to pay us fifty bucks, so we better be *good.*"

We only had half a dozen really good songs, so making a set list was easy.

"Now what?" Chris asked.

"Let's get drunk," I suggested. We pooled together the last of our money and walked down to a Vons market, where we bought a few huge bottles of their cheapest wine. The sun was lowering in the sky.

Chris, John, and I polished off our first bottle in Mrs. O'Neill's garage as we selected our costumes for the night.

"Bring the intern uniforms and the surgical mask for 'Dr. Rock,'" I said. "Just like we did in San Diego!"

"Very cool, very cool," said Chris, his excitement mounting. "Oh, L.A., you're gonna learn *just* how it feels to get fucked!"

"Right on!" yelled John. We piled into the B-210 and took off for the Valley. "There better be *tons* of chicks there."

"There will be," I assured him. "Bla Bla is world-*famous* for its chicks. And these won't be any San Diego country bumpkins, either. We're talking sophisticated *city* girls."

We arrived in the Bla Bla parking lot two hours before the show.

"Fuck," I said. "We're kind of early."

Chris shrugged. "We brought that wine, right?"

We stood around the parking lot, swilling supermarket wine, laughing, growing more and more idiotic as the night grew darker. Meanwhile, the club was almost empty.

"Looks kind of slow tonight," I admitted.

"We'll rock their asses anyway," slurred John.

The time rolled around for Mickey Ratt to rule. We unloaded our gear, hoisted it onto our backs, and made our grand entrance. By this time, a bit of a crowd had congregated. I jumped onstage.

"Hey there, freaky people of the world," I said. "We're Mickey Ratt, and we want to fuck your eardrums tonight. Enjoy."

Immediately, we thrashed into the opening bars of "Dr. Rock." *"You want to take a break,"* I screamed. *"We'd like to take you there."*

John, plastered out of his mind, bashed his drum set with reckless abandon. Chris, a surgical mask strapped around his face, looking like a murderous maniac, began to play his guitar as loudly as humanly possible.

"You want to travel the world," I shrieked, *"I know about these things. . . ."*

As we reached the chorus, we really started to cook. But just then, I opened my eyes and saw the club's proprietor waving his arms desperately.

"STOP!" he shouted. "STOP PLAYING."

Confused, we stopped. We stared dumbly down at him, our instruments still echoing.

"Guys," he said. "I'm so sorry. You're not who we thought you were. You'll have to go home."

"What are you talking about?" I said, still confused.

"You're too loud," the manager explained.

"Are you kidding?"

"We'll still pay you, all right? But you just have to come down off the stage."

I frowned. "How do we know you'll pay us?"

"I promise," said the manager.

"I think we're going to keep on playing until you pay us," I decided. "Chris? John? Let's go!"

We burst back into song as the manager dug furiously in his pocket to find our fee.

"Fucking *totally* embarrassing," Chris mumbled the next day, as we attempted to stave off our terrific hangovers with a grease-laden breakfast of hamburgers, pickles, and eggs.

"At least we got paid, right?"

"They paid us to *stop*."

"Things will get better for Mickey Ratt," I said. "Meanwhile, have some of this delicious meal that I've prepared with money we earned from gigging."

I was ruthless with our schedule, the determined leader of a crack band of musicians. Granted, practice didn't always begin at ten in the morning—or rather, it never did——but we managed to play for several hours almost every single day. We knew we were reaching the correct volume when complaints began to roll in from all the neighbors.

"Egg cartons are the way to go," I told my buddies. "You staple them up to every surface, and you'd be surprised—they work better than professional soundproofing equipment."

Chris eyed me. "Okay, but where are we going to get all those egg cartons?"

"*Victor,*" I said. "I can't believe I didn't think of this before. My old buddy Victor Mamanna works at a meat market, for Christ's sake! If anybody in this city has access to egg cartons, it's him."

Immediately, I hopped into my car and zoomed down to Mamanna's, where I explained my problem to my friend.

"Sure, Pearcy." He laughed. "Go back in the stock room. We got plenty of what you need."

I left my friend's shop that afternoon with great treasures: about a hundred stinky egg cartons, not to mention two heads of romaine lettuce, a pound of pastrami, a pound of sliced ham, two loaves of white bread, and an oval of Muenster cheese, just past expiration.

"I'd eat the cheese by tomorrow morning," Victor advised me, "if I were you."

"I really can't thank you enough."

"Just play your music. You guys are going to be so great."

The next few days were a blinding flash of staple gunning, weed smoking, and purposeful grilled-cheese eating. Our labors complete, we resumed practice, thrashing even harder than before, working tirelessly to extract the maximum amount of power from our instruments. We were working on our band's identity as much as our songs, and, like everyone in the hard rock community at the time, we believed that rebellion, joy, anger, and enthusiasm were all best expressed at full volume.

But not everyone was down for the cause. The force of nature who lived two doors down, Mrs. Schwartz, believed that egg cartons, even those that had been tacked up with true gusto, weren't worth much of a shit when it came to noise insulation. Soon, she sent over her son, a goofy, awkward guy about my age, to investigate.

"Guys, I'm so sorry about this," he pleaded. "But my mom's going nuts. . . ."

I sized him up. An obvious virgin, in desperate need of a blow job. But clearly not a bad guy.

"What's your name, man?" I said, coming over and snaking an arm around his shoulders.

"I'm Phil," he said, grinning hopefully. "Phil Schwartz."

"Well, Phil," I said, friendly as could be, "I'm Stephen Pearcy. And we"—I motioned to the other guys—"are Mickey Ratt."

Phil surveyed the scene for a moment, taking in the tapestries, the drum set, the amplifiers, the microphone stand.

"Are you guys in, like, a *band*?"

I nodded.

"Chris, how about getting a cold beer for Phil, here?"

"Oh, no, thanks. It's a school night," Phil said hurriedly.

"We don't have any beers left, anyway, Stephen. You finished the last one about three hours ago."

"What do you study, man?"

"I'm taking a photography course," said Phil. "No big deal. Just at the community college while I try to figure out what I'm going to do with my life."

"Hey," I said, my eyes narrowing. "We *need* band photos. For publicity purposes."

"Well, I could do that," said Phil. "I wouldn't even charge you or anything."

"This is starting to be very cool, Phil," I said. "This is a very lucky coincidence that we've met—for everyone involved."

Phil smiled, unsure.

"Now, here's what I want you to do," I continued. "Go back to your house and tell your mom that what sounded to her like random, horrible *noise* is actually a promising job opportunity for her son."

"Job?"

"Official band photographer sound good to you?"

"Wow!" said Phil. "Sure does!"

"Then hurry back," I said. "We'd like you to start immediately. We still have a few more hours of practice tonight. This could be a great opportunity for you to squeeze off a few trial shots."

"Right!"

"Oh, and Phil?" I said. "Bring back a couple rolls of toilet paper, okay? We're totally out over here."

They were great days. Nobody knew what the fuck they were doing, yet we were in constant forward motion. We knew it was the right thing to do, not morally, or for reasons of personal growth, but for *the good of the band.* Though I'd sworn I'd never stoop to a level quite this dirty, we needed a new Marshall cabinet, and so, with no other money coming in, I applied for a job at a head shop in Culver City. Three days later, I was appalled to learn that my application had been accepted.

It was a lot to ask of a guy, to toil like a serf in the yuppie wilds of Culver City three times a week, just to bring home a lousy hundred bucks or so. But we had to eat. With pride, I took my first paycheck directly to Victor's, where I bought a bag full of beer and sandwiches.

"Good God, we eat!" Chris yelped. "Great job, Stephen."

He grabbed for a sandwich.

"Wait a minute," I said. "How's *your* job searching going?"

"Pretty good," he said defensively. "I dropped off an application at Toys R Us today. Should hear back soon."

"You gotta be kidding me. A toy store? Dude, that's *embar-*

rassing. You should work at a guitar shop, man. You could talk to the customers about our band. Maybe we'd even find a bass player."

"It's work," Chris said simply.

We were living on the edge, a little too close for comfort. It was exciting as hell, but rubbed our nerves raw. None of us had bank accounts. Multiple times per day, we checked the mailbox, in hopes that one of our parents had sent a letter with a few twenties tucked inside. Mrs. O'Neill offered to feed us, but we felt bashful cadging too many meals from her, seeing as she had yet to charge us a cent for rent. That left girls as our best source for food and gas.

"You are not going to *believe* this," Chris whispered to me, right after we'd pulled off a small gig with some success at Madame Wong's West, in Santa Monica. "I just met a really hot-looking chick."

"Yeah? What's so unbelievable about that?"

"Man, she's a *twin.*"

"Oh," I said casually, my interest mildly aroused. "Is that so?"

"That's not even the best part." He paused dramatically, then shared this: "She works at Cupid's Hot Dogs."

"Sweet God almighty."

Cindy and Stacey, the Hot Dog Twins, came bearing ten-pound packages of frozen hot dogs and endless packets of chili seasoning. They would come over to our garage after work, watch us practice, accompany us in getting shitfaced drunk, and then fuck us. It was a deal that worked out for everyone, except John, our drummer, who was forced to take long, thoughtful walks around the neighborhood during the latter part of those evenings. But then, John ate his fair share of hot dogs. We had him there.

Besides feeding and fucking us, the Hot Dog Twins could be depended on to loan us a little pocket cash so we could fill our cars up.

"Gosh, I owe you a million, Cindy," I said, kissing her absently as she made to go.

"I'm Stacey," she laughed. "But you're welcome."

What would we have done without them? Behind every successful man stands a great woman, but behind every great band? Ten *thousand* women. If you're lucky, that is. I still had my first love, Tina, back in San Diego, but that's exactly where she was: back in San Diego. My heart remained true, while my sexual prowess earned dinner.

My soul was bursting with excitement. I would wake up each morning, smell the odor of Chris's and John's feet, and think to myself, *We're doing it. We're really doing it.* Each moment was packed with potential, for who knew what destiny-turning event might occur in the next day, in the next hour? Persistence had its rewards, and Los Angeles was the place to reap them. It was the land of scumbag opportunity, featuring balding movie executives with actual *phones* in their *cars,* hookers with hearts of fool's gold, and a harsh, bright sun that never knew when to shut off.

"Yet another step in the right direction," I announced one afternoon, returning to our home base after a long day of relentlessly pounding the pavement. "Gentlemen, I just secured us a gig at the Londoneer. We're getting a hundred dollars *and* a portion of the gate."

"The *gate?*" John said. "Uh, isn't that place a tiny café?"

"Look, the point is, we get a buck for every five people we bring in the door."

"We should make two bucks easy," Chris said, grinning. He looked way too pleased, and it set off suspicious bells in my system.

"What the hell are *you* so happy about?" I asked. Then my gaze fell upon the many bags of groceries that covered our floor. I rifled through the brown bags: salamis, grapefruit, pretzels, soda, beer, wine, tall loaves of French bread. The take was enormous.

"Impressed?" Chris asked.

"Who'd you have to fuck to get this?"

"Remember that gig at Toys R Us? I've been working there for almost a week."

I frowned. "Last time I checked, Toys R Us paid $1.75 an hour."

"Yeah, well, I work over in returns."

"So?"

"So, I've been, uh, 'returning' some stuff myself." Chris coughed. "First I steal it. Then I return it."

"You can't do that."

"Oh, absolutely, I can. Works great. And hey, before you get all high and mighty on me, remember those Marshall stacks we've been talking about? Let's make a time to go get them this weekend."

I laughed. "You're evil, dude. Honestly, I didn't think you had it in you."

Chris shrugged. "This is rock and roll, right? The weak have no place here."

I was in no position to argue with that. Immediately, I began to devise more ways to spend Chris's newfound cash. Flashback Threads, located on Sunset in Hollywood, had some way-cool clothes in their storefront windows. It was rumored that a couple of Italian designers were behind their collection. We would start there.

With money in Chris's pockets, we began to gather momentum. A friend of ours from San Diego, Dave Jellison, played bass. We auditioned him in the garage, the Hot Dog Twins watching from the sidelines.

"You can play, sure," I said. "But tell me this: What kind of heads are you working with?"

"Ampeg SVTs," he said. "Four of 'em. You want power? I got what you're looking for."

"I like it," I decided. "You're in."

The pile of equipment behind us onstage grew and grew. Chris and I brought home three Marshall stacks and a bundle of hundred-watt heads.

"Isn't this a little excessive?" Chris wondered. "I'm not so sure we even have room in the garage for all this shit."

"It's excessive. Definitely," I said. "That's the idea."

Soon we were no longer able to cart our gear to and from shows in my Datsun B-210. We enlisted Dennis and Andy Holgwen, both of whom had vans, to come along for the ride as our first roadies. Together we screeched around the city streets at night, snatching folding barricades from in front of open manholes and other sites of municipal construction, painting them black, and stenciling our band's logo on them. I made sure to place them in front of us when we were playing.

"What the hell's the point of *that*?" Dave said.

"Adds to our mystique," I explained.

Our constant drinking and trying to pull chicks in the parking lot before and after every show may have added to our mystique, too; either that, or it made us look like total idiots. But we were having too much fun to give it much thought. That could have been our slogan in those days: *Don't overthink things. Just PLAY. . . .*

We were guided by a shared exuberance, and an incredible amount of luck. One night, after a gig in Riverside, Dennis's van broke down by the side of the highway, forty miles outside of L.A. Every member of our band and crew was shitfaced drunk. No one had money. It was two in the morning. After contemplating for a solid minute, I announced the answer: My B-210 would *push* the two-ton van, from behind. They all called me insane. But somehow, we made it home safely.

"This car is magic," I announced to everyone as we congregated in the O'Neills' driveway, victorious. "Magic, dammit!!"

But I was wrong. It was us. We were the magic.

■ ■ ■

ONE EVENING, AT A BATTLE OF the Bands in Venice, we were approached by two nice Catholic girls who said they loved our sound—Beth Miller and Mellette LeBlanc. Oddly, they didn't seem interested in having sex with us. Instead, they wanted to give advice.

"You should start a mailing list," Beth advised me. "That way, all these potential fans could know when you have your next gig."

"How would one go about doing that?"

"Watch," said Beth. Removing a small notebook from her purse, she began to confidently and professionally approach every paying member of the audience, asking them for their addresses, and writing them down swiftly.

"Impressive," I said.

"I'm just organized," Beth said modestly.

Our team was growing. Mellette and Beth began to attend Mickey Ratt shows regularly. The mailing list swelled to enormous proportions.

"Now, how about flyers?" Beth suggested. "Ever thought about making them?"

"Yeah, I've been meaning to do that!" I cried. "Let me draw something."

That evening, I sat down on my cot in the garage with a fat Sharpie and a piece of white typing paper. Freehand, I drew our first-ever Mickey Ratt logo, adding in my crooked hand all our upcoming dates. The next day, we took it to a copy shop and made hundreds of duplicates. We set aside a pile to fold into thirds, address, and toss in the mail; the rest, we took to the street in the middle of the night, running up and down Santa Monica and Sunset Boulevard with a staple gun, posting our logo everywhere at eye level.

"Fuck, this is *great*!" I shouted.

Beth and Mellette were indispensable to our growth. Right from the very beginning, they made it clear that they were never going to sleep with us. "You guys go through women like tissue paper," Beth admitted. "It's kind of, well, gross." Thus, we were able to shut off that part of our brains around them and treat them as normal human beings.

"Just call us if you ever need us," Beth told me. "We want to help you guys make it."

It was almost too good to be true.

"They're like angels, dude," I told Chris, as we set up our stage show at Madame Wong's East.

"If you say so," Chris said, plugging his guitar in. An hour later, we whipped the Madame Wong's crowd into a frenzy. The posters and the mailing list had worked like a charm: For the first time, an audience appeared to have come to see us on purpose.

"Mickey fucking *Ratt*!" cried one long-haired dude. "You guys are my favorite band. You and the Knack!"

A compliment was a compliment, and I decided to take it. After the show, Chris and I headed to the Troubadour to celebrate and take in a show. We guzzled a bottle of vodka in the parking lot, supplied by a cute little pop tart named Cherry.

"I know about this enormous party tonight," Cherry said. "A couple of friends of mine are house-sitting a mansion in Beverly Hills. You guys want to check it out?"

Chris and I looked at each other. "Will there be more booze there?" I asked.

Cherry looked blank. "I don't see why not."

"Then we'll go," I decided. I swiped the bottle from Chris and poured its remaining contents down my throat.

"All *right*," laughed Chris. We dragged Cherry along with us, staggering happily along the street until we found my Datsun B-210. Chris hopped into the passenger seat and patted his lap.

"I just *love* you guys!" Cherry giggled. She jumped into Chris's lap. Wriggling her butt until she was sitting on the floor, Cherry then twisted around so her knees were on the ground. Her head came to rest in the space between Chris's legs.

"Nice," I said, and I started up the car.

Chris began to receive the tenderest of blow jobs from his new friend Cherry. I pulled out into traffic at 2:30 in the morning—wrong move—weaving across the lanes, the majority of my attention directed to the action going on in the area of the passenger seat.

A horn blared angrily at me. *"What the fuck's wrong with you?"*

"Not a thing," I mumbled softly. "Not a goddamn thing. . . ." I ventured a sly hand onto Cherry's shoulder. She grabbed my crotch.

"Man," moaned Chris. "This girl is something else."

"I'll agree to that." I increased my speed as she unzipped my fly. Some turbulence in the cockpit, but that was cool.

"Hey," said Chris. His tone had changed.

"Yep?" I answered idiotically, my left hand gripping the steering wheel.

"*Stephen*," said Chris, "I think there's a cruiser behind us."

I jolted forward. With a sinking feeling in my stomach, I ventured a glance into my rearview. Red and blue lights flashed.

"Shit shit shit shit shit!" I swerved wildly, pushing my pants upward. "Stop, Cherry! Chris, get your jeans back on. Now!"

Chris grabbed the waist of his jeans and thrust his pelvis in the air. As he did, his crotch caught Cherry's jaw.

"Sorry!" wailed Chris, as he tried to push his dick back between his legs.

I pulled to the side of the road and turned off the engine. Cherry began to sob, from her huddled position.

"Don't worry," I mumbled. "I know how to deal with these guys."

Soon a police officer was tapping on my window.

"License and registration, please."

I smiled pleasantly. "Hello, Officer. How are you doing tonight?"

He didn't smile. "License and registration, please."

"Officer, we could go that route." I tilted my head toward Cherry, crouched on the floor. "Or I can offer you something much, much better."

"*What the fuck!*" hissed Cherry.

"What?" I said. "Well, excuse me for trying. Officer, never mind. I'll get you the paperwork now."

In the end, we got off easy. I got cited for drunk driving, but the car wasn't impounded, and there were no charges of lewd conduct.

We'd been nabbed in rich people's Los Angeles, Beverly Hills, so I got to bunk in the county's nicest drunk tank for a night. It was bearable, even mildly interesting. I learned, for instance, that most people in jail liked to get a lot more wasted than I did. It made for awful breath but great opportunity. When my new buddies passed out and began to snore, I got to steal their cartons of milk. Full belly, everywhere I went.

"Stephen Pearcy?" came the voice. "You made bail."

"Holy shit," I said, grinning. "Just like in the movies. Guys? Hang loose."

Beth was waiting for me on the courthouse steps when I got released.

"Beth!" I said, overjoyed to see her. "You shouldn't have."

She laughed. "What was I going to do? Let you rot in there? Chris told me that you guys got arrested."

"*I* got arrested," I corrected her. "Chris probably got laid."

"Stephen," she said, shaking her head. "What are we going to do with you?"

"Well, it's rock and roll, Beth," I said. "Sooner or later, you gotta do some time."

"You did fourteen hours," she said.

That night, I returned to Mrs. O's garage and passed out. Tomorrow was another day, and I would need my strength. I would need every cell of my being in top working condition, in fact, to continue cementing the legend of Mickey Ratt.

ALL OR NOTHING

BETH MILLER, FRIEND:

I think Stephen was upset that they didn't get their big break faster. He would get mad playing stupid clubs. They did a gig out in the Valley one night and there were about ten people in the audience. He was like, "Whatever. For what it's worth, here's another song." He felt like he was wasting his time with that stuff. He knew he was going to do bigger stuff.

They were always starving, always arguing who was going to take the first shower. There were these condominiums in Marina del Rey that were close, and we would break into them at night and go swimming, use their Jacuzzi, use their weight room. We would have the best time. Stephen, Chris Hager, John Turner, Mellette, and I would spend two or three hours in a Jacuzzi. Stephen would always wrap his head in a towel so his curly locks wouldn't fall out from too much chlorine. That was a big deal.

He was extremely driven and focused—always had that energy and that drive to succeed. Some people never achieve that, don't know how to channel it. And Stephen had it at a very young age. Stephen would never get discouraged. Never! The other guys in the band would sometimes have those moments, questioning whether it would happen, and that was almost sacrilege. You never say that. If you think it, you still don't say it.

If he had any free time, he'd be drawing, doing logos. The Ratt, with the t's blending, that was his design. And he was very into clothes. He knew people who designed and made leather jackets. Everything was leather. Sun's shining, but you gotta wear leather. . . .

He knew a designer with a shop, and we went down there a couple of times, looking at boots, shoes. He would save every ounce of money that he had so he could buy the look. He didn't want to look like a wannabe. He wanted to look like he was there already. And Stephen was so charismatic, he could engage people into doing anything for him. What do you want? A cheeseburger? An outfit? I really should be doing that for you . . . after all, you're you!

There was a great, expensive clothing store in Hollywood called Parachute. The girl who worked behind the counter seemed to have a little thing for me.

"How's the music, Stephen?"

"Pretty cool, Tracy. You should come see us sometime. How's the fashion business? Got any, like, movie stars coming in here?"

"No," she said, gazing at me. "No one interesting ever comes in here. Except for you. . . ."

I hung out with her a little bit, took her to a show or two, and in return, she slipped me some of the latest fashions. Nothing too outrageous or imaginative, not yet: Mostly I wore leather, like Beth said. We weren't really "metal," when it came to how we dressed. In fact, I'd started to think of us as something different altogether. We were Fashion Rock.

"Or maybe our style should be called 'Stun Rock,'" I said to Chris. "What do you think of that?"

Chris didn't care. He was loving life. It was 1981, and he was the lead guitar player of an up-and-coming rock band in L.A. Everyone we encountered seemed to want to be on our team. One guy, who we'd originally encountered in San Diego, made his living breaking into pharmacies. He became one of our best fans. Before shows, we'd meet and shake hands, and he would palm us handfuls of quaaludes and Placidyls. There was a gel inside the pills, and we'd pop a hole in them, then drop them in our beers.

Los Angeles was a town that ran on dreams. For a very long period of time, nearly everyone I met was an up-and-comer, convinced beyond doubt that they were destined to "make it," whether it be as a movie star, an athlete, a dancer, a professional slut, a costume designer, a line producer, a terrible stand-up comic, or a modern artist. As long as there was fame and fortune at the end of the rainbow—or at the Rainbow on Sunset—young Angelenos would do anything short of murder to get there. It wasn't nearly enough to have talent or physical beauty. Everyone had those. You had to be ruthless.

For months, we gave our all at frustratingly small shows at tiny cafés and clubs. Finally I got fed up and vowed to stop dealing, once and for all, with the small potatoes.

"It's just not worth it," I complained to Beth. "Nobody gives a shit if we played the Bla Bla Café. Why should they? I hardly care myself. We need to get some attention, and to start building a real fan base."

"What did you have in mind?" she said.

"The Whisky," I said simply. "When a band plays the Whisky, that's when you know they've made it. That's where I saw Van Halen play, right before they got signed."

"You may not be *quite* ready to get the Whisky gig just yet," Beth said.

"Well, fine," I said. "You're right. We're not quite there. But here's the thing: There's a *system* to the Strip. You go up the ladder, one club at a time."

"Makes sense to me," Beth said. "So—what's just below the Whisky?"

"The Troubadour," I said. "But we probably can't get in there, either."

"Who's below the Troubadour?"

"Maybe the Roxy," I said, thinking. There was a long silence. "And I don't think we can get in there, either."

Beth clucked. "Poor Stephen. Is there any place that's, well . . . entry-level?"

I thought for a moment, then broke out in a huge smile. I had it. "Gazzarri's."

Gazzarri's was a key part of the Sunset Strip. Located only a block or so down the street from the Whisky, just past Doheny on Sunset, it had a cheap cover, a dedicated crowd, and about eight different stages. A different band would play every hour, every evening of the week. Best of all, it was where Van Halen had got their start before graduating to the Whisky. And as always, if it was good enough for Dave and Eddie, it was good enough for me.

The proprietor of the club was Bill Gazzarri, an old mobster-looking guy with white hair and a fedora pushed back on his head. He spoke in a hoarse voice.

"What the hell do ya want, kid?"

"Just to play your club," I said, laughing. "You got the best place on the Strip, Bill. *You* know that, right?"

"Sure, I know that! It's my damn club. Now, what's the name of your band? Mickey what? Mickey fucking Mouse?"

"Mickey Ratt."

"Mickey fucking *Ratt*?" he choked. "Really great. Sounds huge. Yeah, I don't know, kid. We're full up this week. Maybe you should come talk to me next week."

"Okay, I'll do that, Bill."

"Nice fucking outfit, by the way. You're sweating your balls off, right? But the little chickies go for it, so it's worth it? I get it."

I was relentless in pursuing Bill Gazzarri—he was the deer in my crosshairs. Every afternoon, when I knew he was counting his money or sniffing up the skirts of the young girls who worked in his front office, I'd come by to pester him. Eventually, I began to wear down his resistance.

"Fuck, Stephen, you're not going to go away, are you?"

"No," I said. "Bill, just give us a chance, and we will pack this club."

He looked at me for a long time. Then he spoke.

"You'll pack it on a fucking Tuesday night, that's when you'll pack it."

"Are you serious?" I cried, unable to believe my ears. "You're going to let us play?"

"Yeah, why not. Stage eight. Seven o'clock. Go talk to Cathy. She'll book ya."

"Holy shit," I said. "This is . . . amazing."

"Don't get that fucking excited, kid. We ain't paying you." He laughed a hoarse guffaw. "See ya Tuesday."

So we were in. We'd made it onto the Strip, on the bottom rung of the ladder. But it was a pretty fantastic rung. Gazzarri's had history, and not just with Van Halen: The Doors had gotten their start there. Tina Turner had played their main stage. So had Sonny and Cher. We were in the big time now, clad in leather pants and custom-made shoes, dragging mountains of amps and homemade risers and idiotic hand-painted barricades. Never mind that we were still too broke to buy our own drinks when we performed. Some admirer would rise to the occasion. Or we could take matters into our own hands and smuggle in a few warm six-packs inside an empty guitar case.

I'm not sure how it always seemed to work out that we had the money to pay for supple Italian leather pants and nickel-plated microphone stands, and yet still not have the cash to buy a beer at full bar price. But that's how it went. I enjoyed trying to get drunk for free. I played that game every day. Same with eats. Victor Mamanna was still working at his dad's meat market. He could always be depended on to slide me the odd hunk of pastrami.

I accepted the sandwiches graciously. "Vic. Thank you."

"Not a problem. We were going to give it to the dog, but I'd rather feed a rock star."

Something was *happening*. I could sense it. We were manufacturing our mystique, and even if they didn't consciously know it, the people around us could sense we were going places. Right next door to Mamanna's market stood a small grocery store. I peered into the window: A young, dark-haired guy was working alone. I stepped in through the door, ready to push my luck.

"What's up, man?" I said.

"Hell, not much," he answered. "What are you up to?"

"Getting a free case of beer from you," I said, deadpan. "And maybe a bag of ice."

The young guy broke into laughter. "Are you out of your fucking mind?"

"No," I said earnestly. "I'm in a band."

"Fuck, I must be crazy," said the kid, "but yeah, why not? Listen, go around back. I'll toss some shit out the back door to you. I want to get into one of your shows—can you do that for me?"

"Gazzarri's," I said, smiling. "Tonight."

The kid's name was Joe Anthony. He was from Tulsa, Oklahoma, and was a black belt in tae kwon do. That night, at the show, he revealed his deepest secret to me.

"I'm not working at a fucking grocery for the rest of my life." He picked up someone else's cocktail and drained it. "I'm in training to be a stuntman."

"A stuntman?" My mind refused to hear a tidbit like that and not try to figure out how I could turn it to my own advantage. "Forget that. You should be a *bodyguard*. I'm glad we met. Now, when I need security, I'll know who to call."

"Security?" Joe laughed. "Hey, how's that pay?"

Momentum, the most magical elixir in the entire universe, was upon us. We had it, and the other fuckers didn't, and that was that. Mickey Ratt was still an underground phenomenon, but in my mind, it was just a matter of time before we got huge. Los Angeles in the summer of '81 was all abuzz with Dodger fever; lost in a cloud of self-involved musical obsession, I wouldn't have gone to a game if you paid me. The entire east side was a mystery to me. My world was the Strip. And like a gambler beginning the hottest of streaks, I was just starting my run.

We played Gazzarri's every night. Soon we graduated to stage seven, and then to stage six. On a Thursday evening, we might pull fifty people into the club for a show, but that was just the beginning of the party. The Strip was like Woodstock for people who hated hippies. Armies of pretty girls wobbled drunkenly in their fuck-me high heels and black microminiskirts. Tit-hugging spandex tops showcased their perky little boobs, their glitter-covered skin moist with sweat and excitement and sex. Once you got the girls inside the club, all they wanted to do was snort something and fuck, in that order.

"Stephen," Bill Gazzarri shouted, "I'm having a big dance contest tonight. I want you to be one of the judges. How about that? You got time for that?"

"Sure," I said. "What do I have to do?"

"You watch a bunch of chicks take off most of their clothes and dance to some music. Then decide who has the best tits. What the fuck did you think it was?"

It was a very good time to be young and in heat. I judged the Miss Gazzarri contests as honestly as I knew how, and even though a few bribes may have been accepted here and there, I also tried to make myself available after the show to explain my ruling to the women who were not selected.

"Your moves are stunning," I told one fourth-place finisher. "I would just say, work on your expressions."

"Thanks," she said. "Want to go into the bathroom with me and talk about it more?"

Hollywood in 1981 was a pre-AIDS trimfest. Period. You didn't have to be slick, you didn't have to be good-looking. You just had to be *there*. I saw so many people fuck on the lawns behind Gazzarri's that I actually got bored of watching and started to throw empty beer cans at them. Michael Sweet, the lead singer of Roxx Regime, a band that often played Gazzarri's on the same evenings we did, chided me.

"They're having their fun," he said. "Leave 'em alone."

"But I'm *drunk*," I explained. "That means I can do what I want."

Sweet was right, but I refused to take advice on how to behave myself from a dude whose main fashion innovation to date was dressing his band in black and yellow. They looked like glammed-out bumblebees onstage. The Pittsburgh Steelers of rock.

Later, the Regime's emphasis would shift, and their lyrics would transubstantiate. They would become the famous Christian rock band Stryper. But for the moment, they were as fucked-up as the rest of us and absolutely loving every minute of it. Michael Sweet was no stranger to drama. He was always engaged in enormous fights with his sensationally sexy blond girlfriend, who had a weird shtick of constantly wearing a teddy bear attached to her belt. One night, after yet another explosive confrontation, he approached the microphone to begin his first song. A hush fell over the crowd when silently, in a gesture of pure and total penitence, his girlfriend walked onstage and laid the teddy bear at the base of his mic stand.

The pungent smell of marijuana was on every street corner. On Friday and Saturday nights, you might not play until ten, but if you were smart, you'd get to the Strip at four and start handing out flyers, to start getting the name "Mickey Ratt" moving on everyone's lips. Great White was getting popular, too, though in those days, they called themselves Dante Fox. And of course, W.A.S.P. and Mötley Crüe. Mötley was always about two steps ahead of us. One day we were destined to meet.

Gil Turner's Liquor Store was the place to get your booze, and if you wanted to chow down, the Rainbow was the only place to go. It was the spot where you had the best chance of running into other up-and-coming musicians, some of them legitimately famous.

"Let's do the Strip tonight, Beth," I said. "Come on. Are you with me?"

"It's *Monday*, Stephen," Beth groaned. "No one will be up there. What's the point?"

"Beth, Beth. Come on, don't be lazy. I'll meet you at the Rainbow. I'm buying, so bring your appetite."

We met outside the Rainbow at eight o'clock.

"Do you have a table in the kitchen?" I asked hopefully. The true rocker tables were in the kitchen. Everyone knew that.

We were seated, and not five minutes later David Lee Roth walked in with Ozzy Osbourne.

"Watch this," I said to Beth, rising from my seat.

"Stephen," she whispered. *"Don't."*

"Dave!" I called out, confidently. "What's going *on*, my man?"

I had no fear that he wouldn't remember me, or wouldn't want to talk to me. I had all the momentum in the world behind me. Everything was in a flow.

"Stephen," he said after a second, laughing. "My man. Mickey *Ratt*. Love that freaking name."

"Thanks, bro," I said. I extended a hand to the legend who accompanied him. "Hi. I'm Stephen. This is Beth."

"Hello," said Ozzy, his eyes goggling.

"Would you two care to join us?" Beth suggested.

"Why not?" said Dave. We scooted over and made room for them. It was Monday night, family night. It felt real cozy in the booth. When the waiter came, we all ordered chicken soup.

"Best chicken soup I've ever had," Ozzy commented.

There was no vodka swilling that night, nobody getting laid, nobody sniffing blow off the countertops or heading off to the bathroom in groups of eight to do God knows what. The hot topic of the night, instead, was aerobics classes.

"I *love* 'em!" announced Dave. "You think it comes natural? Me jumping around the stage like that? *Hell* no! I owe it all to my classes. I'm even getting *this* dude to come with me tomorrow."

"I'm despising the decision already," said Ozzy. He blew gently on his soup. "I'm awfully fat, you see."

Beth and I drank it all in. Every so often, we'd shoot unbelieving glances at one another, as if to make sure the other one understood just how stupendous this moment was. *Okay, deep breath. We're sharing a table at the Rainbow with Ozzy Osbourne. Let's make sure we appreciate this exact moment. Because everything we ever dreamed about is starting to come true.*

I was getting more and more confident every day, to the point of approaching cocky. One morning, I dressed myself in my sharpest rocker outfit, leathers from head to toe, and knocked on the Schwartzes' front door. Phil's mother answered, clad in a blue bathrobe.

"Yes? What is it?"

"I need to speak to Phil," I demanded. "Your son."

A minute later, the young Schwartz came bobbing out. "Stephen, how's it going?"

"Phil, you said you were going to be our official band photographer. You *promised*."

"What?" he said, confused. "I know, but, I never heard anything else from you. . . ."

"Phil, don't make excuses, it'll just make it worse. Now, we've got a gig tonight, and I'd really like you to be there to document it. Can I count on you?"

"Of course, I mean, all you had to do was ask—"

"Oh, you want money? Well, we don't have any. We'll pay you in beer. And tell you what, if I find some little groupie who's in need of some loving, I'll make sure to send her your way. How's that sound to you?"

"Well, *yeah*," Phil said, his neck growing scarlet. "It sounds good, if you really think she'd even want to talk to me. . . ."

Phil came to the gig that night. He snapped off ten rolls of pictures and even got in a few ass squeezes. We got the shots back a week later. The kid had world-class talent. It was uncanny. We could simply do no wrong.

Then my luck came to a screeching halt. Several months before, Tina, my first love, had moved to New York to pursue her modeling dreams. We'd managed to keep up a fairly regular stream of phone conversations, until one day, I noticed that she had somehow stopped calling me back.

Was she *dumping* me? The thought hit me like a punch to the stomach. I had to talk to her, had to tell her that I loved her. Granted, I hadn't always been faithful to her, but in my heart of hearts, I'd cared deeply about her—I'd always just assumed she *knew*. I called her house in San Diego, the tears beginning to flow.

"Can you tell Tina to call me?" I pleaded. "This is Stephen. It's an emergency."

"You have her number," her father said. "And she's got yours."

I hung up the phone and immediately fell into a full-blown panic. How could I have been such a selfish idiot? I was losing the only woman I'd ever cared about. I had to get to New York. But how? I wondered. I had fourteen greasy dollars to my name.

"Chris," I said. "I need some of that Toys R Us loot. Pronto. It's an emergency."

"Wish I had some to give you," Chris said. "They're onto me, man. Yesterday they moved the assistant manager over to returns."

Desperate, I sped over to the head shop. "I need a two-week advance," I demanded.

My boss laughed in my face. "Steve," she said, "you call in sick half the time. When you show up at all, you're hours late. I'll be honest: Lately, I've entertained the notion of letting you go."

I scanned her face for any sign of sympathy. There was none. "So, no advance?"

Her eyes darkened. "No."

"Fine. You know what? I'm out of here. I quit!"

"We accept your resignation," she said calmly.

I sped furiously back to the garage, racking my brain for a solution. Short of selling sperm or blood, though, I had only one salable resource to my name. My Marshall stacks.

"I'm sorry, my darlings," I told them. "I never, ever wanted it to come to this."

It was like cutting off a part of me and putting it up on the auction block. But I had no choice in the matter. Sweating, I pried my best cabinet from the corner of the garage, hefted it up on my shoulder, and dumped it into the backseat of the B-210, determined to try my luck at the neighborhood's best used-music-equipment store.

"Yeah, I don't know," said the long-haired, bespectacled clerk. "Looks pretty good, I guess. Tell you what, I'll give you three hundred for it."

"Three hundred??" I said, outraged. "Eddie Van *Halen* used this cabinet at the San Diego Sports Arena! Dude, this cab is *cherry. . . .*"

"Jesus, all right," said the guy. "Three-fifty. Will that do? Don't have a heart attack, man."

I boarded the airplane with a tiny bag of clothes—my coolest ones, naturally—and a stomach full of cold fear. I had never been to New York before. Aside from the drag-racing event with Walt in Indianapolis, I hadn't seen much of America.

"Could I get you something to drink?" a sexy stewardess asked me.

"Yes, how much is a beer?" I asked, fingering the few bills I had left in my wallet.

"For you," she whispered huskily, "nothing . . ."

"No, I'll pay," I snapped. No more bathroom blow jobs for Steve! No, this trip—this very *moment*, in fact—would mark the beginning of my adult life. My faithful life. Visions of me and Tina, house-bound, with critters and rug rats, smooching on some boring beige living-room couch in the suburbs, flashed across my brain. *A one-woman man, that's me. . . .*

That weekend in New York turned out to be the most painful, lonely, wretched stretch of days I'd ever experienced in my entire life. Upon arriving, I wandered around the bleak city, confused and lost, freaked out by the towering buildings and the speeding, honking yellow cabs. What the hell was SoHo? Would I know it when I saw it? Manhattan was damp and cold and ominous. It was late evening when I finally found my way to the address Tina had given me months before. A tall girl answered the door. She gave me an amused once-over and then broke the news.

"Tina's not here."

"What do you mean, she's not here?"

"Exactly what I said," she said. "She's gone."

"As in, she doesn't *live* here anymore?" I peeked behind her. "Are you sure?"

"Look, come on in if you don't believe me. See for yourself."

She wasn't there, but her roommate sent me to a cocktail party in full swing where I might find her. Thirty or so glamorous models and fashion-industry people mingled, drinking and flirting. Normally it would have been a dream come true for me. These people were successful and smart, and they worked in an industry I admired. But I was sweaty and out of breath, and not feeling myself at all. I looked around for a while, but there was no Tina.

My plane wasn't leaving until Monday morning. I wandered until I went back to her apartment. I stretched out flat on my back. *So this is what a broken heart feels like,* I mused, surprised at the extent of the pain. *Wow, I'm really not a fan.*

Other guys might have used it for artistic fuel, writing an album's worth of sad songs that night. I just lay there, feeling my heart closing up.

"How was the weekend in the big city, man?" Chris asked. "Worth that Marshall cabinet?"

"Fuck no," I said, tired. "Let's not even talk about it, man. It's over."

Mickey Ratt continued on, destination unknown.

■ ■ ■

"LISTEN," CHRIS SAID ONE DAY. "I'VE been thinking about doing my own thing."

"You *what?*" I said, genuinely stunned.

"Going my own way, man," he said. "Musically, that is. I'm not knocking Mickey Ratt. I just feel like I need to explore my own artistic vision. You've got such strong opinions, Stephen, and that's great. I just have a few of my own, you know?"

First Tina, and then Chris? I was completely rattled. My whole world was crumbling around me. Chris and I talked it over for a while, and we agreed to part ways, though we vowed to stay close friends and offer each other support. And just like that, Mickey Ratt had no lead guitarist.

John, our drummer, hung out for a while, but every other member of my band deserted the ship. When Dave Jellison, our bass player, put down his instrument and went to go work for Van Halen as their lighting technician, I was the only member of Mickey Ratt left standing. Lesser men might have given up right then and there. But the callous jilting gave me strength and determination. *No one is going to take my dream away from me. I didn't move here to fail. I moved to L.A. to make it. . . .*

On New Year's Eve 1982, I gobbled a handful of Valiums, chased them down with a beer, and headed out to the Troubadour to mingle. This would be *my* year, I decided. A slutty brunette with blue eye shadow edging up to her temples flashed me a sultry look; ten minutes later, we were slobbering all over each other in the back corner of the Troubadour parking lot. *It's all or nothing*, I thought, rocking back and forth into her squishy tan thighs. *Rock glory or bust.* The party was still Ratt 'n' rolling.

The next day, nursing the most brutal hangover of my life to date, I recruited four Southerners, new in town, to audition for the band.

"Mickey *Rayutt*?" one sneered. "Ah don't understand that at *all*."

"Actually," I said, my head splitting with pain, "the name of the band is now 'M. Ratt.'"

"Mickey" was yesterday's news: too soft, too cutesy. It was time to put away childish things. "M" had more pithiness to it— more mystery. The Southerners decided to join up. Soon they could be found dragging their lackadaisical asses to practice sessions in Mrs. O's garage. Instantly, our sound changed, transforming from that of a hard-edged, dramatic, flesh-eating shark to that of a soft, trippy rock quintet. Secretly, I couldn't stand the way we sounded, but I didn't have a choice. I had to keep myself out there at all costs.

"I don't get it," Bill Gazzarri said to me. "So you guys are now 'M. Ratt'?"

"As of now," I said, "yes."

"Son, make up your fucking mind," Bill said. "Our audience ain't that bright. We don't want to confuse them."

The new moniker was a little awkward, I had to admit, and not particularly catchy. Sensing I was close, I decided to drop the *M* completely, rechristening the band "Ratt." It was a mature, leaner, meaner name—more adult, harder hitting, and finally fitting for the new image that I wanted strutting around the streets. I also wanted to create a logo for Ratt to look like the one for the band Kiss.

"Ah still don't really care for the name," admitted one of my new guys. "I mean, a *rayutt*? That's a despised animal, man."

"You're fired," I said. "Thank you for all your hard work."

So I was back on my own again. But that didn't last for long: I was too determined, and too connected in the music scene to stay solo for long. Matt Thorr and Jake E. Lee, two talented young musicians from San Diego who had recently made the move up to Los Angeles, were looking for stardom themselves. I let them know exactly where they could find it.

"Hey, I remember *you*!" said Jake. "You were the guy from Straight Ahead Sound. My band Teaser would play with you."

"Yep."

"Well, let's see how we sound together."

Those guys weren't the only members of the San Diego music mafia who'd decided to come up to Los Angeles. Everyone, it seemed, had made the move, from Aircraft, to Seagull, to Teaser, to good old Robbin Crosby.

"How's Phenomenon?" I asked him, when our paths finally crossed.

"Phenomenon is no more," said Robbin, sadly. "But I got a new band, Mac Meda, and we're hot as can be. You were right: Nothing's happening down there in San Diego. I guess we all kinda came to our senses a couple of months ago and decided to get serious."

"I don't want to say I told you so," I said. "But I did."

Robbin grinned. "Stephen Pearcy, always ahead of the game. How's this place treating you?"

"Up and down," I said.

Robbin and I hung out and talked for several hours. He was excited to be in town. But more than that: He was excited to be alive. His unrelentingly positive energy reminded me that you didn't necessarily have to claw your way to the top.

"Hey," I said, feeling generous, "Gazzarri's is practically my second home. We've done at least fifty shows there. I mean, we're more or less the house band. You want me to talk to Bill for you? See if he'll give you guys a shot up on stage eight?"

"Seriously, man?" Robbin said. "Would you do that?"

"Consider it done."

Mac Meda imploded soon after that, and Robbin was left without a group.

"Come jam with us," I said. "Bring that ax up onstage."

"Really?"

"Yeah, really."

And I still remember that first night we played together up onstage. Robbin Crosby was a killer, no doubt about it. Just up there, sweating, growling, a six-foot-four blond oak tree, slobbering all over his new guitar like it was some chick, and every woman in the audience groaning with heartsick desire over the very sight of him, laughing, one hundred percent rock star, riding the crest of our music like it was a cold ocean wave.

And I just had this feeling: He was gonna be our guy.

THE GLADIATORS

THE NEW RATT HAD sex appeal. With Jake on guitar and Robbin coming in to jam, I knew we were onto something special. The drunken cupcakes who packed the Strip couldn't get enough of us. Night after night, they stretched their trembling arms toward the stage and called out our name.

Gazzarri's began to bore me. Too easy. I knew the place so well, I could walk around blindfolded and not bump into a single wall. I wanted to keep climbing.

The Troubadour was the next logical spot. I met Doug Weston, the owner, a flamboyantly gay man who wanted me around for more than booking my band, which I wasn't going for. Book my band, and that's all you're going to book. I fed him a superb line of bullshit, one that would make a used car salesman proud.

"Ratt has a new philosophy of heavy metal."

"Oh yeah? What's that?"

"Slay, steal, pillage, fuck, inspire twenty-chick orgies, all that good stuff," I explained. "But in a classy sort of way, no devil worship."

"Gee," he said, looking dubious. "I don't know."

"Look, man," I said, "we'll bring so much ass into your club that you'll have to look sideways to see anything else."

"Sideways, huh? Well, I've got a slot next Monday night for an opener. Would ten work for you?"

"*That's* what I'm talking about," I said.

Inspired by the new location and a bigger, crazier audience, Ratt was agitated, ready to tear into some flesh. I laid down the guitar, and for a time, I missed it, but whenever I listened to Jake, I never thought twice about picking it up again. Jake E. Lee had moves that not even Eddie Van Halen could duplicate. He had no whammy bar. And yet, his guitar whammied out all the time. It was uncanny. (Warren DeMartini would eventually become Jake E.'s roommate and learn all his riffs and solos, which he would incorporate into Ratt.)

"Jake's like that Jeff Beck guy," I whispered to Robbin. "He must have sold his soul to Lucifer to get those chops."

"Can I make the same deal?" Robbin said, looking on enviously.

A pack of hard-core, truly psychotic fans began to crawl out of the woodwork. Before long, we had our own Ratt army. The soldiers came to our shows, babbled about us to their friends, and passed out our flyers with demented determination. After one packed Troubadour show, a member of our new street team smashed a flyer right into the palm of some freak dressed in full military gear. I took a closer look. It was Chris.

He and I stared at each other.

"What the hell . . . are you wearing?" I said, finally.

"Well, I started a new band," Chris said, somewhat embarrassed. "We're called Sarge. It's military-themed."

I looked him up and down, observing the green khakis, army boots, and close-cropped hair.

"It's the same old rock and roll," Chris explained. "Just, like, in camouflage."

"So, how's that going for you?"

"Well, so far, not too many converts," Chris admitted, "but hell, at least we're trying."

Ratt kicked ass at the Troubadour several times in succession, and a buzz grew quickly. One evening, the top dogs in town came down to take a look: Mötley. Tommy Lee, Vince Neil, Mick Mars, and Nikki Sixx had been famous on the Strip since day one. They were four charismatic fucks who wore huge heels and leathers and tights when they played their offensively huge, cartoonish stage shows. They had a solid reputation for drunken, lewd behavior, and their whole vibe was based on the implicit understanding that they'd sock you in the face as soon as look at you. I respected their look and dug their music, but was prepared to do battle with them.

"Dude," Nikki said warmly after the show. "You guys are fucking *good.*"

I'd expected them to be competitive pricks, but instead, every member of their band was cool. Far from seeking to exclude us or humiliate us, they just wanted to be our buddies. Tommy and Nikki and Vince lived right up the street from the Whisky, in a shitty apartment building that was full of trash, hangers-on, discarded pizza boxes, puddles of half-dried puke, ripped leather jackets, trashed leggings, broken sunglasses, overturned ashtrays, and irregular brown spots on the wall that were as equally likely to have been blood from someone's busted lip, Jack Daniel's from a drunkenly thrown bottle, or the smeared remains of some dog shit.

Anything went at the Mötley House—though boozing, screaming, fighting, snorting, and fucking would sum it up pretty faithfully, too.

"It's krell time, baby," Robbin called out after one show, looking down happily at the fat line of cocaine that had appeared magically out of some chick's purse. "Stephen, come on over here and take your medicine."

"Nah, no thanks. Not in the mood."

"Dude, suit yourself," Robbin laughed, returning his attention to the mirror they'd pulled down off the wall. "It's all good. I refuse to force you."

The Mötley House sucked you in like quicksand. When they threw a party, chicks just poured in, tirelessly wedging their way inside like termites and roaches, jamming through the doorframe with twelve-packs of beer hoisted overhead. Up-and-coming rock dudes dove in through the windows and sprinted to the bathroom, where they pulled down their jeans, banged drugs into the nearest vein, and passed out cold on the crapper. More than once when I was in their house, I merely blinked my eyes twice and returned to consciousness three days later, sprawled out facedown on the living-room carpet.

"Holy shit, what the fuck happened?" I groaned, emerging from one particularly awful party coma.

"You got *laid*, Pearcy!" Tommy told me. "Congratulations, dude."

"Huh?" My head was ready to explode. Each word spoken felt

like a thudding, detonating A-bomb. I massaged my genitals gently: They were swollen and raw. "Where . . . did she go?"

"Oh, she took off, man! Right around the time you started to blow chunks." He sniffed my collar, in his friendly manner. "Yeah, you smell ridiculous, bro!"

Mick, although a hell of a sweet guy, was more reclusive, and Vince was sort of lost in his own universe. Robbin and I were closest with Tommy and Nikki, and we started tripping around with them frequently. Robbin, particularly talented at making up nicknames, soon gave Nikki the title Leader Sixx, apt for the man who'd created the Mötley mystique.

"I'm fucking *Leader Sixx*!" he bellowed, scaring two little wide-eyed rocker preteens who walked the Strip, their hair carefully styled. They jolted with fright. "Do as I *say*!"

Tommy was now Duke. Vince was Sergeant of Arms.

"He's Leader, but I'm the Duke, huh?" Tommy said sadly. "No one respects the drummer. Always the same."

I became Ratt Patrol Leader, or else they'd call me Felix.

"Felix?" I said. I took a swig from my open beer can as we walked the packed Strip, shoulder to shoulder, gawking at all the chicks, pushing flyers into people's chests with tireless dedication and obnoxious swagger. "Dude, why?"

"Don't question it," Robbin said. He stopped in his tracks to stare down a gorgeous chick in a red miniskirt. "Live with it."

Nikki ended up giving Robbin the nickname King. And it was just so perfect. It became his name for life. Nobody called him Robbin after that—it was always King.

"We're like a fucking gang!" Robbin shouted. "We're the *Gladiators*!"

"Shit, yes!" I yelled, getting into the spirit of things and tossing my stack of flyers into the air. They fluttered down all around us, a snowstorm on the dirty Hollywood street.

"Right on, King," Nikki agreed. "If you say so, we're the Gladiators."

Robbin was everyone's favorite, but he was truly my musical brother, accessory to all my Ratt crimes. We schemed at great length and with unbridled enthusiasm about complicated and devious plans for fame and fortune. Robbin was there for me when any emergency arose, and soon one did. One night at the Troubadour, Jake and I got into it, embarking upon a screaming match that soon evolved into a spiteful resignation speech. He was leaving the band.

"I'm going with Ronnie Dio," he spat. "He's a *pro*. I'm outta here."

Dio, a mild-mannered Brit managed by his wife, Wendy, was a decent man, one of the nicest rockers on the planet. But his brand of hard rock was a weird fantasy blend that somehow always returned to goofy man-on-a-silver-mountain themes.

"Fine," I snapped. "Enjoy your Dungeons and Dragons."

Jake departed, and immediately I fell into a catastrophic funk as I attempted to envision Ratt without its resident guitar god.

"Dude, we'll be *fine*," Robbin consoled me, a strong arm around my shoulders.

"No, we won't," I said, shaking my head. "We're done for, man. I'll never find anyone who can play as good as Jake. He was one in a million."

"Come on, Stephen," Robbin said patiently. "You'll see. We'll rebuild."

This was true, but first, we'd fall completely to shit. One week later, Matt Thorr dropped his own atomic missile on my ego and our band.

"I hate to do this to you, bud," he said. "But we're leaving."

Our drummer stood behind him, his arms crossed. "We're starting our own band," Matt said. "We're going to call ourselves Rough Cutt."

"Good luck," I said bitterly. "Hope you make it. You don't even have a lead guitarist."

"Yes, we do," he said quietly. "Chris."

I couldn't believe my own ears. But it was true. Sarge was a casualty, their army fatigues never quite catching on with the drugs-and-vodka-fueled Sunset Strip crowd. Now Hager was joining up with the enemy.

The situation looked bleak: I had paying gigs scheduled, but no members in my band. Only Robbin stood by me. This was our make-or-break moment. And I wasn't going down without a fight.

"Let's fucking *steal* people," I said to Robbin.

"Ratt is in attack mode," he assured me.

We assembled a skeleton crew to get us through the next few gigs, swooping up the bass player from Teaser and a hyper local Los Angeles sticksman with a bizarre Rod Stewart haircut who could barely see out over the edge of his own colossal drum kit—but our guns were aimed on bigger targets. At a show in Anaheim, we shared a bill with a La Jolla band. Their lead guitarist was a skinny, wispy young dude who went by the name of Warren DeMartini. The kid had no "look" whatsoever. In fact, he resembled someone's younger brother who'd managed to sneak up onstage. But minutes into their set, you could tell this was no mistake. The boy could grind.

"You should come up and hang out sometime," I told Warren casually.

"Hang out?" he said.

"You know," Robbin broke in, flashing the movie-star grin that had parted a thousand female legs. "Audition."

We weren't just making idle promises—Ratt had gigs locked in at the Troubadour, and any aspiring musician had to respect that. Warren showed up at the garage a week later, and the young lad promptly rocked our faces off. We wanted him badly, and I told him as much. With a few well-placed ego boosts from Robbin, he was in. He was only supposed to show up for one day, but he never left.

"Now drums," I told Robbin.

"Go."

We auditioned a host of drum warriors, all of whom could hit the skins well enough, but nobody made much of an impression on me until a ruddy blond Ozzy Osbourne look-alike named Bobby Blotzer crossed our paths.

"Man," I said, squinting at him. "I feel like I *know* you from someplace. . . ."

"You probably saw me with Vic Vergat, my old band," Blotzer said. "We've been on TV a few times."

"No, that's not it. . . ."

"Well, we just toured Europe. Say, do you ever make it over there?"

"No, that's not it either," I said. "Dude, this is really odd, but I'm going to ask anyway—have you ever met a guy named Dennis O'Neill?"

"Oh, *yeah!*" said Bobby, his face lighting up. "Hey, I remember *you!*"

As it turned out, Bobby and I had met briefly a few years earlier, through my old friend Dennis. Bobby's girlfriend had been sharing an apartment with Dennis's main squeeze and another chick I used to pull in every now and then.

"Sure, I remember you." Bobby laughed. "That chick you used to bang was so damn hot! Except she had a missing finger, right? She was like Jerry Garcia, man!"

"I never minded the finger!" I cried, "I always said: I'll take her!"

Bobby sat down and played for us. Immediately, it became clear that he was head and shoulders above the rest of the dudes. He clearly had a fat ego to go along with his talent, but Robbin and I were committed to getting a good rhythm section for the band, and we told him so.

"Join us," I commanded.

But Bobby Blotzer was not so easily convinced. Having recently been relieved of his duties with Vic Vergat, he had his sights set on another band.

"They're called Bruiser, guys," he informed us. "And they *rock*."

I had a soft spot in my heart for all bands that rocked, of course, but I'd decided that Bob was our guy, and I'd be damned if any other band was going to lure him away.

"We have gigs," I reminded him. "Solid dates. Big crowds. Can Bruiser say that?"

After a few weeks, Blotzer came to his senses.

"All right, I'll play for you," he sighed, like it was a favor. "And by the way, if you're looking for a bass player, I know a good one."

"Oh yeah?" I said. "Who's that?"

"His name's Juan Croucier. He plays for my best friend, Don Dokken." Bob thought for a moment. "Let's steal him."

Robbin and I fell into step with no hesitation. When Dokken played their next gig at the Roxy, we dressed in our finest threads and made the scene.

"How about letting me in for free?" I asked the pretty girl taking tickets, giving her my best charming grin. "I'm in a band, Ratt."

"Never heard of you," she said, bored. "That'll be five bucks, please."

"I always tell them I'm in Iron Maiden," said Robbin, laughing. "Try it, it works."

With bellies full of booze, we pushed our way to the front of the crowd, spotting the curly-haired Cuban playing the bass.

"He's good," I said, after a moment. Juan Croucier played with confidence, and he had impeccable timing. His backup vocals were strong. "Damn good."

"Yes, I know," said Robbin, frowning. "But those cowboy boots he's wearing, aren't they . . . ?"

"Cow-patterned," I finished for him. It was true. They were leather moo-boots. But we could fix that, unlike talent.

With Blotzer firmly in our corner, we went after Juan with both barrels, giving him the hard sell. It was another tough one, though, because Dokken already had a deal. They were already in the process of recording an album.

"Look, I like you, but you guys aren't signed," said Juan simply.

"But we're *going* to be," I promised. "Give us a try. If you don't like it, you can always quit." Everyone else always had.

Juan agreed to give it a shot, at least temporarily. And just like that, we had created the Ratt nucleus that the world would eventually come to know: me, Robbin, Warren, Juan, and Bobby. Our first gig was an end-of-the-semester campus party at UCLA, and all of us were pleasantly surprised at how nicely we fit together as a unit.

"It's fucking bizarre—we sounded great!" I cried to Robbin, as I poured an entire can of beer over the front of a coed's T-shirt.

"We got chemistry," he answered, nodding.

The beginning of any new relationship is a fucking fairy tale, and this was no different. I found Warren DeMartini likable and talented, like a small, gifted chipmunk. Bob was loud and often hilarious. Juan, spicy and unique. I was sure we'd be signed within a month. Then the owner of the Troubadour, Doug Weston, threw a monkey wrench into the works.

"I don't like your name anymore," he said. "I don't want the word associated with my club."

"What the hell's the matter with it?" I said. "Everyone else likes it."

"Conjures up images of vermin," he said shortly. "Haven't you ever heard that before?"

"People are *coming to see us*," I pointed out, seething. "Dude, we're *hot* right now."

"Stephen, I'm not going to argue with you," said Weston. "Change the name, or find a different place to play."

I went back to the garage, frustrated beyond belief. "Can you believe the balls on this guy?" I yelled. "The whole town loves us, and he can't get with the program. What got up his ass?"

"Probably a gerbil," said Robbin calmly. "Stay cool. I know what we can do."

"You got something?"

"Let's call ourselves the Gladiators," he said. "Simple as that."

Ever resourceful, Ratt became the Gladiators for a week. The name was on all of our tickets and flyers. It shut Weston up, and no one in my band seemed to care. But for me, it signified a shift in identity, and I wasn't about to start over at square one. I made sure to stamp the name RATT in huge letters on all the flyers. Stubbornly, I strung up our big RATT banner behind us, too, when we played. The crowd knew who we were.

The Gladiators nonsense went on for three nights, and then, on a Saturday night, our final show of the month, we sold out so early, turning away so many people that they decided to schedule an extra set that evening in order to accommodate the rest of the crowd.

"All right," Weston relented. "You sell this many tickets, you can call yourself whatever you like."

Finally, we were back to being Ratt, but further improvements had to be made. At our next gig, I nudged Robbin, onstage.

"Take a look out there," I told him. "What do you see?"

Robbin frowned. "A bunch of people."

"People?"

"Dudes," he admitted.

Exactly. Metal was hitting big. Maiden, Priest, Ozzy, and Quiet Riot had the world in the palms of their hands. But heavy metal audiences had far too many guys in them for my taste. I respected the average fat, stoned heavy metal fan as much as the next guy. A fan base is a fan base, and they all pay for tickets. But the truth was, it was not nearly as enjoyable to play to a bunch of long-haired teenage dudes as it was to drive a bunch of sexy sluts mad with desire. We couldn't compromise our sound, of course—that had to remain as hard-hitting and brutal as we could stand it. But we *could* change our look.

Robbin was with me. "The whole Mötley thing, it's just not us. We don't need all that leather, razor blades, and pentagrams."

"Fuck no," I agreed. "Softer and sexier is the way to go. We don't even need to get androgynous—just *unique* looking."

"New-wave swashbucklers?" said Robbin.

"Kinda, yeah, man," I said, nodding, excited. "As if we've been sent from the future, to fight you and fuck you."

"Pirates," Robbin mused. *"Cement pirates."*

From that moment on, that was our look and our motto: Cement Pirates. We strove for originality and color. Our flair was inspired by Adam Ant and Duran Duran. I traded in my leather jacket for thigh-high boots and big puffy pants. Ripped T-shirts, cut by a thick belt, mismatched earrings, and long, wild necklaces. I tried to let fun and spontaneity dictate my fashion choices. I was always ready to trade rings or bracelets with people I'd meet backstage.

Anything went: fingerless gloves, white gloves, black gloves, three belts, a sash tied to the belt, ivory tusks on a sterling silver chain, a bandana around the neck, a heart pin. Sounds faggy, but it really worked. Robbin, who could pull off anything, dressed in black tights and boots, red vests with studs on them, and full-on pirate blouses. We dressed a dubious Warren in clothing of our choosing. Juan and Bob were down with it in the early days, too.

"I feel kinda like a *freak*," laughed Warren, looking at his reflection in the mirror: his eye shadow, his blown-out hair, his costume jewelry, ear clips, and glitter spandex tank top.

"When I was your age," I said, "I was wearing bell-bottoms and a surgical mask onstage. Consider yourself lucky."

I don't know if our fashion choices ever really changed the demographic of our audience. Chicks definitely came to all of our shows, but dudes continued to outnumber them. Still, for the first time, I felt truly authentic onstage, in terms of my look. I'd given myself permission to kind of branch out, experiment, and try new things. True, we weren't going to intimidate too many people while wearing satin, but there was a kind of unburdening in that, too. . . .

With our style locked in, our name defended, and our growing roster of semifamous friends, we were approaching near-professional status. It no longer made sense to live in my friend's mom's garage.

I hugged Mrs. O good-bye and began to stuff band equipment and boxes of clothing into my Datsun. That evening, Robbin, Warren, and I moved into a shabby one-room apartment in Palms, a sector of Los Angeles located just down the freeway from neighboring Culver City. Our new apartment made the Mötley House look luxurious by comparison.

"We don't even get a *kitchen*?" Warren said, looking frightened, as he turned around slowly to survey the twin gas burner and minuscule Philco refrigerator that comprised our tiny kitchenette.

"What do we need a kitchen for?" asked Robbin, plopping himself down, spread-eagled on the apartment's only bed. "We don't have any food."

"We live in a *mansion*," I proclaimed. "Ratt Mansion West."

It was my first real apartment. I wanted it to smell of excitement and wet trim. We soon christened the mansion with a metal bash, inviting the entire Troubadour audience to our pad after one particularly packed show.

"Come on down to our new place in Palms, off National, near Victor's Meats," we shouted, "and *bring booze*!!" Hordes of Ratt bastards and their slutty sisters jammed into our living room. The one-bedroom apartment could seat twenty comfortably, so we stuffed a hundred freaks inside, with more pushing in through the windows every moment. I sat on a corner of our bed, pushed up against the wall, bookended by two platinum blondes wearing leggings and jelly shoes. As they nibbled on my earlobes, I had to choke down two Valiums to deal with the pandemonium.

"Hey, it's Stephen Pearcy! Holy shit. Ever tried Everclear?" some dude asked me. He held up a cup of clear alcohol. I sampled from the cup and nearly cried out. It was the gasoline of liquors. Two hundred proof. Immediately, my gorge began to rise and my vision began to blur. In time, we would come to light the shit on fire and pass it around.

I recollect the rest of the evening as a flurry of images: Robbin snorting an enormous line of white powder off the top of our empty, unplugged Philco refrigerator, its door hanging open. Warren with his arm around a gorgeous chick with hair-spray bangs, one full head taller than him, his nose perfectly level with her tits. David Lee Roth gabbing to a handful of chicks, refusing them all autographs, and instead, perversely, signing the refrigerator. Tommy and Nikki holding court in the corner of the bedroom, taking turns biting each other, Nikki drawing blood, Tommy leaving just teeth marks. Everyone laughing wildly. Cigarettes burning endlessly. Pop radio station blasting the latest '80s rock. The warm glow of rising success in your bloodstream. The feel of being young and on the rise, with a beautiful girl's feathered hair brushing up against your skin.

Clarity returned at dawn next morning. I awoke to find myself sitting upright, back against the wall, shirtless, my expensive fashion metal pants ripped and stiff with dried alcohol and spilled ashes.

Phil Schwartz eyed me. "Stephen," he said, relieved. "You're okay."

"Yeah," I groaned. "Thanks, Phil. What . . . what happened?"

"You had a very nice time," he said.

■ ■ ■

BY THE TIME THE SUMMER OF '82 rolled around, Mötley was starting to break big. They were going out on the road with enormous acts, and when they came back to L.A., they were treated like royalty. I was happy for our buddies; don't get me wrong. But I was jealous, too, and I'm sure it showed.

"Stephen, my brother," Tommy instructed me once, "do not stress! Your time will come, man."

Sure, I thought. *But when?*

Because I was ready now. I was foaming at the mouth, ready for our share of the spotlight. It was time to tighten the pirate belt and start thinking with our heads. We had to be smart. We had to move now. Metal wouldn't be king forever, we all knew that. The move out of Mrs. O's garage had been the right one: We were up on our own two feet, and that gave us confidence, independence. But relocation had been costly, and besides draining us of every last cent, it had stripped us of our only practice space.

Blotzer lived out near the beach. "Listen, Stephen," he said, "I know about a great practice space in the Valley. Let's go check it out. Maybe we can get a discount rate."

We jumped into his car. Weirdly enough, Bob had a Datsun B-210, too. Was it destiny, a pronouncement in the form of afford-able Japanese imports?

"Hey, mind if we make a quick pit stop in Manhattan Beach?" Bob asked me, checking out his hair in the rearview mirror as we slid through traffic.

"Fine by me," I said.

We pulled into a small driveway.

"I just gotta fuck this girl real quick," Bob explained. "It won't take too long."

"Oh," I said. "I'll stay in the car."

"Nah," Bob said. "It's hot as hell. You'll sweat to death. Come on in."

Mildly perplexed, I followed Blotzer to the door. A fairly cute young chick with blond ringlets in her hair answered his knock.

"Bobby! How *are* you?" She made to hug him but he held her at bay.

"Hey, Susie," he said brusquely. "This is Stephen. Me and him are kind of in a hurry—it's band business. So we're going to have to make this real quick."

I plopped down in an easy chair in the living room, turning on the TV. "See you guys in a while," I said, figuring that they'd head for the bedroom.

"Nah," said Bob. "I'll just fuck her right here. Go ahead and get undressed, sweetie."

Susie stripped obediently. I watched as her small breasts, relieved of their bra, popped into view. Bob rolled his cotton shorts down around his ankles and waddled over to Susie, guiding her to the couch. She peeled down her underwear and he mounted her from behind. As he began porking her, I watched, unable to peel my eyes from the train wreck unfolding before me.

"So . . . the practice space . . . is in . . . Burbank . . . in the mall," grunted Bob, as he rocked his wide hips into Susie's backside. She gasped. "It's . . . an old buddy of mine . . . so I'm thinking . . . he'll be cheap."

"Sounds great," I whispered, sinking into the easy chair.

"You think . . . we can afford . . . thirty bucks . . . an hour?" grunted Blotzer.

STEPHEN PEARCY

I began to answer, but suddenly, Blotzer squeezed his butt cheeks together and bucked to a comical orgasm. He withdrew and patted his gal pal on the butt. "Thanks, Susie. I'll call ya, okay?"

"When?" she asked, but Blotzer just pulled his shorts up, nodded at me, and we made for the door.

Bobby's connection had a great rehearsal space: spacious, soundproofed, and located not too deep into the Valley. We could grow as a band there, learning one another's style and idiosyncrasies. Hopefully at some point, we could create a trademark sound. But our problem was the same one we'd been dealing with for months: We had no cash on hand to pay for the space.

"How about you let us jam for a couple of weeks," Bob asked, "and then we get it back to you?"

His buddy wasn't stupid: He'd dealt with bands before. "How about you pay up front?" he replied.

I was beyond frustrated. We'd made it into the Troubadour on pure persistence, but the gravy train had stopped there. To get into the Whisky, you couldn't just be good: You had to be *great*. Tight as a drum. Ratt needed practice hours, period. I racked my head. Who could front us money? My mom? Impossible. She was sending me a hundred bucks a month already, and that went straight to rent at Ratt Mansion West. I was ashamed to ask for more. Well, how about robbing a bank? No, they would recognize my trademark fingerless gloves and ivory tusk necklace.

Our answer came unexpectedly in the form of Wendy Dio, the wife of rocker Ronnie, to whose silver mountain Jake E. Lee, our guitarist, had fled.

"I'd love the chance to manage you boys," she told me, cornering me after a Troubadour gig. She pressed her still-attractive forty-

130

year-old body uncomfortably close to my chest. "You have great talent."

"I don't know," I said, retreating back against the bar in an attempt to create a few inches of space between us. "Don't you manage your husband's band, too?"

"Ronnie doesn't mind," she insisted. "He knows I have my . . . ambitions."

"I can't just *appoint* a manager. The whole band needs to be in on it."

Wendy raised an elegant hand. "Bartender," she called, without once taking her eyes off me, "five Jack and Cokes, for my handsome young friends here."

"Wendy," I said, "what do you know about practice spaces?"

"You'd be surprised," Wendy said.

She fronted us two hundred bucks, more than enough for a week's worth of practice time at Bobby's buddy's spot in the Valley, and in return, she only asked to be *considered* as our manager. But there were strings attached.

"Ste-phen," Wendy sang. "I've got a pair of tickets to a play tonight in Hollywood. Would you mind doing me an enormous favor and accompanying me?"

"A play?" I said, confused. "Why would you want to go to one of those?"

"I'm very boring, I'm suppose." She laughed. "Dress nicely, darling. I'll pick you up at seven."

Mystified, I stood in my underwear in front of the full-length mirror at Ratt Mansion West, trying to figure out what rocker clothes I owned that would also be appropriate for the world of high-class theater. I came up with something fairly off, but acceptable. When

Wendy picked me up in her sports car and eyed me up and down, I realized, *Huh, I'm arm candy.* We entered the dark theater, Wendy squeezing on my arm. *She's married to Dio, dude. No touching.*

The situation was awkward, but I was in no position to alienate Wendy Dio or her deep pockets. She wanted to take Ratt all the way up the ladder. With her enthusiasm mounting every passing day, she soon began to stop by Ratt Mansion West unannounced.

"Ste-phen!" she called. "Darling, are you hungry? Put some clothes on and let's go to the Rainbow, to see and be seen."

She was hitting me at all my weak spots: Money. Ambition. Pizza. I threw on some leathers and allowed myself to be escorted to the Strip. We ambled into the Rainbow, requesting a table in the kitchen.

"Shall we discuss the future of the band?" Wendy said, bright-eyed, when we were seated, running her fingernails lightly over the back of my hand.

"Absolutely," I said. "But first, let me take a piss." I snuck out to the pay phone to make a call.

"Hello?"

"King," I whispered, "it's Stephen. I'm over at the Rainbow with Wendy. She's about to feed me. Quick, call the rest of the boys, come on over!"

"Perfect," Robbin said. "Stall her and we'll all be there as soon as we can."

The scenario repeated itself many times over. In this manner, a band was fed. But the bills for the rehearsal space kept piling up, and I, of course, was always in need of a few new outfits. Soon we'd racked up a sizable debt with Dio.

"You're good for it, darling, don't worry," purred Wendy, one afternoon at Ratt Mansion West, when she'd come over to check up on me. "I *trust* you."

A few friends of ours were hanging out on our couch, smoking weed and talking music. One of them took out a crumpled piece of newspaper, from within which he produced a gram of blow. "Anybody want to do a line?"

"Oh, Stephen and I would like to," said Wendy happily. "We'll just step into the bathroom together, won't we?"

"No," I said flatly—enough was enough. "We won't."

Wendy's face darkened. "Not *interested*?" she asked.

"Nope," I admitted. "Not at all. Hey, look, I'm sorry, but I'm not going there."

Wendy nodded. She waited for quite some time before speaking, and when she did, she didn't mince words.

"I believe this association is over," she said. "Clearly, you're no longer in need of my help."

"Fine with me."

"So, I'll need to get the money I've loaned you," she said.

"I don't have any cash right now, Wendy," I said. "Come on. Seriously."

"Fuck off. I want my money."

"You fuck off," I snapped. "I'll get you your money when I get it to you. I'm sorry it didn't work out, okay? Now split."

Wendy gathered her purse coolly. "We'll be seeing one another soon," she said, leaving.

I sank into the couch.

"Older chicks, man," one of my friends said, chuckling. "They get past a certain age, and they need dick so bad it clouds their whole mind. They stay crazy all the way up to menopause."

The constant rehearsing had an effect on us. We were tighter, more unified, perfectly in step. We scheduled a two-night run at the Troubadour, selling out both shows. Blotzer paced us effortlessly, driving out a heavy beat that stopped only as long as it took him to guzzle a Budweiser in between songs. Juan's thick bass riffs were the perfect counter to Warren's improvisational noodling.

"These new guys sound great," I whispered to Robbin, when we were packing up our gear. "I can't believe how lucky we got."

"Stephen," he interrupted. "I think someone wants to talk to you."

I whirled around, brandishing my unplugged microphone in my hand. It was Wendy. A heavily muscled rocker dude stood behind her, wearing a menacing scowl.

"I want my *money*," Wendy announced. "And I want it now."

"Oh, for fuck's sake," I snapped. "We don't *have* any money, Wendy. I told you that already. I'll pay you—just give me a few weeks."

"You've just played two sold-out shows!" Wendy yelled. "You're due to be paid now, aren't you? You owe me six hundred dollars, Stephen. So pay up."

"She wants her cash, man," her dude added, throwing in a threatening knuckle crack, and taking a step toward me.

"Hold it," Robbin said, stepping in front of me. "Who are you with, clown?"

"Yeah!" cried Blotzer, noticing the confrontation and jumping into the fray. "Are you trying to fuck with *my* band?"

"No one's trying to fuck with anyone," said the muscleman, a bit more carefully.

"You *sure*?" asked Warren, squaring up to the dude, his face barely reaching the guy's neck. "Because from where I'm standing, it sounds like you're trying to put the squeeze on us."

"Yeah!" called out Juan, getting into the spirit of things. "No one steps up to Ratt and lives to tell about it, buddy."

The five of us stood shoulder to shoulder, staring down Wendy and her bouncer.

"I just want the money I'm owed," Wendy repeated, waning.

"Ah, get lost," Blotzer sneered. He tapped one of his drumsticks into the front of the muscleman's shirt.

They retreated, mumbling angrily. The five of us watched them slink out the door, then took a look at one another.

"Goddammit," I said. "*That's* a band."

■ ■ ■

NEEDLESS TO SAY, AT THE END of all that, Wendy got her money. To this day, we're still friends. And Ronnie, you can rest in peace, I would never go there.

As for the band, we were brothers now. Every day was spent writing, recording, experimenting with riffs and lyrics, smoking joints and drinking beers, learning our craft. We had focus and all the drive in the world. In our tiny Ratt Mansion, a clock radio alarm would go off, and Warren DeMartini would roll out from beneath his covers. Lighting a cigarette, he would begin to practice his scales, fingers flying up and down the neck of his guitar. We were headed for greatness.

"I want to write a song about being a gang," I told Robbin. "That's what we are now: a gang."

"Go," he said.

I hunched over a brand-new legal pad, tapping the end of my pen.

Out on the streets, that's where we'll meet, I scrawled. *Get in our way, we'll put you on your shelf.*

Round and round . . . What goes around, comes around. . . .

It was time. We were ready for the Whisky. I was going to get us in there or die trying. I grabbed a phone book and called the club.

"Whisky."

"I need to speak to your booking agent."

"Hold on a sec, let me see if she's here." There was a long pause, and then, finally, a female voice came on the line. "Hi, this is Dee Dee. What can I do for you?"

"My band wants to play your club," I said.

"Yeah, you and everyone else." She laughed. "Who is this?"

"Stephen Pearcy," I said, "of Ratt. Maybe you've heard of us?"

"Uh . . ."

"We were the house band at Gazzarri's for a long time," I said. "Now we mostly play the Troubadour."

"Look, Stephen," she said, "we're kind of busy right now. Why don't you call back next month—"

"Let me come down and bring you a tape," I blurted. "Please. If you'll just listen to us, I know you'll want us to play."

She paused for a long time. "Can you be here in an hour?"

"I'm leaving right now."

I snatched a demo cassette off our kitchen table and sprinted down the steps. I jumped into my B-210, gunned the engine, and shot off toward the Strip. Twenty minutes later, I peeled off onto Clark Street, sliding into the exact same parking space I'd used the day I'd offered a poorly rolled joint to David Lee Roth in 1978.

I will make this happen, today, I promised myself, clutching the demo in my sweaty hand. *This is my time. I will not be denied. . . .*

The booking agent was there to greet me at the door.

"You made it in no time at all," she said, extending her hand warmly. "I'm Dee Dee."

She was an okay-looking chick in her early thirties, with dirty-blond hair and a few freckles on her nose.

"Let's see what you've got," she said, motioning for me to come inside. "Come on in. My office is upstairs."

As we walked up the stairs, I looked around the empty club hungrily, savoring the late afternoon light. *This is where we'll be playing soon,* I told myself.

We stepped into her office. Dee Dee closed the door behind us. She popped the cassette into a deck, pressed play, and slid behind her desk, a thoughtful expression playing on her face.

I knew right from the beginning . . . that you would end up winnin'. . . .

Round and round . . . What comes around, goes around. . . .

"Yeah, sounds great," she said, when the tape came to a close. "Honestly, you guys aren't half bad."

"So you'll have us!" I said excitedly. "Oh, wow, Dee Dee, this means the world to me!"

"Whoa, there. Not so fast," she said. "This is the hottest spot in town. I got ten bands who are lining up to play here. This town works on grease. Know what I mean?"

"Sorry?" I said. "Grease?"

Dee Dee laughed. "I mean, what can you do for me?"

"I . . . don't know," I admitted. "What do you want?"

She pointed at my crotch, a hopeful expression on her face.

"What are you working with there?"

I stared at her, dumbfounded. "Working with?"

Dee Dee smiled and slid out from behind her desk. "You are *really* cute, Stephen," she said, running her fingers along my chest. "Tell you what. How about you let me see what's going on there?"

For a long moment, I didn't know what to say. Then, slowly, I unzipped my jeans and pushed them down to my ankles.

"You're not wearing any underwear," chided Dee Dee. "Naughty, naughty."

"It's laundry day," I managed, before she sucked me up into her mouth and cut off all rational thought.

I left the Whisky fifteen minutes later, drained and confused, bearing the promise of our first show. Tit for tat—we were in, as long as I kept coming around. According to Dee Dee, we were on the right track. Now, to keep working toward our goal.

We played our show and rocked pretty hard, as I remember. But at five o'clock the very next week, there I was: right back on the Strip.

"Dee Dee's upstairs," said the guy at the box office, nodding to me. "Go right on up."

I knocked on the door of her office. "Uh, Dee Dee?"

She swept it open with a dramatic flourish. "Come in, come in."

I entered and closed the door behind me. "I brought you some more songs."

"Wonderful," she said, reaching for my belt buckle. "We'll get to those shortly."

We developed a pattern. Once or twice a week, I would head to the Whisky a Go Go, the world's most famous training ground for up-and-coming rockers, and the doorman would nod at me, then point me up the stairs to Dee Dee. She would compliment us on the last Whisky gig we played, and then she'd service me. Every now and then I'd rifle through the files and see which bands had played there previously—Zeppelin, Priest, and Van Halen—and how much they got. When I saw the tiny paychecks the Whisky was giving out to the mega-bands, I didn't feel so bad.

"How's the Whisky going, man?" Robbin asked me. "Seems like you're putting in the effort. Way to go, dude."

"You have no idea," I groaned.

Dee Dee's casting couch was uncomfortable, and excruciatingly long. She just couldn't get enough. Finally, I'd had it.

"Dee Dee," I said. "Stop."

She looked up, an innocent expression on her face.

"Why?"

"This is insane," I said. "We've been doing this all month. Now, come on. Are you going to let Ratt play here on its own merit, or what?"

"You'll have to earn your time," she said, and lowered her head, going back to work.

"Hey!" I said. "No more. No more dick for you. Look at me. We're a *good* band. I'd put us against anyone. Seriously. We got the power. We got the moves. We got the look."

Dee Dee eyed me crossly. "Gimme."

"No way," I said, holding my crotch possessively. "Not until you give us a *good* gig, on a big night."

"And then you'll give it back to me?" Dee Dee asked. "You promise?"

"Yes," I agreed.

She paused for a very long moment. "Oh, fine. Let me look at my calendar." She scanned the dates for a minute or so. "Two weeks from now, Saxon's playing. You think you're up to opening for them?"

"Are you serious?" I said. "Please tell me you're serious."

"I suppose so," Dee Dee answered. "But you guys better be good, or that's the last time you'll ever play here."

"Oh, thank you!" I cried jubilantly. "Thank you, thank you, thank you! Man, I can't wait to tell the guys!"

She cleared her throat.

"Oh, sorry," I said. "Here you go. Knock yourself out."

ALL FOR ONE
AND ONE FOR ALL

WE WERE IN. IT was August of '82 . . . *and we were opening for Saxon at the Whisky.* L.A. was our world, and the Strip our capital. No longer were we just pissing on the front lawn: Against all odds, we'd been invited inside.

"You nervous?" Robbin asked me backstage.

"Shit," I said, gulping down a stiff drink. "I might be. How about you?"

"I've puked once already, man," Robbin confessed. "I got nerves, bad."

But our fear dissolved when the lights came on. The Saxon gig was like none other we'd ever played. The packed Whisky audience surged violently, trying their raucous best to touch us, punch us, girls grabbing our dicks, crying out with pure rock frustration. We slammed back into them, forcing driving beats down onto their heads, belting lyrics furiously, dousing them over and over in senseless rock abandon. We watched, unbelievingly, as something tighter, meaner, and more powerful than ourselves surged like wildfire out of our instruments. It was larger than us. We just carried it.

The buzz we generated was intensely gratifying. Lines formed around the block to see us, chicks in heels and miniskirts and boys who looked like girls. We opened a few more times, but soon it became obvious that the crowds were coming there for us.

"I'm thinking of booking Ratt as a headlining act, Stephen," said Dee Dee, in one of our midday back-office sessions, which had yet to taper off. "What do you say to that?"

"Works for us," I declared, unzipping.

We packed the house every time we played. Crushes of adoring females crowded around us after shows, demanding to be a part of our inner circle, sweet girls who wore chains and mesh and color-change lipstick, peacock belts, gold pleather miniskirts with high-heeled boots. I recruited the most beautiful ones into the upstairs dressing room, where we discussed the high price of love. The others I set to making clothes for the band.

Custom tights were my new obsession, and the girls ran diligently to their sewing machines. I took their offerings, laid them over two carefully arranged chairs at Ratt Mansion West, and splattered them with fabric paint.

Robbin and I set about creating a "look" for Warren, as if we were two junior high school girls and he was our little doll.

"I'm not sure how I feel about all this *makeup*," Warren pleaded, as we hovered over him before a party at Neil Zlozower's house. The charismatic Zlozower, whose voice sounded like he'd just eaten a pound of gravel, was the most famous rock photographer in Los Angeles. He'd worked with Aerosmith, Tom Waits, Van Halen, Quiet Riot, and more. Zlozower fucked more rock sluts than the bands did, and didn't make any secret about it. If he liked you, it *mattered*.

"Quiet," said Robbin. "This eyeliner I've got going for you is going to look great. Now please, shut the fuck up."

I hair-sprayed our lead guitarist, then shoved him into a knee-length red jacket with immense shoulder pads.

"I don't know, guys . . ."

"Don't worry. You're going to kill," I assured him, patting him on the back.

And indeed, Warren did well for himself that night. Half an hour into the party, a good-looking chick named Kathy, intrigued by the perfect little rock doll, pounced on him. They talked all evening and apparently had quite a lot in common, because they left together. Some weeks later, they shacked up, and he was out of Ratt Mansion West. But it was all right; we had already written several songs that would later become hits.

One night, after playing at the Whisky, I got approached by an older Jewish guy with curly hair, wearing a big smile.

"You guys are *terrific*," he said. "Tell me—you got a manager?"

"No," I said. "Although a few people have tried."

"Listen," he said. "I'm Marshall Berle. You know who my uncle is? Milton Berle. Mr. Television? I got twenty years of music biz experience up here on the Strip. I know bands backward and forward."

"Oh yeah? Like who?"

"Where do I begin? I was at the William Morris agency when the Beach Boys came through. I was their very first agent," said

Berle. "Credence Clearwater Revival, Ike and Tina Turner, Canned Heat—I did 'em all."

"Cool," I said. "Did you ever help out anyone born *after* 1950?"

"Funny," he said. "Great. I like that. Funny's good. Listen, Stephen, I think I can make things happen for you guys. Wouldn't you like that?"

"Things are already happening," I said, pointing to the crowd, still milling about.

"You got a record deal?" Berle said.

"No," I admitted.

"Have you guys ever even stepped inside a *studio*?"

We had previously recorded "Tell the World" with another bass player and the Rod Stewart lookalike drummer for Brian Slagel's "Metal Massacre"—the first metal compilation release, featuring Metallica, Black 'N Blue, Cirith Ungol, Bitch, Ratt, and many other up-and-coming bands.

Also, when we had moved to L.A. in 1980, Victor Mamanna had helped me finance a two-side single, recorded at Lucky Dog Studios in Venice. I would throw them out at shows. They were labeled M. RATT with the Ratt logo on the record itself. They're actually quite a collector's item these days.

"We've recorded," I said. "But a full-length record, that's in our near future."

He shrugged. "Look, do what you want. But I'm not just some schmuck off the street, okay? I helped Van Halen get their start."

That stopped me dead in my tracks. "Excuse me?" I said.

"Van Halen. I was their first manager. Ask around." He smiled, satisfied, and slipped me his card. "Stephen, I'm always around. Give me a call."

I called an emergency band meeting that evening.

"The guy who managed *Van Halen* wants to manage us," I said breathlessly.

Bobby, Juan, and Robbin exchanged high fives. News like this was especially important for Juan, who was still flirting with Dokken and occasionally gigging with them, too. If they broke big before Ratt did, we'd lose him for sure.

"What are the terms?" Warren asked suspiciously.

"How should I know?" I said. "Dude, he wants to *manage* us. This is great news."

"I'm not signing my life away to anyone," Warren insisted.

We met with Berle, who revealed the details of his strategy: Instead of being a traditional manager for our band, he would operate more like a record company executive.

"Meaning?"

"Meaning, I'll still run your fan club and help you book gigs, do all that manager type of bullshit. But more importantly, I'm starting a label, Time Coast Records. If you want, when the time comes, I'll help finance an EP for you guys."

"I don't know," said Warren.

"What don't you know?" Berle asked. "I'll pay for you to get in the studio. I'll distribute your record. I'll get your songs on the fucking radio. And then I'll get you signed to Warner Brothers."

"Sounds like a *plan*," I exclaimed. Me and Robbin high-fived. We had been waiting for this moment for a long time.

Bobby and Juan were on board to sign Marshall's contract, too, but Warren, ever cautious, insisted we take it to a lawyer. A few of the terms were fiddled with to his satisfaction, and then we took it back to Marshall. He donned his eyeglasses and peered at it carefully.

"DeMartini," he said thoughtfully. "Doesn't *sound* Jewish."

"He's a cautious little fella," I explained.

"Ah, what the hell," laughed Berle. He put the contract down. "You guys win, okay? Let's move forward. I want to get you in the studio as soon as possible."

Even with the concessions Warren forced, the terms of the contract were still highly favorable to Time Coast Records. They would own most of the profits if the EP ever did any real business. We were either unable to see that far into the future or, more likely, we just didn't give a shit. We were still drinking Budweiser for dinner. We had nothing to lose.

Berle rounded up three thousand dollars quickly and then came knocking at my door. "You got five days in the studio, fellas. We need six songs for an album. Can you make that happen?"

I'd been biding my time for such an opportunity.

"Absolutely," I told him. "It'll be a snap."

We hadn't been together for long enough to have much new material, so I decided we'd go mostly with Mickey Ratt songs: "Sweet Cheater," "Tell the World," "Back for More." We included "Walkin' the Dog," too, an old blues standard, mostly because Aerosmith and the Rolling Stones had done so, too, on their early albums.

Robbin and I also threw in a new song, "You Think You're Tough," and it really cooked.

"This is our single, man," I said. "I'm sure of it."

"You think so?" asked Robbin.

"King," I said, "this is the one."

Robbin is all over that record. His raw metal-blues solos are featured more prominently than Warren's catchy, complex tinkering. His style meshes with the overall feel of the EP, which, produced over the course of five consecutive all-day, all-night recording sessions, emerged as a harsh, brash, ballsy creation.

"I don't know if the average fucker will like it," Bobby said, popping open a final beer as we dragged our crusty bodies out of the studios and into the parking lot at dawn on Thanksgiving morning, finally finished. "But we kicked some major ass in there."

He was right. The album was mean. And now we needed an image to go with it.

"I know just who to call," said Robbin. "Zloz."

NEIL ZLOZOWER, ROCK PHOTOGRAPHER:

Part of being a photographer in the music industry is picking up on great bands before anybody else does. I picked up Aerosmith and Ted Nugent before anybody else. Same thing with Mötley, Quiet Riot, Ratt, Poison, Guns N' Roses. You want to start working with these bands when they're nothing. You have to have the talent to know who's gonna be big. When I heard "Eruption" by Van Halen, I said, These guys are sick. I want to work with them. I got in on the ground floor. When they grew big, I grew big. I had the ear.

When I first met Robbin, I'd always run into him at Van Halen shows, and Robbin would go "Hey, Zloz, I'm in a band. Here's our tape, check it out," in his big, deep, slow voice. I'm all, "Yeah, yeah, dude, give me the tape, let me fucking listen to it." Of course I never listened to it. And the same scenario went on quite a few times. "Yeah, dude, sorry. I didn't listen to it. Give me another and I'll check it out."

After about ten times of Robbin coming at me, I finally listened to his tape. Like, "Okay, you've been persistent."

*I took it home, put it on. It started with "Sweet Cheater,"
"You Think You're Tough," "Walkin' the Dog," "Back for
More" . . . I was like, Oh my God, I love this. Why didn't
I listen to this the first time? So I called him up, and said,
"Dude, your band smokes. I want to work with you."*

*So honestly, when Ratt started taking off, no, I wasn't sur-
prised. I believed in them.*

"He's in," Robbin told me, arriving at Ratt Mansion West with
a roasted chicken under one arm, a tall pack of Bud, and a sack of
paper napkins. "Zloz is on board."

"Bullshit," I said.

Robbin set the beers down, broke one off, and took a big swallow. "He called me this morning, said, 'Your tape smokes.'"

"Those were his exact words?"

"Yep, and Tawny says she'll model for us," Robbin offered. "You
know, if we want her to."

I stared at him for a moment, unable to believe our luck.
Tawny Kitaen had made the move up to Los Angeles with Robbin, and the on-again, off-again rock power couple had fucked,
fought, and screamed until they could take no more and had to
separate. They no longer operated as a team as they had in their
glory days, but there was still love and mutual respect there.
Tawny was one of L.A.'s hottest up-and-coming sex kittens. She'd
just appeared in *Bachelor Party*. Now she would be on the cover
of our first album.

"Yes," I said. "We want her."

Robbin and I dressed everybody for the shoot. My chick at Parachute supplied us with shoulder pads galore, as well as trench coats,

studded nonsense, ripped seams, puffy pants, wide belts, black bangles, obscene rings, wacky spats, gold ear cuffs, and colorful scarves. Our Cement Pirate look was up and running, stronger than dog breath.

Tawny showed up at Zlozower's on time, looking so obscenely hot I was ready to go off into the bathroom and start yanking it like a twelve-year-old. Neil tossed her a pair of fishnets casually. "Put these on, babe, please," he growled.

Tawny flounced off to the dressing room, and Neil waited until she was out of earshot to speak.

"I want to throw some live rats at her," he said.

"Perfect," I said, hunched over a small pile of pungent marijuana, crushing the buds carefully with my forefinger, so as to prepare the first joint of the day.

Neil continued to explain his vision. "We see Tawny's legs in the fishnets. And then we notice there's *live rats* clinging to 'em. It's real futuristic. Real dark and sexy."

"Where will the band be?"

"The band *won't* be." Zlozower laughed. "Anybody want a beer?"

"Neil, with all due respect, don't you think—"

"Back cover," Zlozower interrupted. "*That's* where you want the band. You guys ain't famous enough to sell records with your pretty faces."

"He's right," I said. You never saw a picture of Led Zeppelin on their covers. Just blimps and lagoons and symbols and weird shit like that. You never even got a *lyric* sheet out of Zeppelin. Just had to listen to their albums three thousand times in a row, stoned off your ass, if you wanted to get a handle on what they were saying.

"I'm with you," Robbin agreed.

"Good," Zlozower continued. "I know a company that's got rats. I'll call 'em, if you guys think it's right."

"Go," I said. "Call. Amazing vision."

We drank for an hour, smoking weed and listening to Black Sabbath, until a man in a dented Toyota van bearing the inscription RENT-A-RAT arrived. Neil took five white rats off his hands: one to represent every member of the band. Tawny emerged in fishnet stockings; I began to have trouble swallowing.

Neil took up his post a few feet away from her.

"Stephen, when I say go," Zlozower said, "I want you and Robbin to throw the fuckin' rats at Tawny." He laughed hard. Neil was one of those people who could get anyone to do anything, and he knew it.

"You cool with this?" I asked Tawny.

She shrugged. Tawny was a true rock chick.

"NOW."

For one amazing hour, Robbin and I tossed rats at the hottest chick in Los Angeles. They clung to her perfect legs, skittering up her thighs. Even the rats were dying for a taste.

With seemingly no effort, with an offhand kind of pleasure, Zlozower got his shots.

"Good work, Tawn," he croaked, lighting up a cigarette. "You're done, babe. Thanks."

Carefully, Robbin plucked the rats from her stockings, tossing one after the other into the wire cage that Rent-a-Rat had supplied. Tawny retreated to the dressing room, smiling proudly.

"I'd gouge my left eye out to fuck that woman." Zlozower lit up a butt. "No offense, King."

Robbin just stared down at the cage, absorbed in whatever was going on down there.

"I thought we rented *five* rats," he said finally.

"We did."

"There's *six* here," said Robbin. "I peeled *six* off Tawny."

We peered into the cage. It was true. Five white rats scuttled about, nipping at one another, but nestled among them was a smaller, filthier black rat.

Zlozower frowned; then he opened up a fresh can of beer. "I guess he lives here."

■ ■ ■

MARSHALL BERLE WAS A HUSTLER. OUR self-titled Ratt EP was immediately pressed onto vinyl and dubbed to cassette. Soon, it was in music stores across the country, selling copies at a respectable clip. To celebrate, Robbin started banging Don Dokken's ex-girlfriend. In a matter of weeks, they were a thing, and he was never at Ratt Mansion West anymore. I'd lost both my roommates. I was a lonely soldier again.

The Whisky gigs continued. With a record out, we began to solidify a real reputation for ourselves. We played several times a month, not enough to oversaturate the market, but enough to certify us as their "house band." Phil Schwartz began to come to every show, and so did Beth and Mellette, trucking equipment, assisting me in setup and breakdown, and usually driving me to the after-parties. When we began doing an early version of our song "Wanted Man," Phil found me a prop gun to brandish, as well as a cowboy hat and spurs.

PHIL SCHWARTZ, CONCIERGE AND SECURITY, RATT:

I kind of fell into working for Stephen. I was this geeky Jewish kid from Mar Vista. I was in that preppy stage of my life—always wearing an argyle sweater. The people that I hung with at the time, that's the way they dressed, so I figured I had to also. I didn't know what the hell I wanted to do in life.

Then I started hanging around with Stephen, and my mom and dad were always, "What do you do with these guys? They just do drugs." I was like, No, I'm not, Mom. I was always kind of the straight guy. And Stephen was the rock star. It's like, we're going to this gig: I'll drive. It's no problem. I didn't need to drink. I was never a big drinker anyway. Not my thing. It was like, he's my friend; I'll take care of him.

And that kind of evolved to the point where it became my job.

One night after a show, Phil helped me break down the gear, and then we headed over to the Mötley House to party. I looked around for chicks. My eyes fell, unfortunately, on Dee Dee.

"Stephen," she said. "I haven't seen you around much lately."

"I've been real busy," I said.

"I thought we might have another meeting soon," she began, "talk about the band's future at the Whisky."

I sidestepped her, slipping into the churning mass of people. Four cups of keg beer later, Phil appeared by my side.

"Your friend Dee Dee wants to take us to another party," he said.

Pearcy kids, Culver City, 1962—Debbie, William, Stephanie, and me.

Celebrating my dad's birthday. It was the last time I ever saw him.

Recuperating in my '70s bedroom with two broken legs.

My first-ever band, Firedome.

Custom-made Explorer and Les Paul, loaded with Bill Lawrence pickups.

I dug my grandma Betty so much.

Mickey Ratt
gig, 1978.

Jamming
with Mike
Hartigan in
Culver City,
circa 1977.

Gazzarri's gig, circa 1981.

Most guys were
strictly Budweiser. I
was versatile.

Custom-made spandex pants.
Early glam, Hollywood, 1981.

A moment of peace.

Me and Johnny Gehring, our first-ever roadie.

Me and Warren DeMartini at one of our first gigs as the real Ratt, at UCLA in 1983.

Bobby Blotzer's enthusiasm was never in question.

Dave Jellison, Mickey Ratt.

Original set list, July 1983.

The boys on the bus.

MTV's Martha Quinn braves the Rolling Hilton.

When Robbin was happy, he was really happy.

Warren and Bobby preparing for a show.

Backstage with the boys from Mötley.

Bob and his new buddy, a Wisconsin state trooper who had boarded the bus to check us for drugs.

Me and the Prince of Darkness.

Billy Squier and me, early 1985.

New Year's Eve, 1984. Celebrating the survival of a hellaciously long tour.

The boys in Hawaii.

With Bruce Dickinson of Iron Maiden.

Terri Nunn came backstage and wrote on our mirror, GOOD LUCK, BOYS, TERRI NUNN. FUCK YOU.

Me and Warren backstage.

Me, Chris Hager, and Matt Thorr.

Robbin, in Miami Vice mode.

Steven Adler, me, and Fred Coury in some Hollywood hotel, 1987.

Robbin's Halliburton suitcase contained an ounce of weed, an ounce of blow, heroin, and a handgun.

Bret Michaels said he'd give me a platinum album one day if we'd let Poison open for us. I'm still waiting.

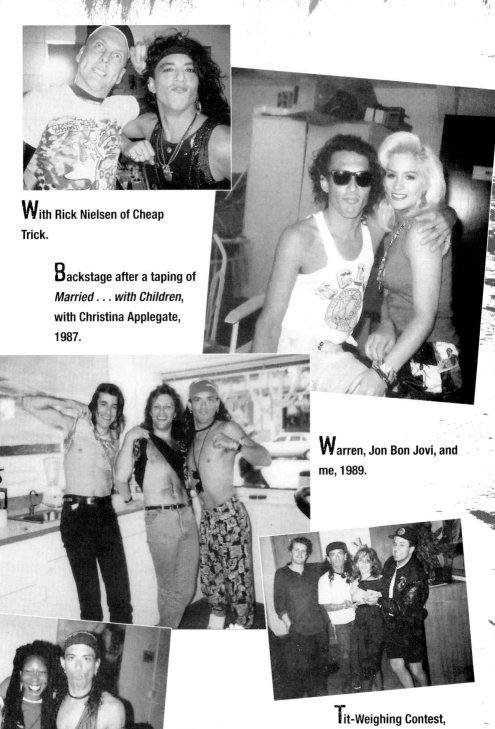

With Rick Nielsen of Cheap Trick.

Backstage after a taping of *Married . . . with Children*, with Christina Applegate, 1987.

Warren, Jon Bon Jovi, and me, 1989.

Whoopi and me, talking metal.

Tit-Weighing Contest, Detonator sessions with Joe Anthony (right).

Holding the girl who changed my life.

Dave Grohl, Jewel, and me.

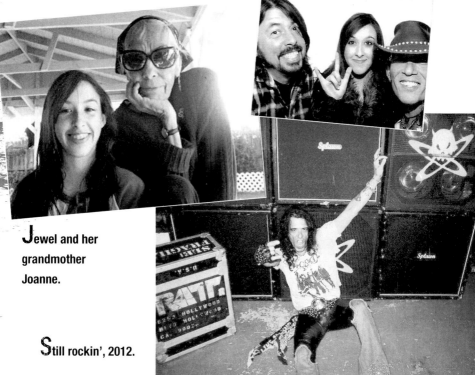

Jewel and her
grandmother
Joanne.

Still rockin', 2012.

"The best party in the world is right here. Tell her that."

"Okay," said Phil. Two minutes later, he was back. "She says we have to come with her, or no more Whisky. She said you'd know what she was talking about."

We didn't need the Whisky shows as badly anymore—we were going to headline the Santa Monica Civic soon, thanks to Marshall and the EP breaking. But still, I couldn't bring myself to just throw away prime gigs.

"Jesus. All right. Let's go. Looks like we have no choice."

We piled into Phil's Crown Victoria, all of us squeezing into the front seat.

"Where's this party, Dee Dee?"

"It's in Laurel Canyon," she said happily. "Oh, this is great. I'm bringing the hottest rocker in town!"

"And the rocker's friend," Phil pointed out, starting up the car, looking behind him carefully, then pulling out onto Clark Street.

"Sure, honey," Dee Dee breathed. She was staring at me, deep in the eyes. "Whatever you say. God, Stephen, I've missed you so much." She tousled my hair.

"Dee Dee, goddammit, control yourself, okay?"

"Why should I control myself?" she breathed excitably, reaching for my crotch. "I want it now, Stephen."

"Hey. That's enough," I said. "Phil, pull over."

"You got it, Stephen," said Phil. He screeched the car to a halt on the side of the road and turned off the engine.

"Thanks, Phil. Now look, Dee Dee, this is *it*. No more. Ratt's earned our spot at the Whisky. We got a record in the stores. I don't have to keep getting blown by you."

"I didn't realize it was such an imposition."

"The first few times, it wasn't. But now I'm starting to feel a little trashy." I crossed my arms. "You want to blow someone, blow Phil."

"What?" Phil yelped.

"What are you trying to do, Stephen?" said Dee Dee.

"It's time for you to try someone new, Dee Dee. Go ahead. It'll be good for you."

Dee Dee looked doubtful. Then she turned to Phil, sizing him up. "Well, he is kind of cute. In a nerdish way."

"Exactly," I said. I turned my head discreetly, so I was staring at the passenger's side window. "Go ahead, you two. Don't mind me. I'll be fine."

"Hey, I don't know about all this," protested Phil, but soon Dee Dee had lowered her head, and all conversation ceased.

Three minutes later, gulping, Dee Dee came up for air. She wiped her mouth with the back of her hand and shot me a dirty look. The drained Schwartz slumped, comatose, over his own steering wheel.

"Are you happy, Stephen?" Her eyes were angry slits. "*Now* are you satisfied?"

I was better than that: I was free.

The EP continued to do brisk business. One evening, Robbin and I were driving home from a club, listening to KLOS, one of L.A.'s rock stations.

"And next up, we got a song from a new group called Ratt—it's called 'You Think You're Tough.'"

Robbin and I looked at each other, stunned. Simultaneously, our mouths dropped open.

"Dude!" screamed Robbin. "We're on the fucking radio!"

"Unreal," I whispered. "Unfuckingreal."

154

We listened, awestruck. My hands were trembling so bad, I thought I'd swerve off the side of the road.

"Okay," I said, before the song was half over. "We gotta change the station."

"Why? What are you talking about?"

"It's bad luck to listen to yourself," I said. "It's like reading your own reviews."

"You're crazy," said Robbin, laughing wildly. "Absolutely fucking insane." His eyes were still wide open with disbelief. We'd made it on the airwaves. Anything could happen now.

I twisted the dial to KMET. And while no one in the world should believe this, I swear it's God's honest truth. "You Think You're Tough" was playing there, too.

"This is unbelievable!" I screamed. "No! It can't be happening!"

"We're on two radio stations at the same time!" yelled Robbin. He stuck his head and torso out of the window of my Datsun B-210. "IT'S TIME TO RATT AND ROLL, YOU BASTARDS! NOW BACK TO RATT MANSION WEST, TO PLAN OUR NEXT RATT ATTACK!"

We'd written the song in a tiny one-bedroom apartment and recorded it in an exhausted frenzy. Now it was hitting. I pressed on the gas pedal and turned the radio up as loud as it would go. Robbin wedged his body further out the window, until he was half in and half out of the car, his blond hair flying behind him, screaming into the wind. We drove like that for a very long time, shrieking and spitting like two half-human beasts, our car disappearing into the night.

■　■　■

ALL THROUGH THE SPRING OF 1983, I heard us on the radio, and it never ceased to thrill me. The same was true of being able to waltz casually into a random record store and check whether our EP was for sale. It never got old. Usually, the tape was there, and if it wasn't, I could bug the clerk about it, ask him to order it. Ratt wasn't famous yet, but we were official. We'd cut a record. People paid for our music. And man, it was just so *weird*.

Here's the thing: You lie awake at night half your life, hoping for something great to happen—marry the hot chick, make a million bucks, play football in the NFL, become a senator, whatever. Most of the time, it never happens. But sometimes it *does*. And when it did for me, it kind of took me by surprise. For a while, I just didn't know how to feel. Grateful? Entitled? Tripped out?

Despite the first taste of success, we were as broke as always, and that tends to keep a man grounded in reality. The initial EP sales were more than fifty thousand, and because it was on an independent label, that meant cash for someone. But we never saw a penny.

"I'm going to crush Marshall if he doesn't give us our dough!" swore Bobby, swerving from lane to lane as we headed down to Long Beach Arena to catch a Scorpions show. Bob knew the group well and had gotten us backstage passes. "I never trusted that guy in the first place."

"Calm down, Bobby," I said. "We're no worse off than we were before we met him. He got us airplay, you know?"

"Do I give a shit about *airplay*?" Bobby looked incredulous. "I am a *businessman*, Stephen. I got a wife and kids to think about here!"

Blotzer was sweating heavily. The front of his shirt was soaked through. He cracked open a Budweiser and swigged deeply from it.

"But if we get airplay," I explained, "then we—"

"I know, I know," sighed Blotzer. "Airplay means we get signed, and that's when we'll make our money. Shit, Stephen, you think I haven't made the connection? I'm not *stupid,* man. You think you and Robbin are the only smart guys in the band? I might drum for a living, but that doesn't make me a *total* imbecile."

Blotzer gulped down the rest of his beer greedily and threw it into the backseat with gusto.

"Fuck, this is gonna be a great show! Scorpions *rule*!!" He extended his left arm out the driver's side window and gave the entire universe the finger. "I FUCKING LIVE FOR ROCK AND ROLL!"

On Memorial Day weekend, Robbin and I headed to San Bernardino to catch Heavy Metal Day at the US Festival. Hundreds of thousands of fans made the trip, too, and for good reason: The lineup was impressive, including Quiet Riot, Mötley, Ozzy, Judas Priest, Triumph, Scorpions, and Van Halen. We were guests of Eddie's, which was the next best thing to playing there ourselves.

"Dude, I can't believe how many people turned out for this," I said, looking out onto the massive, swelling crowd. There were literally more than two hundred thousand fans watching the show.

"It's our time," Robbin said. "Metal is having its moment."

He was exactly right: The US Festival marked the beginning of mainstream commercial heavy metal. Apple's Steve Wozniak had ordered the three-day event by musical genre, and New Wave Day preceded Heavy Metal Day. Bands like Oingo Boingo, Men at Work, Flock of Seagulls, and even the Clash threw down their best stuff, but stacked up against our brothers in arms, they didn't have a prayer. The new wave crowds were pleased to hear their favorite songs, but the rest of us were bored by what had evolved into a fairly tame brand of music. Metal was dangerous, a bit more unpredictable. Simply put, we were the new thing.

Robbin and I decided to try and hang out by the soundboard during Triumph's afternoon set. To get there, we had to crawl for hundreds of yards through a dark tunnel full of intricate wiring. At the end, there was daylight, and we popped our heads up, then lifted our bodies into the tiny space around the board. We took a look at our surroundings. Absolute fucking bedlam. Heavy metal Woodstock. The overheated crowd surged with drunken fervor. The stage was miles away, but anyone behind the soundboard was a sitting duck.

"Yo! It's the dudes from *Mötley*!" one dude slurred. "What's up! Hey, let me get an autograph."

"Hey! Get me in there! Come on, you fags!"

Robbin and I looked at each other.

"Let's beat it," I decided. "I ain't getting hit with a beer bottle."

"Right you are," he said, ducking that enormous six-foot-four frame back into the tiny tunnel.

The entire ride home to Los Angeles, I tried to analyze what I'd seen. It had been a remarkable event, not least because we'd seen our boys Van Halen make that enormous leap from stellar band to true supergroup. They had it all: power, musical integrity, and mass appeal. It bowled me over that I'd seen them rise from playing in front of twenty people at the Whisky to headlining the biggest rock festival of the last ten years.

And while Mötley might not have been on Van Halen's level, at least musically, when you started talking about a force that kids could identify with, they were definitely getting close. Rock and roll had always sold danger and rebellion: Mötley understood that and exploited it better than almost anyone else. They spit-shined the punk ethos, spray-painted it cherry red.

They're cartoony, I thought. *You see the heels, the pentagrams, the hair, the attitude, and you know it's them. They're like Kiss: Even if you don't love their sound, man, you gotta dig all that flair.*

I returned home feeling increasingly optimistic for our chances. Determined not to let the moment slip away, I called our manager and pressed him to redouble his efforts.

"Marshall," I said. "I was just at US, bro. This is our time. The audience exists. I saw 'em with my own two eyes."

"Stephen," Marshall said, "I'm so far ahead of you, it's not even funny. Listen, you think I would have taken you on if I didn't think you had a shot to make it? You think I don't understand the climate out there?"

"Get us *signed,* Marshall," I pleaded.

"I'm working on it," he said. "First, I gotta get you some better gigs. Make you a couple bucks. Whisky's fine, but we want you rubbing elbows with the big boys now."

"Like who?" I asked.

"Gimme a week," he said, and hung up on me.

It was a long week. I ran through the list of my contemporaries. *Twisted Sister: signed. W.A.S.P.: signed. Great White: signed. Black 'N Blue: signed. Ratt? Not there yet.*

I was antsy. I couldn't stay at the Ratt Mansion by myself. It was too quiet. I drove down to the Strip, snapping at the traffic, and popped up to the Rainbow, ordered myself a beer. I sucked half of it down glumly. Then Chris appeared.

"Is this seat taken, sir?"

"Please," I said, sliding my beer to the side.

"How's life, dude?" he asked cheerfully.

"Very good. How's Rough Cutt?"

"Can't complain," he said. "Hey, did you hear? Wendy Dio's managing us."

"Is that right?"

"Yep," Chris said. "Dude, I don't want to jinx anything—but she thinks she can get us signed!"

It was just too much. I pushed away from the table and got up to leave. "Let's talk later, man."

"Hey, what'd I say?" Chris asked.

Something had to happen, and soon. We were sure to lose Juan to Dokken if Ratt didn't step it up within the next month or so. I trusted Robbin to stick with me until the bitter end, but Blotzer and Warren were total wild cards. Other bands, if they sensed weakness, would happily pry them from our grasp, just like we'd done. Los Angeles had never been for the weak, but now the atmosphere on the Strip had begun to tilt toward full-on feeding frenzy. We *all* wanted stardom.

■ ■ ■

MARSHALL CALLED. "WHAT ARE YOU BOYS doing next week? Got appointments at the tailors, or are you ready to work for me?"

"What do you have?"

"You ever been to Phoenix before?"

"No, I don't think so, man."

"Well, it's hot as hell. Tell the boys to take sunglasses. I got you a big gig. You're opening for ZZ Top."

We trucked all our shit to Phoenix, trembling with excitement.

SEX, DRUGS, RATT & ROLL

We'd have a half hour to make our mark before handing the stage over to ZZ Top.

"Holy shit," Robbin said. "You don't understand. I *idolize* these cats. Billy Gibbons is one of my favorite guitarists ever. I don't know, man—are we ready for this?"

We had no choice but to be ready. We blazed through the set with a manic, ripping energy that surprised me. *Where the fuck did that come from?* I wondered as I rushed off the stage, dripping with sweat. The crowd was going batshit. They wouldn't shut up. Thunderous applause rained down from the rafters.

"Dude," Robbin yelled, shining with excitement. "You hear that? They want us to go back out there!"

"We're the opening act. We don't get an encore."

"They *want* it!" he cried.

"Go back out there, you dummies," Billy Gibbons yelled. "Hurry up and give 'em another one."

We hit them with "Sweet Cheater." The crowd swelled up, spread its legs. It was our greatest moment yet.

"Unforgettable," Robbin said, driving back, overwhelmed with gratitude. "I never thought I'd do that in a million years."

That taste of the big time had us riled up. I was ready to go out on the road, and told Berle as much. He pressed me to stay in Los Angeles.

"The industry's here. I'll set up some showcases. Bring people to come see you at gigs."

"We're red-hot," I told him. "Make it happen."

Now I was more than preoccupied: I was obsessed. No longer would I devote precious brain space to ordinary activities, like chewing food. I shoved one sandwich down every day, baloney on white, chasing it with a can or two of Budweiser, otherwise completely occupied with plotting our rise to the top.

"Stephen," one of my semi-girlfriends at the time, Patty, complained, "I *never* see you anymore."

I fixed her with a look. "I'm a little busy here."

"Too busy for *me*?" she said, fingering her gold-link necklace.

"Sweetheart," I said gently, "too busy to shit. I haven't taken one in a week."

Every waking hour was spent thinking about the goal, and our image, and how to market us, how to rise to the top. Phil Schwartz helped me get one hundred promotional Frisbees made: TELL THE WORLD! they said. We opened for Mötley at the Troubadour, hurled the discs into the crowd. Next, I ordered one thousand buttons from a wholesaler in the Valley. They commanded you to BE A RATT! I passed out stickers, matchbooks, and flyers, enthusiastically, tirelessly, dutifully, eventually hatefully, day and night on the Sunset Strip.

I'd been carrying around a rock-and-roll dream in my head for nearly a decade. It was now or never. We had a name. We had fans. We'd built a decent buzz in the industry. But no buzz lasts forever.

"Fellas," Marshall said, "you got a gig at the Beverly Theater next Friday night. Lita Ford's gonna open for you—how do you like them apples? Oh, and by the way, don't get nervous about this, but I got some important people coming to see you."

"Who?" I demanded.

"Don't worry your pretty little heads, okay? Just go out there and keep doing what you've been doing."

Tempers were short that week as we rehearsed. Bobby and Juan sniped at each other, but Robbin was there, as always, to keep the peace between all of us. The night of the gig, Marshall came backstage with bad news.

"Lita's not gonna play after all," he said. "She doesn't want . . . well, she doesn't want to open for you."

"What, is she too good for us?"

Marshall shrugged. "Look at it from her perspective. She's made it already. What's she doing opening for a bunch of nobodies?"

"What's that supposed to mean?"

"Hey, it's her loss. And think about it this way, it's more stage time for you guys. You think you can stretch your set another hour?"

"We don't give a shit," I said. "We'll play the same songs twice, if we have to. She'll end up opening up for us anyway." Which she did—an arena tour, years later.

"Terrific," said Marshall. "Now go out and kill."

It was a night to remember. Warren and Robbin were so in sync with each other, riffing so brilliantly and effortlessly, that I thought they were going to go off somewhere and get married. Juan and Bobby's bickering dissolved instantly under the lights, and together they formed a mean, ugly rhythm beast. And I screamed my lungs out, jumped off our cabinets, and strutted around the stage with a passion that I had rarely felt before.

Backstage felt like a party, some kind of arrival. It was one of the best nights of my life, even before the official-looking guy walked in alongside Marshall Berle and stuck out his hand.

"Fellas," Marshall said, "I want you to meet Doug Morris."

Robbin and I looked at each other.

"Hello, Doug," Robbin said. "What can we do for you?"

I leaned forward, my jaw tense. Was this our moment? My stomach felt sick.

"I'm with Atlantic," Doug said. "And well, there's no reason to beat around the bush, right?" Then Doug Morris said the words that would change all of our lives.

"We'd like to offer you boys a deal."

I've been high a lot in my life. Some kicks were natural, some chemical; some based on attention, some on trim, some even on pain. A lot came through music. But this moment, backstage, sweating, still catching our breath after the best show of our lives, sticks out to me, unrepeatable, unforgettable. All I remember is my head and my heart exploded with joy.

THE THREE P'S: PUSSY, PARTY, AND PAYCHECK

"YOU DON'T HAVE TO seduce the whole world to be happy, Stephen," one of my therapists in rehab, Dr. Roberts, said to me one day, as we were sitting in his sparsely decorated office.

"I'm a flirt, man," I said. "I can't help it. By the way, that reminds me, I've been trying to talk to your receptionist. She's giving me the cold shoulder, though. What's up with that?"

"Let's focus on relationships, Stephen," Dr. Roberts suggested. "It sounds like you've gone through some real emotional pain in the past. Is that fair to say?"

"I'd say I've gone through real physical pain," I corrected him.

Dr. Roberts looked up, concerned.

"I don't want to gross you out," I said, "but when we went to Japan in '87 for the Dancing Undercover tour, I came down with a case of VD that was absolutely *unholy*. Some guys might have thought it was worth it, because I caught it through a vicious three-way with two smoking international model chicks I picked up from the Lexington Queen. I think they were German. Ever heard of that club? Every rocker from the eighties knows about the Lexington Queen."

"No," said Dr. Roberts. "But this is a perfect example of how some relationships, particularly those based on sexual conquest, often lead to a short period of satisfaction, followed by long periods of emptiness. . . ."

"This conquest was followed by a long period of my dick dripping," I explained. "It just wouldn't go away. I called my doctor back in the States. 'I think I've got something.' He's all, 'Go to the doctor, you idiot!' But I was afraid of the Japanese docs, so I just sat on it. I stopped banging groupies completely. And that's when the guys in the band knew something was terribly wrong.

"Eventually, I was like, Fuck it, I'm going to the Japanese docs. But when I got to their office, it was like an assembly line. I move to one guy, he tugs on my balls. Move to the next, he draws some blood. The next one gave me some pills, and I'm out of there. But I was still boozing heavily. I didn't get better. Meanwhile, in three days, I'd be going home with a dirty dick to my girlfriend."

"You had a girlfriend?"

"Sure," I said. "Look, in those days, if we weren't married, then we were free men. Even if we *were* married. I went to Vince Neil's bachelor party, before he married that Sharise chick, the stripper from the Tropicana, okay? Tommy Lee had a bachelor party for Vince that was absolutely *insane*. Tommy rented a big huge private yacht in the Marina, it was the coolest thing ever. You had to have a fucking *laminate* just to get on board. The who's who of rockers were there, and all the waitresses and bartenders were female and fully nude, and Tommy's going around handing everybody dollar bills to give to chicks. Talk about a fucking send-off! At the end of the night, we took Vince up on the roof, cheering like crazy, put him in the center, and twenty or thirty chicks got on their hands and knees, circled around Vince, each one of them planting their face and tongue in the next one's love triangle. Just going to *town*."

"What's your point?"

"My point is," I said seriously, "there was so much goddamn trim around in those days, it just didn't make much sense to any of us to stick to one woman. You could try, and we did, but it never lasted for long."

"Which is how situations happen, like your case of gonorrhea," said Dr. Roberts.

"Yeah, and see, I started being *real* careful after that. My doctor gave me the best advice: 'Always look in the mouth,' he said. 'If the mouth's filthy, then you got a filthy snatch.'

"That guy was my man! I called him Dr. Rock. I credited him on every Ratt record. He fixed my dirty dick. Took a month, but he did it. That was probably the longest month of my life. Total deprivation. I can't believe my chick didn't break up with me. I had to make up excuse after excuse after excuse. 'Not in the mood.' Or 'headache.' But it never happened again, because, like I said, I got smart after that. I started giving them the rocker taste test."

"Taste test?"

"The rocker taste test, man. As you give 'em a hug, slip your finger in, then sniff it, around their neck," I said, my eyes bright, remembering. "Sometimes it smells like *rhino*."

"Stephen," said my therapist. He closed his eyes. "I think we've done enough for the day. Meanwhile, please stay away from the receptionist."

■ ■ ■

THERE WAS NO TIME TO CELEBRATE getting signed. We had a gig in San Francisco the following night. Phil Schwartz packed a car full of gear and beer and drove us north, toward our destination, the Keystone Theater. We were giggling like excited children. A *deal*. With *Atlantic*.

"It's insane, man. When I hear Atlantic, all I can think about is Rolling Stones and Led Zeppelin. . . ."

"Now Ratt!" cried Robbin.

I was in a fucking state of ecstasy. We all were. San Francisco had a strange glow to it that weekend. I staggered through the summer fog, shivering my nuts off, dressed in paint-splattered spats and tennis shoes, a joint behind each ear. One moment I felt wide awake, then caught in a dream, then unable to discern between the two.

"They're gonna give you some money now," Marshall told us when we returned. "It ain't much, less than ten grand a piece, so don't get happy. Don't be stupid with it."

But telling me to be smart with cash was like telling a fat chick to take it easy on the Sara Lee. Suddenly flush, I ran around town, demented, squandering my newfound cash on trinkets, gasoline, liquor, trash. A week later, they asked for all of it back.

"Accounting error," Marshall said. "Sorry."

I turned over what I had left and immediately went back to being constantly broke. It didn't matter. I knew how to get by. I had girlfriends. They fed me, they stroked me . . . you get the picture.

"Now, are you guys ready to get back into the studio?" Marshall asked us. "Ready to make a hit?"

"Marshall," I said, "by now, you should trust us."

In hot August, we teamed with new Atlantic Records staff producer-writer Beau Hill, and the six of us set about slaving for ten long weeks at the Village Recorder in West L.A. The result was *Out of the Cellar,* a ten-song album bearing three singles: "Round and Round," "Back for More," and "Wanted Man."

"How'd we do in there, Beau?" Robbin asked, exhausted beyond all belief, when it was done.

"You all were great, I promise you," said Beau. "Seriously, I think we got something special here."

I wasn't completely convinced, though.

"If it doesn't sell," I worried, "we might not ever get the chance to make another one."

"Stephen," Beau said, "it'll sell."

By late December, the album was mixed, set to be released by the spring. I paced around in gold spandex in Ratt Mansion West on Christmas Eve, nervous and tripped out, turning a tiny snow globe over and over in my hands, watching the white flakes fall with agonizing slowness. Our record wouldn't drop for three months. What the hell was I going to do in the meantime?

Marshall made that decision for me, when he came to us, excited. "Fellas, MTV is where it's at. And you're not the worst-looking band around, right? So let's put you in front of a camera and see if we can make some magic."

We all were into it. At that point, Marshall held the keys. If he had told us to jump into a huge pile of dog shit and roll around,

we would have done that, too. For my part, I loved having someone around who was willing to tell us what to do—as long as I had
the last word. I'd been scratching and clawing for too many years,
booking our gigs, a slave to the unrelenting voice inside my own
head. The yoke of responsibility was gradually starting to slide off
my shoulders. It felt like a huge relief.

"I got *great* news for you, too," Marshall confided to me. "We've
secured a big guest star for the video."

"Who?"

He grinned. "My uncle, that's who."

Milton Berle was a television legend, and he was not exactly shy
about letting everyone know about it. When Uncle Miltie came on
set, his word was law. The poor bastard who'd been hired to shoot
our video essentially had his job swept out from under him.

"What the hell do you mean, you haven't *got* a two-shot yet? Do
you even know what a two-shot is, you amateur prick?"

Our director was stunned, but the band was laughing so hard
our sides hurt.

"Milton," Marshall suggested, "how about you let the crew do
what they need to do. Then we'll start filming the band, what do you
say?"

"No chance," Milton said. "Listen, you schmucks need some
humor. I'll tell you what, I'll play two parts for you. I'll put on a goddamn *dress* for you. This is how much I love my nephew. You owe
me big for this, okay, Marshall?"

Making the "Round and Round" video was a blast. Milton Berle
cracked me up, in drag or out of it. I was so curious about his era.

"Hey," I said, between takes. "Milton—did you really bang Mar-
ilyn Monroe?"

"I'll let you use your imagination on that one," he said, giving me that famous smile.

"Everyone says you've got the biggest pecker in showbiz. Is that just another Hollywood fable, man?"

"Boy!" He looked to his nephew. "Your fucking singer asks a lot of personal questions! What's his problem?"

Marshall shrugged. "Kids. Right, Milton?"

Milton inspected me closely.

"When I was growing up," he said, "if you had pretty hair like that, you'd be considered a real *faygelah*. You know what that is, Stephen? That's the Yiddish way to say *homo*."

"Cool," I said, unfazed.

"Amazing," sighed Milton. "He doesn't even know what the hell I'm talking about. This is our future."

I wanted to get Milton a hooker as a present for doing the video for us, but our budget was so tiny, we had nothing left over to spend.

MARSHALL BERLE, MANAGER:

In the early 1980s, the music industry was in a real boom period. It was like a gold rush. When MTV came along, it really started making stars out of bands like Ratt. MTV was the model that helped break a lot of bands.

We shot the "Round and Round" video in one day. We had a very small budget, twenty-five thousand dollars. Milton came in there, and he took over the whole set. Told the director where to put the camera, told him where to light everything. It was awesome. The band loved it. And it turned out to be the right thing. Before the video came out on MTV, "Round and Round" was turned down by radio. Nobody would play it. And then when the video came out, we did the press, and it made all three networks. "Mr. Television is now Mr. MTV." And it just took off, and then radio jumped all over the single. That video propelled the band into the national spotlight.

When MTV first came down the pike, '81, '82, all you had to do was show up with a video, and they would play it, because they needed content. And then after Ratt had these huge hits, and Def Leppard, Mötley Crüe, it was simply a matter of having the record company's promotion people contact MTV and submit the video. It was not that hard to get a video on MTV. As it got later, in the late '80s, it got a little more difficult, because the style and the music was changing. That was the death of heavy metal, and hair bands like Ratt.

For a while, though, in the record business, everyone wanted a Ratt, everyone wanted a Mötley Crüe. It's funny, because when Van Halen came out, you'd think everyone would have wanted a Van Halen. Well, that didn't really happen, because the punk and new wave scene was coming right at the same time. But when Ratt came out, boy, every record company wanted one just like 'em.

■ ■ ■

IN FEBRUARY, WE BEGAN TO TOUR. The album would come out in stores in March, and so the idea was to generate a little prerelease buzz. Our aims were modest, and our road crew small: Phil Schwartz, a buddy of ours named Road Dog, Johnny Road Rat, Marshall, an accountant, the driver, a few lighting and guitar techs, and that was about it. Most of us managed to squash into one bus.

"Dude, this is pretty amazing, right?" I said to Robbin as our journey began. We lodged ourselves in the back of a big old Eagle bus, hopping up and down in our bunks like kids on the way to school. "Do you know how long I've dreamed about having a bus? Man, do you know how much *trim* we'll get on this bus? Are you *getting* that?"

Robbin agreed wholeheartedly. "A sex ship this grand needs a proper name."

"Y'know, you're right, man. Let's see. . . ." I thought. "How about . . . Starship Pussy Whistle?"

"Hmm," said Robbin, unconvinced.

"The Vagina Diner?" I asked.

"How about the Rolling Hilton?" Robbin said.

King's word was law, and the Rolling Hilton it was. We even christened it as such. Eventually Marshall found a painter with airbrush skills to emblazon the side of the bus with a giant Strat, Warren's guitar at the time. A Flying V, Robbin's choice of instrument, crisscrossed it.

"Absolutely beautiful," said Robbin. "Let's hit the road."

On the first leg of our tour we headlined small five-hundred-to thousand-head clubs, then went to open-arena shows for Billy Squier. An amazing experience—but our real enthusiasm was reserved for the Hilton. The magic bus was split into two regions: a large front lounge with seats, where the grown-ups could conduct business, and then the back area, set off by a folding door, where the band was free to drink, snort drugs, and play Pong. For music, we employed a weathered Sony double-tape-deck stereo that worked on cassettes (Blotzer dominated the deck when drunk, insisting on playing the Beatles for ten-hour stretches—"because they were four *geniuses*! Fucking brilliant, every last one of them"); for communication, a semi-functional two-part detachable cell phone with an enormous portable battery; and for comfort, a cheap AC system that sucked in the hot air from the towns we passed, gave it a quick hit of Freon, and then blew it into our sweaty faces.

Our bunks were coffinlike. They stacked three to a column, six feet and no inches long, shielded from the outside world only by a polyester curtain. No DVD players or tiny televisions in our bunks: There was a small yellow bulb coated in plastic, a thin rubber mattress, and that was it. If you awoke in the middle of the night, disoriented, and tried to sit up, you'd smash your forehead into the bunk above you before making it six inches.

The fuck if I cared. I thought it was the greatest thing I'd ever seen.

Did I give much of a shit if someone's foul toes were in my face when I woke up? No, I certainly didn't, because being awake and on a moving bus, however groggy, meant it was officially party time. It was time to crack the first beer of the day, roll the first joint, and get down to the serious business of catching a decent buzz. The coffin bunks were useful for other purposes, anyway: When we opened for Squier in Erie, Pennsylvania, after the show I stowed a cute, exuberant blonde onto the bus.

"So this is how rock stars do it!" she giggled.

"Yep. Welcome to the Rolling Hilton," I said. "Watch your head." I guided her back to my middle bunk and wedged her inside, closing the curtains but for a tiny gap, through which her lips pooched out.

"Pearcy," Bob asked. "Play Pong?"

I pulled my pants down around my ankles and received the blow job of a lifetime while losing to Blotzer at Pong. "And yet, part of me feels like I won," I said. I zipped up my pants. "Hey, King, come back here for a second, I want to talk to you."

Robbin appeared, grinning. "What are you bad dudes up to back here?"

I nodded my head toward the bunk. "There's a present inside there for you, buddy, if you ask nice."

It was on that tour that the underwear and bras started flying onstage. At first, I found it confusing: Only rarely had our fan base at the Whisky and the Troubadour stripped off their panties and tossed them into our faces. Now, twenty to thirty pairs a night regularly ended up onstage by the end of our set.

Soon I realized we had the opportunity to do something special, and I began to gather up the G-strings, the lingerie, the cotton drawers, and the bikini panties after our set. I brought them onto the bus, tied them to the luggage racks. You walked back to the john to take a piss, and it was like beating your way through the jungle. Silky, filmy lace dragged across your skin from every direction. Soon the Rolling Hilton had the subtle aroma of a whorehouse.

Our bus was a motorized fuck factory on wheels, driven by a long-haired Southern good ol' boy who never seemed to sleep a wink. It was a perfect fantasyland, built for rockers, raw and nasty, lacking many of the amenities that today's bands might take for granted. For example, no one was allowed to take a shit in the bathroom—though, drunkenly, many of us did. The primitive plumbing simply couldn't deal with a man-size turd. The stench would linger for days.

"You guys, stop shitting in the john!" our driver yelled. "You're choking my pipes. If you need to pinch a loaf, do it in a plastic bag, okay? Then when we stop at a rest stop, you can just throw it away."

I followed our driver's advice that afternoon, and went to the crapper to squeeze out a giant shit into a white plastic bag. Tying it off, I waltzed through the bus, slapping my band members across the arms and chests with my fresh bag of turds.

"Pearcy! What's the matter with you, man?" Robbin said. "Are you that sick?"

"Rotten bastard," cried Bob, covering his face with his hands ineffectually. "Christ, Stephen, what have you been *eating*?"

Drugs, weed, and alcohol got us through the long highway treks. And maybe a hit of acid. I stared out the window, pleasantly stoned, watching America's roadways and cornfields roll by.

We were starting to generate our first money and it felt good. Naturally, we had to waste it as soon as possible, lest we be mistaken for responsible human beings. Drugs were the most efficient way to do it.

"Hey look!!" yelled Robbin, Juan, and Bobby. "It's SNOWING!"

The dummies had pooled their cash and bought an ounce of blow, and in a drunken show of brotherhood, they were snorting the entire pile at once, Scarface style. Robbin tossed the excess in the air, laughing like a maniac the whole time.

The crowds weren't enormous in the clubs and theaters, but they were responsive. We played a show in Detroit where I saw a clutch of teenage chicks literally *crying*, reaching out their arms toward us like we were gods. Like . . . really? I never understood that kind of adulation. I really wasn't into music for that. But hey, I'd take it.

Soon road life began to blur, and everything smelled like gasoline and lingerie and weed and shit. The Rolling Hilton felt like a nation unto itself, governed by a completely different set of rules than the outside world. But you had to be careful: Cops were out on the prowl, and a bus with enormous guitars airbrushed on the metal siding was an obvious target.

One evening after a show, we were pulled to the side of the road. Schwartz was pushed out the door and made to go talk sense to the cop.

"You boys were going a *little* fast," he said. "Say, who you got on there, anyway?"

"It's the band Ratt," Phil said.

"Ratt? No kidding. One of those metal bands, right?" The officer stroked his chin, fascinated, and put his ticket book away. "Heck, I'd like to meet them, if you wouldn't mind too much."

"Well, okay," said Phil. "Give me one second."

He leaped back on the bus.

"Guys. Wake up. Stow all your shit. The trooper wants to come on the bus. He wants to *meet* everyone."

Suddenly we were wide awake. We shoveled our weed and cocaine into their appropriate canisters and shoved them beneath our mattresses.

"Officer!" cried Bobby. "*So* nice to meet you!"

"Beer?" I asked, working up a good shit-eating grin.

"No, no, thank you." The officer laughed. "I'm on duty."

"Sir, I just had a great idea. How would you like a pass to the show tomorrow evening?" Robbin asked. "Come hang out with us backstage?"

"Hell, you know, I'd like that!" said the cop. "I've never been backstage before."

"There may be a few nude chicks there," I said jokingly. "Are you cool with it?"

"I'm cool with it," said the officer, crossing his arms over his stomach.

"Would you let one sit on your lap?" asked Robbin. "Are you allowed to do that?"

"Oh, yes, sir," said the officer. He looked excited. "Yes, sir. You bet. If you're off duty, you bet."

There was plenty of money coming in, but we flushed that down our nostrils, lungs, and livers as soon as possible. Enjoying one of the three P's more than the others, there was lingerie as far as the eye could see.

When spring rolled around, things started to change. Our album dropped, and the initial sales were encouraging. I was ready to make the slow and steady climb, but then, out of nowhere, Ozzy's people got in contact with Marshall. Their opening act wasn't working out—how would we like to come out on the road and open for the Prince of Darkness?

"Holy SHIT!" I yelled. "You gotta be *kidding* me."

All of us were blown away. No matter who you were, if you listened to metal, or rock music in general, you had to understand that Ozzy was as good as it gets. We added a few more crew members to our entourage, took out another bus, and struck out in search of the big time.

"We really appreciate you boys coming out on such short notice," Ozzy said, when we arrived at the first gig.

"We had to kind of pull out on Squier," I admitted. "But it's worth it, man. You're . . . well, I mean . . . you're Ozzy Osbourne."

"Rumors of my greatness have been wildly exaggerated," Ozzy said. "Come along. Let's start the drinking."

We toured with Ozzy in Canada, Europe, and the U.S., nonstop. Ozzy was a strong partier, but we did our best to hang right in there with him. One night, at the Mondrian, Bobby and Ozzy and I came stumbling down the hall after a forceful night of drinking. As we passed rooms, we came across several pairs of shoes that had been put out to be shined.

"Watch," said Ozzy. "I'm going to shit in those loafers."

He dropped his pants and laid a huge, stinking shit. It was the most rancid thing I'd ever smelled. Bobby and I collapsed, literally crying with laughter. I was shaking so hard, I felt like I was going to have a seizure. Ozzy was so into it. He woke his wife just to tell her. "Sharon, darling, I've just shit in a pair of shoes." It was a proud moment for him.

Opening up for Ozzy meant that suddenly, we were playing in giant houses, in front of enormous crowds. The sight of all those screaming maniacs inspired me, so I began to take a Kodak Disc 4000 camera out onstage with me each night.

"Peoria," I yelled into my microphone. "Smile!"

I snapped off picture after picture of the roaring crowds, for no other reason than to have a memento, the stage pyrotechnics illuminating their screaming faces like the perfect flashbulb. These were some of the biggest groups of people I'd ever seen in my entire life, and there I was, stamping around in front of them. Who knew if I would ever play to a larger house? *Out of the Cellar* might sink like a stone. I wanted something to show to my grandkids besides the size-40 silk teddy that got left behind in our lighting guy's room in the Highlander Inn in Madison, Wisconsin. When I had finished playing photographer, I whipped the cameras off stage right, toward a waiting Phil Schwartz. Sometimes he caught them. Other times they found the wall and smashed into a million pieces.

"Boston!" I screamed. *"Are you ready for some fucking RATT 'N' ROLL?"*

The arena shook with the collected frenzy of fifteen thousand screams. Standing up in front of them, riding on currents of blinding light and the manic energy of raw guitar, I twisted my body through the swells and rushes of our songs, entering into the mindlessness of the moment, feeling my soul blossom with purest bliss. I was leading my troop into battle, each and every night. It was happening for us. Finally, it was happening.

■ ■ ■

OUR TOUR WITH OZZY WAS WAY too short for me, lasting only a couple of months. Then Marshall got us a monthlong gig, opening for Blue Öyster Cult, one of my favorite bands growing up. Summer was fast approaching and we felt we'd done a rather good job of getting our name out there. We felt like a few weeks off might be in order, to relax and regroup.

"Are you fucking joking?" Marshall said. "No way is Atlantic going to want to stop now. Your album's just starting to climb."

It was true. By the time June 1984 rolled around, "Round and Round" was constantly being played on MTV, to the point that I was almost embarrassed (I do a few too many awkward high-kicks in that video to feel real good about it). The ensuing success of the single had propelled the album onto the charts. Many were the days in the back of that bus that we all huddled around the latest *Billboard* magazine, checking our chart position.

Our success was so immediate, it was almost frightening. I had been prepared to put in years of steady, solid touring work

SEX, DRUGS, RATT & ROLL

in order to earn any kind of name recognition whatsoever. But after only a few months, Ratt was starting to become a household name.

We got booked at an outdoor festival in Michigan, with a host of other rising metal bands: Mötley, Scorpions, Quiet Riot, and W.A.S.P., among others. Everyone pulled into town, parked our buses next to each other's, and began to drink. Enormous thunder-clouds began to gather; soon, it was storming, out of control. A sound tower was knocked over; the dirt parking lots were seas of mud. We pulled the Mötley boys onto our bus and broke out the standard: a little Jack, a little smoke, and maybe some pills.

"No fucking *way* we're playing today," Nikki declared. We all sank back happily into the cushions of the Rolling Hilton.

"I think it's time for a trip to the doctor's office," I said. "Anyone like to join me?"

"Oh God, yes," my friends said gratefully, extending out their palms for a healthy serving of opiates. We proceeded to chomp pre-scription pain relievers for the next hour. Soon I had entered into a fugue-like state, where faces began to blur beautifully, and all voices came through a soggy, sexy ocean of sound.

And then, wouldn't you know it, the fucking sun came out.

"Gentlemen! Chop chop! The gig's a go. Sound check in five. Come on!"

Somehow, I harnessed enough endorphins to get myself out onstage, and from there, my body had sufficient muscle memory to know what to do.

The record kept climbing the charts. By July, we had scurried our way into the top thirty. Berle let us know that we weren't going to open up too many more shows: Instead, we were about to start headlining them. Good news. Now we could shake the trim tree that much harder.

What we had was just *obscene*. We were *greedy* with the trim. All you had to do was snap your fingers, and they were yours. If you wanted to get laid twice in a day, you got laid twice. If you needed more, then you took more. It was truly a numbers game, and at a twelve-thousand-person show, the numbers never once let us down.

See, they were on the hunt for us, too. The audience didn't just want to get fucked up and bang their heads: *They wanted to meet the band.* For dudes, the dream was to smoke a joint with us and talk about guitars; for chicks, it was to form some sort of romantic connection, get to know us in a way that few others could. Night after night, we granted a few lucky ones their wish. Usually, the chicks I ended up with weren't true groupies, per se: I wasn't overly fond of shady broads with loud mouths and loose lips. Instead, they tended to be sexy, down-home chicks, girls who lived regular lives in Memphis or Houston or Beaumont or Phoenix or Charlotte. When a big rock band came through town, it was like Halloween for them, their big chance to throw on their sluttiest costume. If the stars aligned perfectly, they might even get a chance to remove it.

That was my job: to align the stars.

Every night, before the show, I passed out thick stacks of backstage passes to my soldiers, Phil and Road Dog.

"Go find me the best of the bunch," I instructed.

They slogged through the parking lot, sizing up the pack and slapping backstage passes into the back pockets of the prettiest, most pristine specimens. I liked blondes, brunettes—you name it, I licked it, and they knew this. Hot is hot, and as I learned across the years, it can come in any flavor. When the show was over, Phil would herd the thirty or so chattering ladies into one small holding room, where they'd mill around excitedly, waiting for me or Robbin or whoever else felt like popping their head in there.

I'd stick my head in for two or three seconds, tops.

"Let's see . . . I'll take . . . blue top . . . and red halter. Thanks! Have a good night, everyone."

Poor Phil would have to deal with the disgruntled castoffs. It wasn't fair, I know. But that was how the cookie crumbled. None of this was fair.

But it was the crew who, unbound by the normal standards of human decency, made the true magic happen. In San Antonio, Texas, our sound technicians produced two ample-bodied sisters who dreamed of putting on a show for the boys in the band.

"Come aboard the Rolling Hilton," they suggested. "We'd like to introduce you to Brutus."

Brutus was a six-foot-long, flesh-colored double-headed dildo, with a tip on each end the size of a grown man's fist. The young ladies went right to work on Brutus, gyrating up and down, laughing, sucking on each other's tits with couldn't-give-a-shit nihilism worthy of a coming apocalypse.

The freak show attracted much instant attention. A buzz grew. The parking lot was electric with zit-faced excitement. Random fuckers from all four directions swarmed the bus, opening acts and road crew, hustling up on the roof, prying open our pop-top, just to get a look. It was the show after the show.

"I'll do anything to get backstage." It was a refrain that the crew guys heard every day, and it was music to their fucking ears. In a parking lot, true sluttiness knows no bounds. Once, I saw a gorgeous brunette sidle up to Paul, one of our riggers. Paul knew the drill.

Being a reserved sort of fellow, he led her over to a Porta-Potty, so as to take care of business in private.

Five minutes later the happy couple emerged.

"How about those passes?" the brunette reminded him.

"Sure," said Paul, "only, it's my buddy's birthday, so maybe you could take care of him, too."

Thus another jaunt to the Porta-Potty. Ten minutes later, Paul's friend emerged, looking faint. The brunette emerged seconds after him, looking smug.

"She treat you all right?"

"Holy shit," his friend mumbled. "I'd say so."

"Okay. Here ya go," said Paul, slapping a couple of passes into the brunette's hand.

We watched as the cutie took off running, elated. A hundred yards down the way, her boyfriend waited.

"She take care of business?" Paul asked.

"Oh yeah."

Soon the brunette reached her man and, waving the passes wildly, jumped into his arms. They were backstage bound. They hugged, triumphant, and then launched into a deep, soulful tongue kiss.

"Yecch!" I cried, laughing. "What the fuck?"

"I guess I leave a pleasant aftertaste," Paul decided, leaning back happily.

While we were getting ours, poor Phil wasn't sleeping. He would lie awake all night, as we rumbled from Augusta to Savannah to Columbia to Raleigh, staring at the cheap shelving of the bed above him while we boozed and screamed and then slept like babies. Phil would work for hours in the morning, dead tired, organizing our luggage, tagging the equipment, trucking the instruments onstage for us, and then, inevitably, in the late afternoon, as the partying was beginning to gear up, Phil would fall asleep involuntarily on one of the seats. That was our cue to fuck with him.

"Jesus, this is great. Watch this." Mike, our carpenter, unzipped his own fly, tiptoed over to Schwartz, and laid his hairy testicles on Phil's forehead, like a tiny hat.

I almost died from laughter. "Get a camera, please, someone get a camera. . . ."

Phil stirred, his mouth open, then quieted again. I snapped away on my Disc camera, nearly hysterical.

Phil sputtered awake, apoplectic with rage. "You sons of bitches!" he shrieked, clawing at the air. "You dirty rotten . . . I ought to slam every one of you!"

We laughed for days and days. The moral of the story was clear. Never fall asleep first on the bus.

The months rolled on, and Atlantic showed no sign of taking their foot off the tour pedal. We bounced from arena to arena, the audiences only getting bigger. Money really started coming in, more than we could spend in one place. It was now time for the guys in the band to talk about getting accountants, people to manage our funds. Robbin and I needed them more than anybody else, as the other guys had their wives and girlfriends taking care of their shit.

Our hotels started getting nicer. Small mobs would congregate in the lobby when we'd check in. Road Dog and Phil began to act as crowd control, beating back the swarms of women so the band could pass. Robbin and I looked at each other sometimes, unable to believe this was really happening.

"King?" I said, noticing the model-hot blonde who was eye-fucking me with the deepest desire all over her face, a ripped Ratt T-shirt barely covering her gorgeous torso.

"Yes, Felix?"

"This could end any day, right?"

He nodded. "Any day. You're so right, brother. Let's seize it while we got it." He whispered into Road Dog's ear, pointed toward the blonde and her equally smoking-hot friend. We would see them upstairs, immediately.

ROAD DOG, CREW:

When I went out with them, I was clean and sober. I still am clean and sober. That's the only reason I got hired by Ratt. Those guys, Warren and Robbin and Stephen, they knew me from San Diego, and they knew that I was insane when I drank. I mean, it was not good. I'm not a nice person. It was not cool.

But there wasn't a moment when Stephen wouldn't be smoking a joint, have one behind his ear, and one behind the other ear, and make sure he had enough to roll another one. I mean, that dude, he never quit smoking.

Did he get excessive? Yeah, he got excessive when it came to partying. He could outdrink and outsmoke a lot of people. Guys like Dee Snider would just stand there and watch him, going, Oh, man. The opening acts would roll up, and Stephen would sneak up to me and say, "See if they have any-thing, man. See if they're holding." That was one of the terms you would always hear: "Is William around?" For William Holden.

Summer melted into fall. The band began to feel the first signs of being fried. Night after night, we headed out onstage, looked around at each other and the crowd, and experienced the strange déjà vu that comes from playing the same set, with the same people, in the same environment, so many times in a row.

"How many shows have we played?" I asked Blotzer, who always seemed to know.

"Hmm, let me think," said Bob. "A hundred and sixty or so?"

It was enough to make your vision blur. Juan wore the same leather pants onstage every night. After the show, he would roll them off his dripping, sweaty body, and place them up on top of our luggage rack. One night, by accident, I touched them and recoiled in horror: They were stiff as a board.

ROAD DOG:

The crew usually gets more pussy than the band, if you can believe that. But it was always on the quantity, not quality basis. We were in Allentown, Pennsylvania, boring as hell, and I had grabbed these two wild-looking chicks—blond, sadistic. And they were into each other. So they're going at it in the back of the bus, and the whole crew's watching. And [road manager] Charlie Hernandez and I, we go get Stephen's wireless microphone. We turn it on and give it to them to pleasure themselves with. Over the PA sound in there, you could hear this moaning and groaning.

And then Stephen came in for sound check, and he was like, Oh my God. Nobody cleaned this?

The nation was awash with Ratt fever. You could see it on their T-shirts. After shows, audiences would wait for us to leave the parking lot, then trail us in their cars. It was flattering, at first: convertibles zipping up alongside the bus, chicks flashing us their tits, their boyfriends waving and cheering us on. Then it got strange, or annoying, and when the cars simply wouldn't give up, it became a menace to our safety.

ROAD DOG:

One of my duties was to patrol the hotel floor and make sure nobody without a pass got upstairs. One time, in Cleveland, I was walking around, and I found a naked girl in the stairwell. And I look at her, like, not really sure what to say.

"What are you doing?"

"I'm waiting for Stephen."

"You're waiting for Stephen. Well, Stephen uses the elevator."

She figured with so many people crowding in front of the elevator downstairs, she might beat the odds by hanging in the stairwell. I just told her to get her clothes. Just, come on, please get out of here.

I started to dream about returning to the soft and cushy confines of Ratt Mansion West. Los Angeles felt like a million miles away, and I began to miss everyone. I missed my mother, my brother, Victor Mamanna, and Mrs. O'Neill. I missed the Whisky and Bill Gazzarri and my Datsun B-210. How could my favorite town in the world possibly be surviving without me?

One evening, homesick in Colorado, I was roaming around our

hotel hallways with Gary, one of our guitar techs, late at night, looking for trouble. Outside of Blotzer's room, passed out, moaning in
drunken dementia, was a very unconscious rock chick groupie.

"That's so Bob," I muttered, shaking my head. "He'll get them
all sloppy in order to get what he wants, but when she's blotto, he'll
say, 'I don't like that slop in here.'"

Gary returned to his room, seized two large pillows from his
bed, and walked back to the drunken princess. There he placed
the pillows on top of each other. Together, they formed a stack ten
inches high. I eased her hips on top of the pillows, so her ass was
sticking in the air.

Gary took a condom out of his pocket, unwrapped it, and began
easing it over his index and middle finger.

"What are you up to, you freak?" I said.

"I'm a bad person. And I need a hand with this."

"I think I'll just sit here and watch and laugh about this later."

Gary eased Bobby's cutie's jeans down off her hips and rolled
her green lacy underwear down her thighs. Her little starfish winked
at us.

Gary began to work the condom into her ass, plunging his fingers in slowly, until they'd reached the third knuckle. Trying hard
not to laugh, he extracted his fingers with the deftness of a surgeon.
A couple inches of rubber trailed from her, like a latex tail.

"Good night, sweet girl." We patted our friend on the back. "I
hope you enjoyed your night with the Blotz."

We pulled her jeans back around her waist and left her there
in the hallway, ass propped up in the air, with a surprise for her to
discover later.

ROAD DOG:

They threw underwear up onstage constantly, and Stephen would pick the underwear up and smell the crotch of it. Well, this one night, man, I mean, it was a pretty good crowd, probably fifteen thousand or better, and he picks a pair of underwear up and smells it. I thought he was going to throw up. Whips that thing over to the side, and there was stuff inside the crotch of those panties that nobody could even describe.

I want to say it was pus or something, man. Just . . . crusty. Gross looking.

Stephen was awful careful about whiffing panties from then on.

It was great fun. But after a while, I started thinking, is this all there is? Are these tales ever going to reach the tender ears of my own child? (And little would I know what the future would hold. Payback is a bitch.)

Dizziness began to rule all of my waking hours. Each set sounded the same. My middle bunk, in the back, felt more and more prison-like. We needed the tour to end. But the dates dragged on, with little or no respite in between. Day after day. Week after week. Month after month. Would this party ever end?

We had done two hundred shows in a single calendar year. By December, it was time to go home. We all knew it.

"Marshall, we're done, man," I said. "Take us off the road."

"Ah, fine, I guess you've earned a break. Do the month, and then you can go home? Does that work for you?"

"How many more shows?"

"Just sixteen! You can handle that—right?"

Fuck yeah, I could. I would rarely cancel a show. I played through the flu, sore throat, sprained ankles—it didn't matter to me. My voice is what it is. I never claimed to be some operatic singer. I considered myself the party director who wrote and sang party songs, for those who wanted to Ratt 'n' Roll.

We staggered toward the finish line. I had memorized precisely how long Bobby's drum solo was, knew Warren DeMartini's favorite room service items. Our bus driver's beard seemed to have grown six inches since February. It dragged over the steering wheel as we barreled from state to state.

With six nights to go, I felt a strange itching in my armpit.

"Christ," I heard Robbin mutter. "What the hell's biting me?"

Blotzer had it, too. "Pearcy!" he yelled, clawing his crotch. "What did you do to me?"

"Nothing!" I cried, leaping to my feet, bare-chested. A silk teddy dragged against my face, blinding me. "What the hell is happening to us?"

"It's obvious, dammit," he yelled. "This bus has crabs."

Somehow, we dragged ourselves through the last batch of concerts. At our very last show, a fumigation tent was erected around the Rolling Hilton. Enormous billows of blue smoke surrounded the bus, as we watched gravely from the parking lot. It was the end of our first tour. We were going home.

NO GUTS, NO GLORY: A FISTFUL OF PLATINUM

WE HEADED TO MAUI for Christmas '84, as a band and as a Ratt family. The mission: to decompress from a hectic year on the road.

"We'll work on material for our next album here," Warren said. "Surf in the morning, write in the afternoon?"

"With the peace and quiet we've got here? We'll be done in two weeks," I said.

But the best-laid plans of men and Ratt often go awry. One morning Bobby's drum tech happened to wander through a field. His heavy foot sank deep into a cow flop, but then he stopped short, noticing something. He parted the dry dung, revealing a small gathering of mushrooms, which he sniffed curiously, then inspected with a roadie's eye. Psilocybin.

The fields were full of shit-covered goodies. We collected them excitedly, our fingers filthy from our efforts, gagging from the stench.

We washed them in the sea, and the Maui sun dried out our batch in a day's time. Every morning thereafter, Robbin and I would roll out of our luxury bungalows and brew a potent mushroom tea. It was the foulest potion I'd ever smelled. I guzzled it down, nonetheless.

"Now I'm gonna puke," I warned Robbin.

"Yes, *puke*," he encouraged me. "That's how you activate a trip. Then let's hit the jungle. It's time to communicate with sacred entities."

I couldn't help but ask myself, "Aren't we here to work on a new record?" At that time I had a steady girl, a beautiful blonde I had met at a Ratt video audition. Everybody had somebody with them—a wife, a girlfriend. I ended up sending mine back to L.A., as I was trying to get serious.

But there was not much writing happening on Maui. Just tripping and watching things melt into fractals, or swimming in the aquamarine ocean waters, contemplating the beginning of time and our newfound success, trying to surf, digging into the hot sand with a beer or two, smoking good Hawaiian weed with the local bikini beauties.

The world becomes a smaller place when you travel endlessly. We would run into Billy Squier, Bruce Dickinson from Iron Maiden . . . what, was everyone going to Maui for vacation in 1984?

The nature vacation recharged me somewhat, energizing me to the point that I felt ready to hit the studio and do the next record, and go back on the road with a vengeance. That's when we would take an unknown band, Bon Jovi, on the road, on the Invasion of Your Privacy tour. More on that later. It wasn't until the Dancing Undercover tour, when we got back to Los Angeles, that I would find a house to buy. I uncovered one in Laurel Canyon, a gorgeous three-level custom-designed party pad positioned on a steep and secluded lot, aptly titled the White House. Clearly, it had been designed by a bachelor architect with no regard for function. And I used it as just that. The girls, the rockers, my friends, musicians—the place was the ultimate party pad. And it came equipped with one very famous neighbor, just up the road. About half a mile uphill was Eddie Van Halen.

"Welcome to the neighborhood," Ed said, slapping me five, on one of my first days in the giant new home.

"Dude, it's so *quiet* up here," I said. "I'm used to L.A. being dirty and crazy and smoggy and full of people. I don't know if I'll be able to get used to this."

"Yeah, you will," Ed said. "You'll get used to it real quick."

Eddie was living with his TV-star wife, Valerie Bertinelli, who I would occasionally see hanging out at 5150, his studio. She tried to keep him on a tight leash, but now that I was in the neighborhood, Eddie felt hopeful he had found an ally in depravity.

"Stephen," he said, my first week there, as I was still unpacking boxes. "I need a favor."

"Anything," I said happily. If Eddie Van Halen asked you for a favor, you were going to give him a kidney.

"Let me keep some vodka at your house. Valerie doesn't like me drinking too much."

"Dude, of course. My freezer is your freezer."

"Cool," he said. "I promise I won't abuse the privilege."

Many were the mornings where I rolled out of bed around noon, wandered out onto the large back deck that jutted out from my master bedroom, and attempted to come to terms with the life of a new Laurel Canyon homeowner. It was a life where birds chirped and the air was crisp and cool. I loved it. And yet I missed the rabies-infested squirrels of my youth. Had they vanished forever?

Then I'd hear the *whrrrrr* of an expensive moped heading down the hill, coming closer, and finally stopping in my driveway, and I'd know it was time for me to be a good neighbor.

Eddie was always apologetic.

"Aw, man. Thank you so much," he said, pulling open my freezer door and removing a bottle of vodka. "Have one with me?"

"Love to," I said, finding glasses. "And listen, it's no problem."

"It *is*, man. I feel like I'm imposing. Listen, Stephen, let me tell you what I want to do. Let me keep a bottle in your bushes, okay? That way, I won't have to bother you, you know?"

"Dude." I laughed. "It's not a bother, I told you. You don't have to keep your shit in a hedge."

"But what if I come by," said Ed, looking concerned, "and you're not home?"

Valerie wasn't a bad person; she just had bitten off a little more than she could chew when she fell in love with the most famous rocker on the planet, who just so happened to have a taste for party that rivaled some of the best. Most rock wives just sort of looked the other way and rolled with the punches, but Valerie was too strong a presence, not to mention a star in her own right, to look the other way. So she tried tough love with Eddie, but that made them more like a little boy and his mom than an adult couple.

I remember going out to dinner with them soon after moving into my new house. I brought along my girl, Britta, who had been in a couple of our Ratt videos.

"Who's your friend, *Stephen*?" Valerie asked icily, as we sat down for sushi on Ventura Boulevard.

I nudged my dining companion gently. "Introduce yourself, babe."

"Hi," she giggled, extending her hand, decorated by a fingerless lace glove: high fashion, at the time. "I'm Britta."

Valerie's face and mouth formed the shape of a smile, though it was not what I'd call warm, exactly. "Should I assume you two met at some *club*?"

"Steve and I met at one of his video shoots," Britta said. She drew closer to me. I kissed her lightly on the lips.

The topic sufficiently explored, we turned to our menus, except for Ed, who continued to stare wistfully at Britta.

"Eddie?" asked Valerie expectantly.

He broke his gaze. "Yeah, baby?"

"What are you eating?"

"I'm not hungry," he mumbled. You couldn't blame him for needing to look. Britta was a model and an aspiring actress. Gravity had touched nothing on her body. I don't think Valerie liked any girl around Ed—let alone one of mine.

After the tours, I would always reward myself with a car. After the Cellar tour, I was off and running to the Porsche dealership. The Datsun B-210 had served its purpose, and now it was time to put it out to pasture. I had always wanted a brand-new 944 Turbo, black.

The guy at the dealership looked at me funny when I showed him the car I wanted.

"Yeah, sure."

"No," I said. "I want that car right there." And I paid—in cash— and drove out that day.

And I continued that process every year after each tour, until I had a nice stable of Porsches. One time at the White House, Fred

Coury, drummer of Cinderella, stayed with me for a while, and brought another black Porsche. We'd wake up and go, "Hey, what Porsche are we going to drive today?" They were all black. A tough decision.

My new car drove so fast and so smooth, I felt like I was back on the drag strip.

"Mom," I said, "you dig driving fast, right?"

"I try to go the speed limit, honey. It's safer that way."

"Listen, stay right where you are. I'll see you in a couple of hours." I barreled down Highway 5 to San Diego, picked up my mom, and took her out for a spin in my new wheels.

"It's very lovely," she admitted.

"Want one?"

"I have a very nice car of my own, honey, thank you."

She fought me tooth and nail, but in the end I would not be denied, and I managed to drag her into the closest dealership. We left in matching 944s, honking at each other, then flying off in opposite directions.

I was in love with the little Porsche. In the first few weeks of owning it, I tooled around Los Angeles constantly, soaking up sun, testing out my new toy. I had a car phone, and the temptation to talk on it at all times was nearly irresistible.

"King!" I yelled, my hair flying behind me, doing a hundred and forty on the freeway. "What are you doing? Come out with me, let me show you my new Porsche."

"Nah, man. I'm going over to Nikki's. We're going to hang out there for a while."

I got the message. Robbin had money now, too. He had never been overly interested in fancy houses, or expensive toys. Robbin was about the moment, diving into it, and testing his limits. He was all about excess and drugs.

I couldn't stop speeding around town, though. And I couldn't keep my hands off that car phone. It was one of those shoebox phones that cost a fortune and weighed about ten pounds. "Chris! What's new?"

"Not too much, man. Welcome back."

Chris and I had pretty much washed the slate clean after the Mickey Ratt split. Now we were closer than ever. We had history together—and anyway, it was easy to be buddies when things were going so well for both of us. Rough Cutt had been picked up by Warner Brothers. In the spring of 1985, they were gearing up to record their first album under the supervision of Tom Allen, who'd produced one of Judas Priest's best records, and they were also about to go on the road with Dio. I took my Porsche over to the Record Plant to hang out and watch them lay down tracks.

"Sounds pretty great in there," I said, when Chris came outside to smoke a cigarette.

"Thanks, dude," he exclaimed. "Hey, *nice* wheels."

"There's a phone in there," I said, "if you ever want to use it."

Walking around my vehicle, inspecting his reflection in the perfect finish, Chris said, "Remember back in San Diego, when you used to say, 'We'll be putting cocaine on our cereal instead of sugar'?"

"Oh yeah." I laughed. "Of course. That was dumb."

Chris looked at the Porsche, and at the Record Plant behind him. He stubbed his cigarette out on the ground. "Well, brother, we ain't that far off."

With the label pushing us, Ratt began to meet and write again. Atlantic wanted to get us back out on the road as soon as possible. It became a year-by-year process. Off the road; into the studio. On the road; back to the studio. If we had an album to flog by the time we were on tour, so much the better.

"We're gonna invade the houses of America." Robbin laughed. "Housewives, too. Lock up your wives and daughters."

Beau Hill joined us again in the studio, and we recorded our second album, *Invasion of Your Privacy*. Our single "Lay It Down" led the way. The album wasn't a major stylistic leap from *Out of the Cellar*, but it was a solid effort. It faithfully represented what we offered our fans: short, rowdy, blues-inspired metal tunes, presided over by our resident guitar genius and backed by an unrelenting rhythm section. I was excited for the day it would come out in stores.

We began to gear up mentally for what would be another long journey out on the road. Robbin and I began to discuss who we wanted to take out there with us as an opening band. Openers were key. You wanted them to be different enough from your group so that you could get a crossover effect in the fan base, luring people to come see you who normally wouldn't have bought the ticket. But you also needed them to be similar enough that your two musical flavors didn't totally clash when you put them on the same bill.

"I hear there's this one group from Jersey that's starting to break," Robbin said. "Apparently they have a singer who all the chicks go nuts over."

"Who's that?"

"Bon Jovi."

We gave their album a listen, and Robbin was right, it was perfect for us. . . . Little did we know, that little band from Jersey would be so hugely successful, even to this day. We had Marshall float the idea to Bon Jovi's management. *Tell your boys to come out on the Invasion tour. . . . Let us show you the world of the Rolling Hilton. . . .*

They agreed, and we all started to pack our bags. A few weeks before we were scheduled to go out, I heard from Vic that our old friend Joe Anthony was laid up in the hospital, with a punctured lung. I decided to drop in on him.

"Joe."

"Stephen, man. Hey, thanks for coming to see me."

"Joe, when I was fifteen, I lived in one of these hospitals for a year. I know how it feels to shit into a bedpan, okay?"

"I just have a punctured lung," Joe said. "I still shit like a regular person."

"Oh yeah," I said. "How'd it happen, by the way?"

"Stunting," he said. "I was out on this movie that's coming out next year, *Legal Eagles*. Robert Redford's in it. So's Debra Winger. I was jumping out of some moving car, and I fell wrong. Now I don't know if I'll get work anymore. Coordinators don't want to hire you once you're hurt bad—you reinjure yourself, and they're liable."

"Listen, Joe, what are you doing when you get out of this spot?"

"Driving a limo, probably," Joe said glumly. "I've been doing it off and on for the past couple of years in between stunt gigs. It's not the worst job, I guess."

"Well, look," I said. "Forget all that. We need extra security on our new tour. How about you consider coming out on the road with us?"

"Seriously?" said Joe. "Man, you don't have to ask me twice. You just got the newest member of your team."

We were ready to set sail. March of 1985, Ratt and Bon Jovi kicked off the Invasion tour. From the very beginning, it was larger than the Out of the Cellar tour. Bigger stages, bigger production values, multiple nights in arenas, and consistently sold-out shows of fifteen thousand people or more. Every single night, it was lighters flickering and fists pumping the air, and the girls were everywhere. We could do no wrong. Soaked with sweat and swept up in the energy and the momentum, we felt like Zeppelin or Aerosmith up there. Of course, we weren't—but I'll tell you, in 1985, it sure felt like we were close.

ROAD DOG:

During the Invasion of Your Privacy tour, the women were absolutely nuts for Stephen. There were many times when fifty women were lined up in the hotel lobby to see him. Stephen was the kind of guy who'd come in, look at them, take his pick, and make me move the rest of them out. "Make sure they hit the elevator." It was funny, because we still shared rooms in those days, and if you drew the short straw and had to be his roommate, you were screwed. Stephen wouldn't let anybody in the room until he was done. You were left standing outside.

He had his favorite strip clubs, like Shotgun Willie's, in Denver, that was a five-stage strip club, but truthfully, he didn't need a strip club. He had whatever he wanted, when he wanted it. It was like a remote control for him: He'd just point and click.

In New York City, at the height of Invasion of Your Privacy, Ratt was on top of the world. We were staying at the Helmsley Palace. I'll never forget it, because their beds were so comfortable . . . you couldn't even sit on the bed, because you'd just want to go to sleep. So me and Stephen go out one night. We get a limo and head over to the Limelight. At that time, it was the big rock-star hangout. They had VIP rooms where Billy Idol and Steve Stevens and quite a few other rock stars were hanging. It was an area nobody could even get to.

Well, Stephen's severely trashed. And Stephen, when he gets trashed, he don't really tell you a whole lot. He just kind of says, "We're leaving." Or, "We're leaving. Bring that chick." He never bothered to explain much. So we left and came back to the hotel. And I'm sitting in the room and there's an earthquake. New York has an earthquake. The place is rumbling and shaking. It must have woken Stephen up, because right away, I got a call on the phone. "Where the fuck is my little black bag?" I asked, "What little black bag?" He says, "The one I had with me tonight!" So I call the limo company, and thank God, they had it. Stephen had thirty thousand dollars cash in there, just in case he ran into something he wanted to buy.

The Limelight was the best. The booze was flowing. Just waterfalls of vodka, splashing in my face. I tried to pay, but the bartenders just laughed at me. "Round and Round" took on a new, more literal meaning.

I had a little fame now, for whatever that was worth, but it was manageable, and fun. People recognized me as someone out of the ordinary, but you could tell most of them didn't know my name. In other words, I looked the part of what they wanted a rock star to be—long hair, glammed-out, generally drunk, hand on someone's tit—but the question was . . . which rocker was I? *Nikki? Paul Stan-ley? The guy from Judas Priest?*

It was kind of perfect. Kept me mildly normal, but still got me in behind the velvet rope.

In the Limelight, you could always count on some actual famous people being there. I loved watching them. They reminded me of animals in the zoo, eyes darting all over the place. One evening I saw Simon Le Bon, of Duran Duran, and I almost spilled my drink all over myself in my excitement.

"Simon!" I said, approaching him. "Hey, I'm Stephen. Enormous fan."

"Thanks so much," he mumbled. Simon Le Bon didn't look too interested in talking, but I ventured on.

"I'm in a band, Ratt." No reaction. "Hey, I would just love to get a picture with you, man—what do you say?" There was a professional photographer bouncing around the room with a Nikon on a neck strap, asking the famous people if they'd like to get their pictures taken with the other members of their strange club.

"Nah, that's okay," he said.

"Hey." I laughed. "I promise it won't hurt. It'll just take a second."

"What are you, deaf? I said no."

Simon Le Bon had always been someone who I'd looked up to, fashion-wise. I was into Duran Duran's sense of theater, too: their willingness to embrace kitsch while still maintaining a great amount of musical integrity. When they were running on all cylinders, they were one of the most complete, impressive pop groups of the 1980s.

But now their singer was being a dick.

I shuffled away and approached the photographer. He whispered in my ear, "When I give you the sign, run up to Simon." I jumped next to him, placed my arm around him, and said cheese.

"What the hell is—"

SNAP!

Thanks, Le Bon! You were my hero and always will be, you crusty fuck!

Weirdness begets weirdness. That goes double when you're partying in New York. The city is dark and full of roaches, and freaks who wish to stay on beat must booze heavily. I sucked down a gin and tonic, jammed into the Limelight bathroom, sequestered myself in a stall, and gobbled a Seconal.

An hour later, the midnight chimes were striking, and I was vibrating at a high frequency. I was approached by a woman and her twelve-year-old daughter.

"Pardon me," the woman said pleasantly. "Do you have a moment?"

"Sure," I said, extending my hand. "I'm Stephen." At this point, I was blitzed enough to be anyone she wanted. I kept that to myself.

"I'm Jaid Barrymore." She motioned to her kid—a cute, chubby, brown-haired girl. "This is my daughter, Drew. She'd love to meet you."

I squinted, confused. "Hey there, Drew."

"Hi, Stephen." She smiled in this charming way.

Then it hit me: *This was the girl from* E.T.

Jaid backed away a couple of feet, and me and Drew chatted for a little bit.

"What's a kid like you doing up this late?" I said.

She snorted. "I stay up till three every night. This is nothing."

"Have you ever been to a nightclub like this before?"

She laughed again. "Stephen! I go to clubs *all the time.* Don't you know *anything?*"

She was kind of a charming kid. Really adult. I realized how drunk I was and pushed my glass away from me. "Oh, sorry."

"What are you *sorry* about?" She giggled. "I love drinking."

"Oh," I said. *I love drinking, too. Hmm . . . can I say that?*

She looked around the room. "The Limelight is really awesome. But Studio 54 is even better."

"Can you get me in sometime?" I joked.

"Of course," Drew said, serious. She snapped her fingers. "Simple as that."

I laughed, and then she did, too. She was a pretty cool little person, even then.

"Drew would love a picture with you, Stephen," her mom said.

I brightened. "Rad! I would love one with her, too."

We got the photographer's attention, and he snapped off a couple of mementos. Jaid laid her head in my lap, so she wouldn't be visible in the picture.

Life kept accelerating. Our visibility was spiraling out of control. Fans swarmed the hotels before shows, falling victim to rock mania. We checked into our rooms in Little Rock, Arkansas, and pushed past the seas of manic, grabbing hands. Finally we made our way upstairs. Unlocking the door to my room, I sighed, relaxing onto the bed: alone at last.

"Stephen?" The curtains parted.

"What the fuck!" I screamed. "Who are you?"

"I'm so sorry," said the young woman, tiptoeing out, shamefaced, from behind the curtain. She held a Sharpie marker in her hand. "I just . . . really wanted to meet you."

"This is breaking and entering! I could have you arrested!"

"Please don't. I'll leave right now." Shyly, she extended the marker toward me. "But first, could you sign my tits?"

It was a lapse of all sense and judgment, and we were the beneficiaries. Backstage at the Little Rock show, Sweet, Sweet Connie Hamzy herself waltzed in, the most famous rock groupie of all time. She wasn't bad-looking, but then again, she didn't look exactly fresh, either. Her eyes scanned the room restlessly until they found Robbin. When she saw King, her entire face lit up.

"You might be the handsomest guy I've ever seen in person," she said, smiling. "I've already done the crew—honey, let me show you what I do."

Robbin had a few in him, so he just shrugged and let her unbuckle his pants.

I sat there, about ten feet away, watching with a mixture of horror and fascination. Soon Robbin's expression began to change, from casual drunk, to amused horndog, to enraptured monster. . . .

"She's a *freak!*" he whispered, laughing. Connie was going to town on him. She put a lot into her work, moving with such speed and fervor that Robbin nearly lost his footing several times.

Finally she swallowed him down. Wiping her mouth with the back of her hand, she gestured to me. "Now you."

"Nooo!" I said, laughing my ass off. "What you just did to my friend right there, that was as close as you're going to get to me."

But she kept after me. You don't become the world's most famous rock groupie by giving up easy. In the end, she hounded me so relentlessly that finally I was forced to bring her off to the side for a little talking-to.

"Connie," I said. "You don't want what I have."

"Oh," she said seductively. "I wouldn't be too sure about that. What is it?"

"Diarrhea dick," I said chummily.

That shut her up.

There was sex fever in the air. Joe Anthony, quickly finding his tour legs, learned the tricks of the trade from Phil and Road Dog. Soon he was in there with the best of them, slapping out passes like high fives.

"The band would like to have you as their special guest," said Joe, flashing his trust-me, I'm-from-Tulsa smile. "And if they don't pick you, then I'd be happy to fill right in."

But we hardly needed our team to recruit. Other guys, caught up in the hysteria of the parking lot, would do it for us. One afternoon, having driven through the night from Pensacola to our next gig in Fort Lauderdale, we passed on getting a day room at a hotel. Instead we just pulled into the parking lot at the arena, to try to catch an hour or so of rest there.

"Excuse me?" A knocking came at the door, gentle but insistent. "Pardon me?"

Joe answered it. It was a skinny guy and a voluptuous, beautiful woman wearing an off-the-shoulder blouse, a miniskirt, and a pair of boots. "What's up? The band's sleeping, man. No visitors."

"Sherry here would really like to come on board for a little while," explained the guy.

Joe looked her over carefully. She was drop-dead gorgeous. Only a fool would have refused.

"Well," he said, "what'd you have in mind?"

"I want to do a little show for the guys in the band."

"She's a really wild girl," added the guy. "Isn't that right, honey? Aren't you a wild one?"

She smiled, nodding, her chest bouncing up and down.

"Well, all right," Joe said. "She can come on up for a while. You gotta stay outside, though."

The guy nodded. "Absolutely. I have no problem with that. I'll be right here."

"Who the fuck are you, anyway?"

"Her husband," said the guy. "*Huge* fan of the band."

The lewdness, the moral oddity. After a while, it all went to your head. How could it not? Halcion, Valium, Darvocet, and Percocets took the edge off. The boys liked krell, but I was studying at pharmaceutical college. We all had our interests.

Ratt hopped from arena to arena. Then we went to Japan. We were already being treated like royalty in our own country, but what we experienced over there was another thing altogether. Truly, it was like being a Beatle. Those fans were so dedicated, so intense, and ultimately, so completely insane. They came bearing homemade gifts and trinkets and stuffed animals and dolls in our likeness and unique watercolor portraits, all pushed into our arms by crying black-haired beauties. Most impressive of all, we seemed to have been assigned separate groupies for each member of the band.

"Dude, how is this possible?" said Joe. "I got groupies for *me*. How do they even know who the hell I am?"

They were incredibly organized. Zlozower, our favorite rock photographer, came along to snap off some pictures. Like Joe, he had his own clutch of adoring fans.

"I don't know what kind of groupie would choose the goddamn photographer," he growled, "but I'm not complaining."

Mr. Udo, Japan's legendary rock promoter, treated us like we were stars there. The tiny man walked around town like he owned it. Three passions ruled his heart equally: women, rock and roll, and sumo wrestling.

"You come see sumo," he demanded, on one of our first nights in town. "Man cannot know Japan until he sees sumo."

He arranged for us to attend a spirited match, where massive behemoths wearing colored thongs tangled like enormous, pissed-off walruses. From our vantage point, the flabby spectacle was kind of unnerving.

"Bobby," I whispered, "look—that guy's even fatter than you are!"

"Suck it," said Bob calmly, sipping his beer.

JOE ANTHONY, SECURITY:

Before the AIDS thing broke out, Udo used to take us to these bathhouses. It's like a massage parlor, and you go in, strip down, you have like four chicks on you who are nude, and you're in a Jacuzzi, and they wash you down with their pussies. . . . It blew my mind. They'd put their pussy on your fucking leg, a chick on each leg, and roll all over your legs and all over your body, your head and everything, washing your body with their pussies. Then they'd sit you on this little stool that's got a hole in it for your balls to drop down and they'd fucking massage you and put baby oil on, fuck you and suck you and put you in a pretzel position. . . . It was just fucking incredible, especially for a kid like me.

They'd whip you around, crack your back, crack your neck, the next thing you know your legs are over your . . . she's got your balls in her mouth, one's tonguing your butt . . . bringing you drinks and sushi . . . just crazy.

The Japanese women were very quiet. Very shy. Until you got them behind closed doors. Then they were fucking animals.

As musicians, we were holding our own. But as friends to one another, the seams were starting to show. Our constant touring and the grind we put ourselves through to make our name was beginning to take effect. Robbin was our peacemaker, the man who you could count on to extend an olive branch. The rest of us took our turns being crusty, irritable fucks.

Bobby, Juan, and Warren were all married. They had family responsibilities to worry about. After a few months of constant partying and sleeping on a tour bus, your bandmates probably start to look less and less appealing, compared to some vision of your wife in your comfortable bed at home. I got that.

I never tried to be an asshole, but the truth was, I was one once in a while. I was obsessed with getting my quota. Occasionally I could be a loud drunk. But then, I was nothing compared to Bobby, who lived to scream and yell and be stupid, or snap his fingers in restaurants at the waitstaff.

"Hey! Come on!" yelled Blotzer, in restaurants across the land. "Hey, how about some *service* over here?"

Robbin developed a saying: "He who dines with the Blotz is a fool." You just can't insult the service and send your food back three times in the course of one meal, generally acting like a loud, self-important jerk, without some member of the waitstaff taking that burger you keep sending back and hocking a gob of mucus in between the lettuce and the meat. I mean, that's what I would have done.

Bobby and I had different blind spots. When we saw the other guy acting like a total asshole, we never hesitated to call him out on it, but when we did the same idiotic shit ourselves, neither would cop to it. We started to bicker pretty bad around the Invasion tour, and never did manage to turn it all the way around.

The tour wound down without major incident. We found ourselves back in Los Angeles, with more money than we knew what to do with and increasing notoriety within the rock business. It wasn't uncommon for me to withdraw a thousand dollars a day from the bank and then try to figure out a way to piss through it. Limo adventures were always a fun way to waste money.

Life looked good from the back of a white stretch limo, arms wrapped around two gorgeous blondes with dangling earrings and cocktail dresses riding up their thighs. Our limo drivers understood the rules of the game, too: They knew if Robbin was going out to pick up Nikki, they'd have some heroin and blow and whatever booze they wanted on hand. For me, you had to stock the limo with a gram of blow, because chicks always wanted it, and booze, and a bag of weed. And well, if you got a couple of pills, you might as well bring them, too.

Chicks and drugs and booze: It wasn't a complicated formula, but frankly, that's what made us happy. It was fun to share with the young rock dudes, too, kind of do for them what Dave and Eddie used to do for me. I'd take out Andy McCoy, from Hanoi Rocks; Mike Tramp, from White Lion; Tracii Guns, from L.A.

Guns; and Steven Adler, from the up-and-coming Guns N' Roses, all the time. I actually bought Tracii a guitar once—he didn't have a guitar at the time, so I took him to Guitar Center and said, "Pick one." Steven in particular was a really nice guy. He used to come over to my house in Laurel Canyon quite a bit. One day, he was looking all hopefully at the platinum record we'd gotten for *Out of the Cellar.*

"I just want *one* of those," he said wistfully. "I swear to God, my life will be complete if I just get one of those platinum albums."

"You got a tape?"

"Yeah."

"Throw it in."

We listened for half an hour without saying much at all.

"Steve?" I said, finally, when the cassette had clicked off. "You're gonna be fucking huge. See that album? You're going to have a *wall* of those."

There was always something strange to do in Los Angeles, a town where if you felt like it, you could use whatever fame you had like a tool. One evening Joe and I headed down to the Stock Exchange, a good club downtown. We'd landed the second-best table in the house for ourselves and our dates, when the air pressure in the room lowered, somehow. Immediately I understood: There was royalty afoot.

Then I saw him.

"Holy shit, Joe," I whispered. "Don't look over. That's Michael fucking Jackson."

Joe looked over at the table, which was a few down from us. He squinted for a moment. "I actually know that guy."

"What the fuck are you talking about, you *know* him?" I said.

"When I was working at the limo company," said Joe, "I used to drive for him every now and then."

"Get out of here."

"It's true. Actually, I mostly used to drive Bubbles around."

I looked at him blankly.

"His chimp," Joe clarified. "Bubbles was a trip. I used to have to take him downtown to this tailor, to get fittings. Michael liked to dress him up in little sailor suits. We'd always stop off and get him a carrot juice—that was his favorite drink. And you know those plastic clowns, that have sand in the bottom, that you punch, like a Weeble? Bubbles had to have one of those to smack around, or he just went fucking nuts."

"So *introduce* me to *Michael*," I begged. "Please, Joe, I really want to meet him."

"I don't want to do that," said Joe. "He's a private dude. Come on, Stephen."

"As a friend, I'm asking you this favor."

"Ah, hell," Joe said. He lumbered down to Michael's table, then pointed over toward me. I ran my hand over my date's leg, mostly just because I could. She had an amazing thigh, perfectly formed.

"He'll see ya," said Joe, sitting down heavily. "Don't slobber all over him, okay?"

Unsteady feet brought me over to the young idol. His hair was perfect and unmarked, bearing no sign of the recent Pepsi incident, when it had caught on fire during a commercial on a lot in Culver City.

"Michael," I said, reaching out my hand. "Stephen Pearcy. Giant, giant fan."

Michael looked only slightly uncomfortable. "Hi. It's so nice to meet you."

"I won't take up too much of your time," I assured him. "I won't even sit. Unless you want me to."

"No," said Michael sweetly.

"Would you like a beer? I'll bill it to my table."

"I don't drink," said Michael. He smiled. He had a charming smile. "Thank you, though."

"Oh yeah! I read that somewhere. You don't drink." I just stood there, hovering over his table, gaping. "No drinking."

"Michael has enjoyed meeting you," said a dude who was standing behind his table, wrists crossed, in traditional bodyguard fashion.

"Oh!" I said. "Sure!" I backed away from the table, grinning hugely. "Hey, Michael, feel free to come over and sit with us later, if you feel like it!"

"He's good," the bodyguard said.

JOE ANTHONY:

Sometimes I'd drive way up to Rancho Cucamonga, and pick up this little girl named Gail, who was ten years old. I used to pick her up and drive her out to Michael's house in Encino. He also had a condo over in Westwood, over on Wilshire. And I'd drop this kid off. Then after the weekend was over, I'd pick her up and drive her home.

Michael would call me in the car, and I used to think it was the girl's mother. You know? "Hello? Let me speak to Gail." I remember her saying to me, "Hey, Michael told me to tell you to roll up the partition and hang up the phone." I'd hang up the phone and roll up the partition, and they'd talk on the phone for an hour. God only knew what the fuck they had to say to each other.

It was a heady time. I'd drink four beers, turn on the radio, and hear the band. I'd snap it off, find a joint to smoke, turn on the television, and see myself there. There was no place to run. I tried to be a good guy and stay connected to my peer group, keep smiling, keep it social. It was so odd to be around so many people in the public eye, though, grinding their teeth with ego and coke and desire. Once you were famous, you were damned to stay that way. You started to mostly interact with people who shared the same condition.

One evening I found myself at some club in Hollywood, trying to make conversation with Billy Idol.

"Stephen, mate!" he screamed in my ear. "DO YOU HAPPEN TO HAVE ANY BLOW ON YOU?"

"Yeah," I said. "Sure."

Billy's eyes got big and excited. "Then let's leave this fucking place and go to my flat and DO SOME!!"

We sped to his apartment in a limo. We parked and Billy turned to me. "How about that blow, then, mate?"

I handed him the packet.

"Listen," he instructed me, sliding the gram of cocaine into his shirt pocket, "don't pay my wife any mind. She's in a *very* shit mood."

His wife hovered in the doorway to greet us. She was tall and gorgeous.

"So?" she snapped. "Where the fuck were you?"

"With Stephen," he said, pointing at me. "Say hello to Stephen." He walked past both of us and noisily shut the bathroom door.

"I've been waiting for you for FOUR HOURS!!" she called after him. You could hear Billy turn the bathroom fan on.

Seething, his wife crossed her arms and turned to me. Her face was sour.

"Who the fuck are you?"

"I'm no one," I said vaguely. "I'm in a band."

"And how do you know my husband?" she asked.

"We . . . ran into each other," I said lamely. "At a club."

"*Fucking* musicians," she said, stabbing her finger into my chest. "You *fucking* musicians. You have to fuck every twenty-one-year-old cunt in high heels that you meet, don't you?"

"Stephen." It was Billy. Full of pep. "Shall we go?"

"Yes," I said. "Just in time."

His wife hung in the doorway, staring hatefully at both of us. She had her pose down just perfect, just absolutely beautiful, but her performance was wasted on Idol. He was way too geeked to recognize anything but his own pounding heartbeat.

We drove back toward the club. Why the fuck we had to go to his house to do blow when we could have done blow with Vince and Gary Busey in the bathroom at the club was still a mystery to me. . . .

"Hey, could I get the rest of that gram, man?"

"Ah, mate," said Idol, apologetically. "I did the whole thing."

Our driver stopped at a red light and we peered at the street signs.

"But," I said, confused, "we were only at your house for three minutes."

"Yes," said Billy. We were both silent for a second. Then the light went green, and the driver stomped on the gas pedal.

THE GOOD, BAD, AND THE UGLY

BIG JOHN, "ROCK OF LOVE," RATT AND POISON SECURITY:

By the time 1987 rolled around, the Sunset Strip was absolutely crazy. Fucking madness. You ever see that movie that Penelope Spheeris made? Decline of Western Civilization, Part II. *Watch it, it tells the whole story. I was up on the Strip a lot in those days. I was still a fan at the time. One day, I watched Bobby Dall from Poison beat the shit out of this guy with a steel fucking pipe.*

They were still a relatively small band at the time. I think they had just changed their name from the Spectres to Poison. Anyway, some guy kept on covering up their flyers with his band's shit. Finally Bobby caught him at it. He followed him in his car to a Quik Stop, and then he just fucking ambushed the guy. Beat him senseless with a steel fucking pipe. "Who the fuck are you to cover my band flyer?!" he kept screaming.

I couldn't tell you why Bobby had an industrial fucking vacuum cleaner pipe with him. But he certainly did. I'll never forget that curvy plastic tubing flailing out behind him. It was brutal. Absolutely brutal.

And someone goes to the guy afterward: "Hey, you just got your ass beat by a chick."

By the mid- to late '80s, metal was no longer fringe music. This wasn't the US Festival, when it had reached a point of mainstream understanding: It was the beginning of full-on oversaturation. Roving gangs of dudes in eyeliner jammed the Strip, strutting around in acid-washed jeans, leather jackets, and bandanas, pimping their bands from underneath umbrellas of back-combed hair. Riki Rachtman's Cathouse was the club to go to if you wanted to see or be seen. I made periodic appearances there, making careful notes on the scene that seemed to have exploded out of control.

Apart from Robbin, I never saw my bandmates in Los Angeles when we weren't in the studio, recording. We spent so much time together on tour that I think we all felt relieved to take any break we could. Eddie Van Halen was still stopping by my house frequently to knock back his vodka in the mornings. (He actually got busted for drunk driving leaving my place on that bike one day. I don't think he rode it anymore after that.)

Often when I was on the road, my drummer from Mickey Ratt, John Turner, watched my place. He used to get a shock every now and then when Ed would knock on the door.

"Eddie Van Halen's at the door!" he said when he called me.

"Let him in," I said. "He just wants a drink."

My shopping had not evolved much since the days of living with Mrs. O'Neill. A typical trip to the store would net me two and a half cases of beer, several bottles of Merlot, a quart of vodka, and milk, for health. At least once a week we would have parties that left a massive footprint on my home: hundreds of beer cans crushed and thrown on the floor, cigarettes stubbed out on coffee tables, coke residue on every flat surface, half-smoked joints sprinkled in among the pizza boxes.

The disorder didn't sit well with me. Contrary to what the rock stereotype might be, I couldn't stand to live in filth.

"I'm having trouble keeping it together," I confessed to Robbin. "We're on the road so much, man."

"I know," he agreed. "We have no idea how to be normal people."

I had always been immature, but when the whole world starts buying your album and inviting you to present at the Grammys, looking the other way when you show up trashed and slobbering, well, you truly lose all desire to grow up. Robbin was even less grounded than me. He had some house in the hills, where he kept his expensive guitar collection and all his weird impulse-buys, like new bicycles with the tags still on them, but mostly he felt happiest when he was bouncing from woman to woman, trading his love and affection for room and board and three hot meals a day. For a time, he lived over at Vicky Frontiere's, whose mom owned the Rams. Her home was well known as a rocker crash pad. Tawny was always dating some famous guy, but she and Robbin still had love for each other, and some nights he stayed with her, too.

"I think I get *lonely* living by myself," he said.

"Shit," I admitted, "I do too. And I get weird."

"Weird?"

"Dude," I said, "I've gotten into this terrible habit of waking up, thinking I'm in some hotel, and just fucking spitting on the walls of my own goddamn bedroom. I feel like a crazy person. But I just can't stop doing it."

"I'll tell you what we need to do, Stephen," said King, finally. "You and me need to take a walk somewhere. Doesn't that sound *healthy*? Let's go on a hike."

But Robbin and I never embarked on any hikes. The closest I got to getting out into nature or getting any exercise was lying on a deck chair poolside at the Sunset Marquis with a margarita in my hand. I loved the Marquis dearly and spent incredible amounts of money to stay there any time I could. And if it sounds insane to rent a bungalow in a luxury hotel for weeks at a time when you already own a house located about four miles away, let me just explain that by this point, *Out of the Cellar* had gone two times platinum, and *Invasion* was on the verge of selling more than a million, too. We had publishing revenues, merchandising deals, and a portion of the gate at every show. Money was pouring into our hands faster than any of us could spend it.

The Sunset Marquis was where I felt most comfortable in those days. I ended up staying there so long, they gave me a bungalow instead of a room. It was like a hut, set off from the main building, and I brought my dogs there and really settled in. A cute lead singer from a very popular New Wave band came knocking on my door one day. A little too late, I figured out she was involved. But the deed was already done. Robbin saw me having so much fun, he decided to get a room of his own. He and I became like permanent fixtures there, the bull-goose lunatics of the insane asylum. Often Robbin walked around the halls fully nude in the middle of the day.

"Cover yourself, sir!" a surprised clerk yelled.

Robbin just looked down his belly, shocked to find he had no pants on.

"Hey. Right, I'll go do that."

He also enjoyed showing up at my bungalow, unannounced, and asking to use my bathroom.

"Why?" I said, suspicious.

"Boy, I sure do have to take a shit," he admitted.

"What's wrong with your bathroom?"

"I prefer yours," he said, simply.

Then he would push past me, smiling, take a shit with the door open, and walk out without flushing.

He tried to fuck women he'd met half an hour earlier at the Marquis bar on the grass right outside my bungalow; he sniffed coke openly off the top of his fist in the hallways, launching into endless, rambling discussions with the guys who'd come to steam-clean the carpets. He was a force of life, a glammed-out Viking who could line-drive a fastball 350 feet to dead center field.

ROAD DOG:

Robbin was my hero, man. He would do certain sexual things, and he would call me on the phone and say, "You gotta come see what I just did." I mean, he was proud of it. Used to walk around naked all time. Robbin pissed on the road manager on the bus once. We laughed until we were about to have a heart attack.

Robbin was the nicest guy in rock and roll. The nicest guy. He and Stephen were best buds. They were partners in crime. But Robbin was always the one who ended up in the public eye getting caught.

I mean, I start talking about Robbin, I end up wanting to cry.

Robbin's room at the Sunset Marquis was right beneath Rodney Dangerfield's, another longtime guest. Dangerfield was on a hot streak, coming off his role in the movie *Back to School,* and he had more cocaine and eighteen-year-old girls coming in and out of his room than a Colombian drug lord. But he was still an old guy, kind of crusty. And geriatrics, as a rule, don't generally take kindly to heavy metal blasting up at them at all hours of the night.

"Turn down that fuckin' rock music, punk!" the comic screamed, pounding on Robbin's ceiling. "I said, turn it down or I'll cut your balls off!"

"Rodney, man, come on down and party with me," Robbin called up. "We're having a great time in here!"

"I got my own fuckin' party going on, son," Dangerfield yelled. "I got trim in here that would make you sick to your stomach. So for the love of God, *turn that damn music down* and let me enjoy myself, will ya?"

They were both too likable to remain enemies, and soon grew to appreciate each other. In the mornings we would all commiserate over Bloody Marys by the pool.

"Rodney," said King, "man, I just want to apologize. I'm going to keep the noise to a minimum, from this day on."

"Well, all right," said Dangerfield, his eyes popping and goggling as he turned his head to and fro, checking out the bikinis. "Finally, you're coming around."

"How about coming out with us, Rodney?" Robbin said. "You know? Next time Stephen and I head to Long Beach Arena to catch Maiden, you come along, huh?"

"Keep dreaming. I got business over here. I got chicks lined up waiting for me. Long Beach Arena. Come on."

We loved those old-school Catskill comics, and seemed to have a strange connection with them. Our alliance with Milton Berle was still going strong. Robbin and I were frequent guests at the Friars Club. Many were the nights that we sat in full rocker regalia and watched Phyllis Diller or Johnny Carson get ripped a new asshole in celebrity roasts.

"Dude, this is *so* cool," I said to Robbin, sucking back the free booze happily. "Old-school Hollywood. And Miltie's the grand poo-bah, you know?"

Robbin shook his head in mock regret. "'Round and Round' *made* that guy. Now, he never writes. Never calls."

Miltie loved the band. He was always telling us, "Keep comedy in your work. Keep things jovial." One night, Milton took a moment to single us out in the crowd. "My nephew's got a band, some of them are here tonight. Say hello, you rat bastards."

Robbin and I waved from our seats, honored.

"They're a really, really nice group of gay guys. I wish them well. Really do."

Atlantic, eager to capitalize on our popularity, soon shoved us back into the studio to record album number three. Beau Hill was there once again to produce, and together, we created *Dancing Undercover*, which featured the singles "Dance" and "Body Talk."

"Body Talk" would end up being featured in the Eddie Murphy film *The Golden Child.*

While we were recording, I always went out at night and tried to meet the new up-and-coming guys, if only to stay abreast of the competition. One afternoon, Steven Adler took me up to the house that he and the rest of his band, Guns N' Roses, had rented in the Hollywood Hills. The place reminded me of the old Mötley House, trashed beyond all recognition. Although it was about two in the afternoon when we got there, I was stepping on people still laid out from the night before.

"Party never stops, huh?"

"I guess not." He shrugged. "Hey, come on out to the balcony. I want you to meet Axl."

His lead singer was outside, hovering over the keg, coaxing the last few drops of beer from the plastic tube.

"Hey, bro," I said, extending my hand. "I'm Stephen, how's it going?"

"Hey," said Axl. He just sort of said it. He stood there, looking kind of distant, with his bandana pulled low over his eyes.

It was a cool little scene, though I wouldn't say it was overly welcoming. Axl went back to pumping his beer, I went back inside, and a short while afterward, I left.

A couple of nights later, Steven invited me to the Troubadour to see Guns N' Roses. I was mingling backstage with my rock brethren and their chicks, a drink in my hand, a Vicodin in my gut, when out of nowhere this girl came up to me and said flirtatiously, "Aren't you Stephen *Pearcy*?"

I grinned. "Guilty."

"Well, Stephen," she said, "you have something on your shirt."

I looked down, surprised. Food? *But I'm on an all booze-diet. . . .*

When I did, the chick lifted up her hand and popped me on the underside of my nose. *Bonk.*

"Hey," I said. "That's not funny."

"What do you mean?" she said, concerned. "I'm so sorry, I didn't mean to hit you. And you *do* have something on your shirt—look down."

I looked down, and she did the same trick again. *Bonk!*

"Now look, dammit," I said, "nobody bonks me! Okay? I took *karate* when I was a kid."

"What's that got to do with anything?" she sneered.

"It means I'm not afraid to *bonk* you back," I said, tweaking her nose with my forefinger and thumb.

"What the hell's wrong with you?!" she screeched, holding her nose, outraged.

People started to cluster around us.

"What's going on, Stephen?" asked a security dude, a guy I knew from previous tours.

"This woman bonked me," I announced to the room. I pointed at her. "Get rid of her."

"Sorry, Stephen," he said, in a low voice. "We can't."

"What do you mean?" I said. "She bonked me."

"Dude—that's Axl's girl."

Oh, great, I thought. *So Axl Rose's chick bonked me. And I bonked her back. And now the whole world's gonna know about it. Just fucking great.*

On another night not too long after, I headed to the Cathouse, looking for thrills and maybe some trim. Joe Anthony with me. He and I walked in the door, smelling the odd scent that permeated the building.

"Hair spray by the gallon," I said. "Super fluffy in here."

"Damn shame when the guys are looking tighter than the chicks."

A weird aura of doom spiked the air along with the Aqua Net. Riki Rachtman had some of the best up-and-coming talent sprouting up in his club: L.A. Guns, Faster Pussycat, Lickety Split, Shiver Shiver, Jetboy. But there was something odd about it, as if metal had passed a critical point, and had now begun to approach the status of a *cartoon.* . . .

"You know, Joe," I said, as we approached the bar, "I almost died last night. Drank some weird alcohol out of a jar with cow balls in it."

"What the hell, Stephen?" laughed Joe. "Do you need to be supervised at all times?"

"It's an idea."

We ordered beers and shots. We'd been at the bar for about ten minutes when Riki Rachtman approached, smiling. "Yo, Stephen," he said, "Axl's here."

"Oh, okay," I said. "I met that guy. I'm real close with Stevie, his drummer. I'll go say hey."

"Where is he?" Joe asked.

Riki pointed to the sound booth. "Right in there."

The sound booth was super small, about the size of two telephone booths. We made our way to it, knocked on the door, and the security dude let us right in.

"What's *up*, fellas?" he said, smiling. "Come on in." He nodded at Joe. "What's up, man?"

Inside, it was crammed so full, there was hardly any room to move. The club DJ was in there, as well as the security guard. Then there was Joe and me and Axl, and a chick who was with him.

"Axl, how's it going?" I said.

He didn't answer. Just gave me this little push in the chest.

Now, I'm a jolly guy. I never have beef with anybody, and I don't expect static. So I just thought it was a rock-star push: you know, mutual respect, right?

"Hey, what's up, man?" I said, trying again. "I'm a good friend of Stevie Adler. I think we met once—"

"You like this?" snapped Axl. And then he reached over and *bonked* me.

"What the hell's your *deal*, man??" I said, offended.

"Why'd you mess with my girl at the Troubadour?" he accused.

"You got it *backward*," I said, outraged. "Dude, she bonked *me.*"

"Well, how about you pick on someone your own size?" he said, all threatening-like, all "Welcome to the Jungle." "Huh? *Pearcy*?"

And he reached back and tried to shove me.

Joe intervened—he caught Axl's hand. But I was pissed. I'm thinking, *What the fuck is going on here? I've done nothing to this dude.*

We lit into each other, raining a torrent of weak, girlish blows that repeatedly missed their marks. It was downright embarrassing. Joe and the security guard tried to intervene.

"Stop, guys! Guys—stop it!"

They moved to separate us, but then Axl's chick jumped on Joe's back and wouldn't let go.

"Goddammit," yelled Joe. "Get off me!"

He swung her around in circles, trying to hurl her lean weight from his body, but she dug in, all nails.

"Come on," I said to Axl, "Let's go! Let's take it outside!" There were beads flying, screaming, yelling.

"YOU GUYS GET OUTTA HERE! NOW!" yelled the security guy, annoyed. He used his giant body to push me and Joe out of the booth. Axl's girl hung gamely to Joe's back, but the guard peeled her off like a used condom. "Stop this shit, you idiots."

Me and Joe found ourselves, disheveled and confused, standing outside the sound booth, totally befuddled, trying to figure out just what the hell had gotten Axl so pissed in the first place.

"What the hell was that all *about*?" I said.

Joe shrugged. "Man, I don't know."

"But I *respect* that dude!" I said, frustrated.

"Can't fight for shit, though," observed Joe.

Half an hour later, Axl finally emerged. I began to say something, but he just shot me that look of death and went: "PEARCY."

Then he smirked and walked on by. It was just like that Seinfeld episode: "NEWMAN."

To this day, every time I run into Axl, he goes: "Pearcy." I reply: "Axl."

Years later, Steven Adler explained the whole thing to me.

"Axl thinks you had something to say to his old lady at the club." Well, just for the record, I didn't know who she was. I would have been respectful if I did.

Or not. I was loaded, so who knows?

JOE ANTHONY:

I actually did see Axl land a punch once.

I was working for a limousine company, same one I worked for when I drove Michael Jackson's monkey.

Axl was dating Stephanie Seymour, and I got a call to go out to Malibu, for New Year's Eve, and pick up Stephanie and her mom and a bunch of different people. And I guess her mom got kind of drunk and started telling Axl what to do. And Stephanie came up to Axl, because Axl was giving her mom shit, and Axl turned around and fucking knocked Stephanie out. Like, clocked her right in the fucking face. Knocked her ass out.

And as soon as she hit the floor, he yelled, "Everybody get the fuck out of here! This party's over." Everybody left, just like that. I'll never forget that. It was like: whoa.

■ ■ ■

WE HIT THE ROAD FOR THE Dancing Undercover tour with a larger crew than ever before, including three buses, five truck drivers, two sound guys, two carpenters, a bass tech, a guitar tech, a drum tech, riggers, six lighting guys, a set designer, a wardrobe girl, a pyro-technician, a production manager, a tour manager, a tour accountant, and plenty of security. We were top-heavy from the moment we set out, with the band having taken out complex contracts with travel agencies, legal teams, insurance agents, merchandising corporations, even our bus and truck companies. Everyone wanted a piece of the pie. And all we wanted to do was Ratt 'n' roll. I just wanted to keep the party going.

When I look back on it now, I can kind of pinpoint the third tour as the period when we began the transformation from young guys in a band to a corporation. Oh, we were still having fun out there, for sure, but it just wasn't as *new* anymore. It was one hell of a thrill to get out there and sweat and scream in front of thousands of people, but our sets were a little less dynamic, and, frankly, we'd begun to move through the paces. We had a system for everything: for exciting the crowds, for getting our chicks backstage, for scoring the drugs that we felt like we were entitled to. Frankly, once in a while, I would have preferred to catch a movie, know what I mean? After all, I was getting on in years. I had just turned thirty.

But there was no way we were going to catch a movie. The machine was off and running, and we were at its service. They shuffled us off to Cedar Rapids, Iowa, to play at the Five Seasons Center, and then to Bloomington, Minnesota, to do the Met Center, then to Milwaukee to rock the Mecca Arena, then boarded a bus to Chicago to do the Rosemont, and then finally truck all the way back to Indianapolis to play for the raging crowds at the Market Square Arena, and not a day off in between.

"I'm not trying to be a dick about this," I said. "But it seems like we're traveling in *circles*."

"You guys got one job to do, Stephen," our tour manager told me. "Play, okay? Otherwise, let us take care of the itinerary."

People ask why so many rock dudes have drug and alcohol dependencies. Part of it has to be the road. I mean, sure, you could pull off a tour sober, if you really wanted to, punching the clock day in and day out like a mature, responsible adult, but the travel is so deadening, so monotonous, that without some kind of spice, the room service all starts to taste the same. The hotel decor begins to get to you. Soon you can no longer discern the difference between the Stouffer's Five Seasons or the St. Paul Hotel or the Pfister Hotel or the Hyatt Regency or the Seelbach or the Peabody or the Ventana Canyon Resort or the Mulberry fucking Inn. They all morph into the same four walls, a giant television, a bed that other people fucked in last night, and a toilet warmed by the asses of countless traveling businessmen.

I tried to make it fun. Not just for me, for all involved. And if that meant trying to get the doe-eyed concierge at the Ritz-Carlton to sneak up to my room after her shift and take a bubble bath with me, endangering her own job in the process, then *so be it*. Back-to-back-to-back shows made my vision blur. Only immature hijinks could straighten me out.

Poison was out with us for the Dancing Undercover tour, opening up our shows and enjoying their first taste of success. Bret Michaels, C. C. DeVille, Bobby Dall, and Rikki Rockett had talent, and we liked them pretty well as people, too. Robbin and I had gone to some Poison shows in Los Angeles, and we'd agreed: "There's something about this band."

I started hanging out with Bret, taking him on limo rides. One night, we ended up at his apartment playing beer pong games, doing blow, smoking—standard procedure. I happened to have my video camera there, and I set it down and let it film hours of us entertaining ourselves. That night, Bret was *begging* to open up for us: "Hey, man, please, can we do a show, come on, man, we'll do anything!" To this day, that tape is a big part of their history, yet I couldn't give it away to them. Maybe I'll put it on eBay—let someone else in on how they got their start.

One night we were hanging backstage after a show, just being total idiots, drinking, smoking weed. One of our techs, John, was just finishing a Slurpee cup that he'd half filled with vodka.

Instead of putting the cup down, John took the lid off, unzipped his pants, and started to piss into it.

"Dude," I yelled. "Come on! Pull those pants up! Your *aroma*. Don't you ever shower?"

John ignored me. He filled the Slurpee cup halfway with hot piss and passed it to me.

"What the hell do you want me to do with this?"

"Piss in it?" suggested John.

In drunken times, disgusting notions seem somehow appropriate. I rolled down my skintight white spandex pants and pissed into a Slurpee cup full of another man's piss. Then Joe did it. Mike, our carpenter, followed.

And then the cup was full, on the table, yellow and stinking— seventy-two ounces of tour piss. You could smell it from a mile away.

"Well," said Joe, "who's gonna drink it?"

I totally died laughing. Maybe it was a drunk thing. I'm not sure. But I scurried away and found a fifty-dollar bill in my dressing room, ran back out there, threw it down. "Not me. But whoever does is welcome to *my* cash."

A shower of bills followed. They piled up next to that cup of warm piss. Twenties and tens and fives. Soon the pile grew into a pyramid. Joe counted it, his voice rising with a barker's enthusiasm. "Two hundred and ten bucks here, ladies and gents, two *hundred*—"

"Watch out."

Riki Valentine, Bret Michaels's personal assistant, cut Joe short. He picked up the Slurpee cup. Then he chugged it in one fluid motion like it was an ice-cold fucking brew.

Riki wiped the piss drops from his lips, dropped the cup, picked up his money, and walked out of the room.

Dead silence. I think we were all in shock.

"That piss was so stank it had a crust on it," someone said finally, and we all walked away a little older and wiser.

We all thought, *This guy is a fucking freak*. The next night, we told him we'd give him a hundred bucks if he ate one of those urinal cakes. Well, the sick bastard did it. He got another hundred bucks.

A few nights later, we paid him another hundred bucks to drink an ashtray full of butts that we poured some beer into. He took it down. Granted, this guy was making some bread, but he was out of his mind. Go figure. He was working for Poison. Out of all the crazy opening acts we've had, Lita Ford, Joan Jett, Queensrÿche, Bon Jovi—we knew how to pick them, and they did us well—Poison took the cake. In weirdness, they took the cake.

The rules of the road were such that we constantly tried to take advantage of one another's weak spots. For Blotzer, this was women. He was just a secretly sensitive son of a bitch, like a lot of us, and if a groupie was especially pretty, or showed him a lot of love and attention, there was a chance that he'd come out of his hotel room glowing with pride.

Well, one of our best tricks was to find a tall, slutty groupie with dyed blond hair and black roots—these are easy to find at Pittsburgh and Cleveland shows, especially—and have her suck off as many crew guys as possible; ideally, the ones who never showered. Then we'd steer her over to Blotz.

"Guys," he'd say, emerging from the back of the bus with a post-coital rock strut, "I just met someone, and dammit, I'm almost afraid to say it, but she's *really special*."

"Bobby," I'd say seriously, "man, I hate to be the one to tell you this, but I hope you didn't kiss that girl."

"Why?"

"She just deep-throated ten crew guys."

"Agh! Agh! Agh!" Bob would cry, wiping his lips with the back of his hands. "You *bastards*. Fuckheads! I'll get you for this."

This tour lasted just as long as the other ones did, which is to say, forever. We hauled our asses from Atlanta to Landover to Philly to New Haven to Boston to Worcester to Providence to Binghamton to Poughkeepsie to New York City to Troy to Erie to Johnstown to Utica to Rochester to Lansing to Muskegon.

Bret tried to drink as much as me and Robbin and Blotz. We pulled him into our lair and threw down the gauntlet. Bret hung tough for a time, but as the hours wore on he began to stagger. Sometime into the second consecutive night of boozing, snorting cocaine, smoking powerful joints one after the other after the other, and eating muscle relaxants like Pez, he started looking kind of green. I told him not to be embarrassed. The next night, Bret collapsed onstage, and the fucker almost *died*. It was dangerous to hang with Ratt. But worth the risk. That was our motto. Anyway, who knew Bret was a diabetic?

In Montgomery, Alabama, I got my first death threat and had to wear a bulletproof vest onstage for several shows. It didn't quite go with my costume, but what the hell was I going to do about it? *I'm gonna kill Stephen before the drum solo,* the scratchy note read.

We always went on, no matter what. Rock and roll is a dangerous profession, as Marshall Berle used to say. They threw cue balls at me some nights. Bottles of piss. Flaming rolls of toilet paper. I have a Chinese throwing star on my desk, next to my computer—someone got it confiscated from them at a show in Marin. I mean, a *throwing star?* Why someone would go to a show to injure the entertainment is beyond me. When we'd open for Ozzy, he'd be getting death threats nightly. He'd cancel shows, too. Nobody's immune to fear out there.

One evening in Salt Lake City, Robbin wandered outside after a show, smoking a roach. He immediately was arrested and the city's by-the-book cops hauled him off to jail. We ended up getting him sprung on some technicality, but the band was wary of it ever happening again, so we hired a former DEA agent to accompany us on the road, in case another incident of the sort occurred. Our guy was a strange fucker, quiet and definitely crooked. Once I overheard him talking to a sheriff buddy of his about some guy they were going to "get rid of." *Okay! I wasn't supposed to hear that. I'll be leaving now, gentlemen.*

Robbin was the same old lovable giant, but he was a little less reliable, onstage and off. Before every show, you could see him puking at the side of the stage. He was pretty into heroin—by now, he was no longer smoking, he was slamming it—and we all knew it, even though we tried to pretend that it was still at the fun-and-games stage. Once in a while he'd fuck up onstage, and we'd pretend it was no big thing. Warren had already sort of begun to rule up there, as far as the guitars were concerned. So hey, no biggie, right?

But shit just got progressively stranger. We came through L.A. to do the Forum, stayed for a couple of nights, and on our way out, Robbin came to me with a confession.

"Fuck. I just got a threatening phone call from O. J. Simpson."

"What the hell for?"

"He says if I don't stop seeing Tawny, he'll cut my hands off."

I frowned. "That's crazy." I said.

"It's not good."

"I didn't know you were still seeing Tawny," I said.

"Oh, once in a while," Robbin admitted. He held up his hands and we both looked at them. They were nice hands.

"I guess I also didn't know O. J. was seeing Tawny," I said, after a moment.

"Well, he's married. But he keeps Tawny on the side. He got her an apartment in West L.A. that he visits a couple of times a week."

"And were you just at this apartment?"

Robbin nodded.

"I probably wouldn't do that anymore," I said.

"I know this sounds really stupid," Robbin said, "but I always kept Tawny in my heart. She was my first love. You don't just forget that."

"Yes, you do," I said gently. "When an NFL running back threatens to cut your hands off, you do."

Our lives felt surreal: sometimes repetitive, sometimes exceptional, always inebriated, often irritating. Every morning, I would wake up, begin to drink, smoke a fat joint, then wait for reality to come at me in waves. In Boston, we played the Garden. Returning to the bus, we discovered that Robbin's metallic Halliburton suitcase had been stolen.

"My fucking *dope* was in there, man! This is out of control!" He was so furious that anyone would fuck with his drugs.

He started stomping around and smacking the walls of the bus.

"Someone got a serious score, all right, huh, King?" Bob said.

"Man, I will seriously *fuck* with the guy who took my shit! I'm not standing for this shit *at all* right now!"

"Hey! Chill out, man! King, stop!" I yelled. "Stop it! It could have been worse, right? I mean, did you actually lose anything else?"

Robbin stared at me. "Just ten grand cash, that's all, and my fucking gun. That's all, dude."

"Oh," I said quietly. I didn't know he carried a gun.

We never caught the guy. It wasn't like Robbin could file a police report. Not even our DEA freak could help with that one.

I was having a good time, but I wasn't what you'd call happy. The unceasing sameness of the road turned the everyday into the banal and the banal into a bizarre maze. You look at one thousand coffee-makers in one thousand hotel rooms, and after a while, they begin to seem deeply linked.

MONKEY ON OUR BACKS

JOE ANTHONY:

Dunno if you remember when you were a little kid, but my mom had a little recipe box. It was alphabetized—a file box, but it was smaller. I had one that was from A to Z, and I had a Polaroid of each chick that we hung out with. I'd put down her name and her phone number, and we'd rate them. The next time we were in that city, I'd call them up. Have them come down. Guaranteed to have a good time.

Man, I used to have so many fucking great pictures. But I had a girlfriend many years ago, and the fuckin' bitch went through my shit. Found all this personal shit I had up in a shoebox and got pissed off and threw all the shit out. Same thing happened to Stephen. He had these itineraries with women, how they looked, color of their eyes, their hair. And one night, he and I were out in Hollywood somewhere. We

used to go to a place every Thursday night called the Spice
Club. It was on Hollywood and La Brea. Every Thursday
night, Sam Kinison would show up, and Billy Idol. Every-
where you looked, there was fucking rock guys. They did an
all-star jam every Thursday night.

Anyway, Stephen was sharing his place with this chick
on an on-again off-again basis. I drove him home, and he
called me on my way home. He told me on the floor of his
pad, there must have been like one thousand pictures and
itineraries that she found while he was out. She got pissed
off and laid it all out on the floor, so when he walked in, it hit
him right in the face.

■　■　■

IN THE END, THERE WERE JUST too many of them. Girls who
were fly-outs. Girls from the in-store signing with great tits.
Girls who just wanted to fuck, despite being married or having boyfriends—and we didn't want to know about it. Girls who
smiled too long. Girls who smoked Menthol Virginia Slims. Girls
from the South who used clever homespun sayings. Girls who
played guitar. They all had one thing in common: They were so
freaking hot.

There was just one problem. By late '87, our shtick had started
to feel like a joke even to the guys who were doing it. When we got
onstage to perform the official mating anthems of Reagan's America,
puffing our feathers out like peacocks, raising V-shaped guitars to
the sky, choking on a toxic cloud of stage fog, even we kind of knew
the door was closing.

Me and Bobby really started to give each other shit around this time. He and the guys liked to have their fun with coke, and hey, more power to them. But when it's four in the morning and someone's blasting "Ruby Tuesday" for the fifth fucking time in a row, singing along in his rowdy drummer's voice, it can begin to get on your nerves.

Blotzer was a nation unto himself. Everybody liked him for the first ten seconds that they met him, then rapidly changed their minds when he said something shitty. Blotz liked stand-up arcade games, like Asteroids and Zaxxon, pumping his quarters into them at any opportunity. He loved Trans Ams and the loud sounds they made. He drooled over speedboats, taking the money earned from his first publishing royalties and buying a sixty-thousand-dollar model that he named *Ramboat: First Blotz.*

"Stephen! Fuck, man, let's bury the hatchet. Okay? Get back here. Do a line with me."

He bellowed through a megaphone backstage and on the bus. He *golfed* at every opportunity. His solo, which involved a six-pack of Budweiser being slowly lowered from the ceiling while he beat the shit out of the skins at every conceivable angle, was always an issue. Blotz thought the Bud was hilarious. The rest of us, who had to watch it go down night after night, weren't so sure.

"Come on, Stephen. Stop being so high and mighty. Do you really need sleep? I mean, seriously, *how many hours does a man need to sleep?* Come on back here and do a line with me, okay?"

Blotzer stood out from many of his contemporaries for the fact that—though he drank steadily and enjoyed his blow in a recreational kind of way—he was never an addict. Blotz was too controlling, too conniving to let some substance run his show. He was clearheaded, brash. Even intelligent. He would not, however, under most circumstances, ever be mistaken for a very generous guy.

"Cocaine is fun but it's *useless*," said Blotz, his nose white, teeth chattering in the Freon of the late-night bus air-conditioning. "I basically only do it so I can drink more." And drink more he did.

At the next night's show, Bobby was looking rough. He was hungover, sweating, his face haggard and green. He kept trying to get my attention.

"Stephen!" he screamed. "NO SOLO!"

Bobby's drum solo was his moment in the sun. When he was in the mood, he lived for it. And as corny as I found the slowly lowering Bud, it was often my favorite part of the show, too, because at that point I could always smoke a joint or have a few drinks, and then come out refreshed for the second half of the concert.

"Stephen! Dammit!" he repeated. "NO SOLO!"

YEAH, SOLO. I nodded happily and danced across the stage, feeling the vibe of the night. *YEAH, SOLO!*

"LADIES AND GENTLEMEN," I screamed into the microphone, "BOBBY BLOTZER ON DRUMS!"

"You fucking homo. I'm going to cut your *fingers* off after this show, Stephen. . . ."

Poor Bob, having to sweat it out in front of fifteen thousand people while we filed off stage right and enjoyed a couple of fresh Jack and Cokes and a nice fat spliff. Robbin and I would smoke anytime, anyplace on that stage. And I swear, my buzz never felt sweeter than when my drummer was experiencing a gut-punching hangover.

Ratt was a family—five brothers and Marshall, our shyster cousin. We loved each other, at least as much as five selfish guys can love one another. Success will get you through a lot of years with minimal friction. But now the friendship wasn't really there anymore. All for one and one for all? Hardly. We'd come together as mercenaries, and that's how we began to treat each other.

Robbin was with us, but at the same time he wasn't. Increasingly, he was distant, and you rarely saw him sober. Sometimes, it affected his playing, and I found myself wanting to say something about it. You know, not exactly like "Hey, don't ever do that stuff again." More like "Dude, why are you in so much pain?" But I was usually pretty messed up myself. Wisdom and caring didn't exactly flow freely from my heart.

It was a fucked-up time, rotten in many ways. I drove over to Nikki's house one afternoon when we were in L.A., just to say hello. I felt a little weirded out when some other guy wearing no shirt answered his door.

"Hey," I said, confused. "Where's Nikki?"

"Who the fuck are you?" he said.

"I'm a friend of Nikki's. Who the fuck are *you*?"

"Nikki's out of town right now. Can I help you?"

"Hold up, baby," came a voice. "Let me handle this."

The dude shot me a dirty look and retreated into the house, and then Vanity came out, hands on her hips. She was supposed to be Nikki's girlfriend at the time. We stared at each other without speaking. I got the picture pretty quick and took off.

But what the fuck was I going to say, you know?

Girls come into the picture already thinking you're a cheat just because you're in a band. But some of us are pretty straight up and don't bullshit around out there—like Juan. Now this cat was real devoted and faithful to his girl. Some chick would zero in on him and go, "I'm taking that fucker down!" And he'd sit and talk for hours with her. At two in the morning, we'd see her down in the hotel bar, all disappointed.

"What happened? Weren't you just with Juan?"

"That guy just talked my ear off for hours! About his horse, his kid, his guitars. I just wanted to get laid!"

"Not a problem, come right this way," Joe or Robbin or I would tell her. "We'll take care of business right away."

But that could come back and bite you sometimes. Some woman I'd slept with on the road several times got in touch with me to let me know I was the father of her unborn child.

"What do I do?" I asked my lawyer.

"Just let me talk to her," she said. "I think I can make this go away."

The chick just wanted ten grand, in the end, and I had my lawyer give it to her in cash. We'd gotten off cheap and we both knew it. She didn't want my kid, or me—she just wanted my money.

Greed was the vice of the day, pride a close second. Sex rained down on my head, with so many blow jobs that I couldn't decide if they were sexual anymore or just something wet on a specific part of my body. At night I often dreamed of intense rainstorms, and a feeling of joy and relief would flood through me. But invariably, when I awoke, the relentless sun would be shining in my face.

Robbin met a hot chick from Texas named Laurie Carr at an in-store signing, and he began courting her. Soon they were dating. She came to Los Angeles and within a few weeks had become a *Playboy* Playmate. A couple of months later, Robbin married her. I was happy for my brother, but selfishly, I couldn't help but feel all the more alone. All the guys in my band were hitched now: I was the last man standing.

Playgirl magazine approached me and asked me to be in their July issue. Only a drunk or an idiot would have agreed. Luckily, I was both.

"I ain't getting naked," I told them. As if that made all the difference in the world. "No cock shots."

"Of course not," their managing editor assured me. "We'll put you in a nice little black thong. You'll look like a Chippendale. Pretty cool, huh?"

"Yes," I said, confused. "No. I don't know."

"David Lee *Roth* will be on the cover," he assured me. "It'll be very rocking."

The shoot was casual. Kind of trippy. I stumbled in high on a codeine pain reliever and a female photographer hustled me in front of her camera, then kept on trying to get me to show her my package.

"Just pull it down. It'll only take a second. Then we're done."

"No way," I said, stepping in front of her backdrop. "The only way I would *maybe* consider it is if you promise to come back to my place and party."

"I'm married," she said apologetically, snapping off a few quick shots in a businesslike manner.

"Thong stays on," I said.

One night, en route to a party in Malibu, Joe crashed my Porsche. We spun around four times in the middle of the street and rolled up onto the curb, with all four tires flat. A normal person would have gotten down and kissed the pavement, thanked his lucky stars just to be alive. Somehow, I didn't feel blessed.

The following week, I dragged myself into the dealership to have the car detailed and repaired. They gave it back to me fourteen days later, with one problem: It wouldn't quit making this odd clicking noise.

"We're so sorry, sir," the manager said. "We'll work on that for you."

"Nah, forget it," I said. "I'll take a new one."

"A new one?"

"Yeah," I said. "That 930 Turbo looks good. You got it in black?"

"Of course, sir. That's our newest model, so, as you might imagine, the price is a bit high at the moment—"

"How high?" I laughed.

"Thirty-five thousand dollars."

"You know what? That's perfect. I'll have my accountant send over the money right now."

It was powerful and strange to be able to walk into the Beverly Hills Porsche dealership and leave with a brand-new car, just because I felt like it, and not even feel the extraction from my bank account. It made me want to smash up this car, too. My own internal dysfunction was getting harder and harder to ignore: an odd clicking noise.

I pushed back the creeping feeling with pot, Valium, and late-night TV. In early 1988, Joe and I embarked on our Jägermeister phase. Jäger worked off a potent recipe in those days, and their black alcohol obliterated both memory and conscience. Joe and I knew a chick who worked for the company, who would often bring us their boxed set, which included a massive bottle and six free stemmed glasses. In no time at all, I had hundreds of stemmed Jäger glasses in my kitchen. They all sat there silently, eyeing me, just begging to be smashed to bits.

My three-tiered home felt increasingly useless. Occasionally when I left town, I let a cute young girl from the neighborhood have the run of the place. We didn't have a romantic thing going on between us. I just liked the way she moved.

"I have a confession to make," she said. "I . . . well, I had a boy over while you were gone."

"That's okay." I laughed. "As long as you didn't, like, have sex in my bed."

"Oh." She was silent for a moment. "We did have sex in your bed."

"Oh," I said. I considered the news for a moment. "Well, that sucks."

"And actually, it wasn't a boy. It was Dennis Quaid."

"Dennis *Quaid*?" I whispered. "But . . . why?"

"He's so gorgeous. I just couldn't say no. You're not mad, are you?"

I needed a change of scenery. I leased a fully furnished corporate-style apartment, smack-dab in the center of glamorous North Hollywood. What the apartment complex lacked in soul, it made up for in blandness. Beige was everywhere you looked: on the walls, on the towels, on the sheets.

For a week or so, I felt steadier. I purchased a tub of multi-vitamins from a health-food store in the strip mall around the corner, and in the mornings when I drank my first beer, I sniffed them curiously. One morning, I dared to swallow one. It turned my pee a vibrant shade of yellow. That's when I knew that they were making a valuable difference.

I was headed back on the road to normalcy, maybe, or at least something approaching peace, but then the dreaded call came from up above:

"Time to cut another album, fellas! You up for it?"

Simply put, that was the last thing that any member of the band Ratt wanted to do. We'd recently split with Marshall, arguing—

surprise, surprise—over money. (Is there anything else a band and their manager would argue about?) We'd taken on new representation, Allen Kovac. We needed rest, and we needed perspective. We did not need to be forced back into the studio to make a washed-out, shitty album, created by five dudes who were starting to feel jumpy at the sight of one another.

But Atlantic stayed on our ass. We might not have been their most talented musicians, but we'd always been able to deliver the platinum hits. The monster was hungry again. It needed to be fed.

Hoping to push us in a new direction, the label axed Beau Hill as our producer, and they brought in Mike Stone instead, who had enjoyed major success in the studio with Queen, Journey, the Rolling Stones, and Asia, among others. He was meant to provide contrast to our band's bad habits. Too bad he was already precisely on our level.

"Fill that shit up . . . fill it up . . . perfect!" Robbin said on our first morning together. He held up a tall glass of vodka. "Mike? You take yours neat?"

Reach for the Sky was messy, and it took way too fucking long to make. I always liked the way we sounded when we punched things out. It represented what I thought of as our sound more faithfully: At our best, we were brash and loud and imperfect and fun to listen to.

But the dominant style of the time had begun to lean toward overproduced, multitracked guitar and synth heroics. We followed right along. I missed Beau, who had been full of ideas, organized, and active, a sixth member of the band for whom perfectionism was no burden. Mike was more laid-back, and I got the impression he wasn't overly concerned with how the album ultimately turned out, either.

One day, I came in to do a vocal scratch for one of our tunes. He watched me from behind the glass.

"Okay," called Mike, when I'd finished. "How do you like it?"

"What do you mean?" I spoke into the microphone. "I just sang it. How did *you* like it?"

He shrugged agreeably. "Sounds great! Ready for the next one?"

I was confused. This wasn't how I'd done it with Beau. I'd bounced ideas off our producer, and he'd given me his opinion, and we'd gone on from there. This wasn't the way to make a good album. You couldn't just take the first thing you did and lock it in.

"You know what I'm considering?" Juan told me on one of our breaks. "Doing the bass on *keys.*"

"But why?"

"A million reasons," he said, smiling brilliantly. "Crisper sound, truer notes, more control . . . need I say more?"

"But every *note*? Won't that take a ridiculous amount of time?"

"Who's in a rush?"

None of us were, exactly. What was the hurry? The fan base couldn't get enough of us, right? So Juan was granted his strange wish, and he put his guitar away. But the recording studio cost an ungodly amount of cash every day that we were in it. And the more we fucked around, boozing, arguing, and generally being children, the more money we burned through, and the more we really started to resent one another.

By then, I had bought a new house in La Costa, in San Diego. It was just me, alone in this big old house with my two dogs. I'd call the studio to see what was going on—and to my dismay, nothing was going on for months. By then, I was working alone on music. I would rarely write lyrics with the band—how could I write lyrics in a room full of people I had grown apart from? I preferred hiding out, grabbing the demos, and doing my own thing—and the band always gave me shit for it.

"Can you come on *time*, Stephen? I mean, truly, is it *that* hard for you to do?"

"Bob, this is rock and roll, if you hadn't noticed, not a Boy Scout meeting. I'll show up when I show up, all right?"

It was a painful time. Nerves really frayed. Animosity was brewing between us, and it showed in the music. We sent the tapes into Atlantic. Doug Morris sent them right back.

"This is absolute shit," he said. He was livid. "What are you doing in there? We can't sell this, not in a million years."

Stone was yanked immediately, and Atlantic brought Beau Hill back to save the day. Together we managed to whip the album into shape. "Way Cool Jr." and "I Want a Woman" were our singles—and the funny thing was, despite the kicking and screaming and stomping of our feet that we went through to create them, they're some of my favorite Ratt songs. Juan's bass *did* sound good when he played it on keys. And for all of his fucking pouting and finger-pointing, Bobby played the drums as well as he ever did. They were impossible to get along with at times, but I was surrounded by an all-star cast of musicians, and I could never ignore it. As the decade had progressed, competition had surged. Each member of Ratt had responded by getting stronger at his craft, not weaker.

Except for Robbin. It was on *Reach for the Sky* that we all started to notice a difference in his playing. He could still make the guitar do what he wanted, and he was never going to lose that gift he had for melody, and for writing songs. But he was spending long hours locked in the recording studio bathroom during our sessions. You never saw him sober. He was always drunk or wasted, and when that's your life, your focus is generally not on improving as a musician.

One evening, soon after we'd finished recording *Reach for the Sky*, Robbin and I were slated to present at an award show. I showed up early at his house with a limo and a model chick, ready to catch a decent buzz and then head out on the town to make the scene.

When I showed up, he answered the door, buck naked, pupils dilated, and back hunched.

"Come on," I said, laughing. "Get your clothes on, man. I got my date in the limo—is your old lady ready to go?"

He didn't even appear to recognize me. A hostile expression crossed his face, and he just shook his head angrily. When I reminded him about the fact that we were presenting, he told me to fuck off. Then he took a swing at me. I ducked under it, completely unable to believe it was even happening.

"Fuck!" I yelled. "Wow, I'm *gone*, man! You're crazy."

I went back to the limo, totally in shock. We'd never even had words before.

We went out on tour and played up and down the whole East Coast: D.C., Virginia Beach, Philly, Boston, Hartford. We came into New York City and landed at the plushest hotels.

We crisscrossed the country and the world, occasionally returning to L.A. to let the guys see their kids and wives, and to let me practice my drinking. Though my castle palace was a solid, quiet place to stay, I continued to enjoy going to hotels in my own hometown, if only for the perverse thrill of feeling like a paying guest in my own life.

JOE ANTHONY:

You know the Century Plaza Hotel, over there on Avenue of the Stars? It's one of those five-stars. All suit and tie, snooty. Presidents, leaders of other countries, when they come to Los Angeles, they always stay there. One night, Stephen and I are cruising around with some chicks, and he wants to get a hotel. So he gets a hotel room THERE.

One thing leads to another and you've got me and Stephen and these fucking chicks in Stephen's room. I think one of the girls set him off: "All you rock stars, aren't you famous for throwing shit out of hotel room windows?"

He got up, grabbed a TV: "You mean like this?" And chucked the TV off the fucking balcony.

And next thing you know he's throwing all kinds of shit out of the twentieth floor: a chair, a desk. I was like, "Come on, dude! You can't be doing that. You might kill somebody!" Thank God it was all landing on a roof, lower down, on an adjacent building. They caught wind of it of course, and he got a hell of a bill.

Why would a person want to do that? Because he can.

The months passed and we made another album, *Detonator.* We recorded it in a small studio right on Melrose. Desmond Child, the famous songwriter, was called in to work with us. He'd written "Dude Looks Like a Lady" for Steven Tyler. The label hoped he'd work similar magic for us. We barely noticed he was there.

Robbin was falling apart. He was frustrated and often sobbed. His fingers were swollen and he moved slowly, clumsily. For the first time you could notice the beginnings of a belly swelling over his belt.

"I can't *play*, man. I can't fucking play."

"What do you mean, man? That sounded pretty good—"

"The fuck it did!" yelled Robbin. "Everyone's always lying to me, and I swear, I'm so sick of it. I'm over it, man! You guys know I suck, so why not just say so?"

He had never been an angry guy before. Now he could snap into a rage at the drop of a hat. In seconds, the outburst would turn to shame, and he'd be apologizing, breaking down in tears. It was scary. The real Robbin was in there somewhere, but he was buried underneath a lot of layers. King didn't even make it through the recording of the album. He went off to rehab for the first time instead.

"I gotta do it, sorry," he mumbled. "You guys can see I'm starting to lose my fucking mind. . . ."

We were all supportive. "Dude, it's the best thing for you. We'll see you on the outside. Clean."

"Can you wait for me?" he asked, embarrassed. "To finish the album?"

How could I have told him no? That would have been heartless. A guy inside needs something to hope for, to motivate him.

"Sure," I said. "Not a problem."

Needless to say, we didn't wait. Warren came into the studio, and in a matter of days, he'd recorded all of Robbin's parts, easy as that. As much as it killed me.

JOE ANTHONY:

That's one of the best albums they ever did, and it got no fucking recognition whatsoever.

The record company wasn't behind them. Things were starting to change. After the album was done, we had a

record-listening party. Stephen gave me a pocketful of
cash and I organized the whole thing and got strippers and
lesbians—turned the whole studio into a model shoot. It
was just fucking insane. Jon Bon Jovi was there, and C. C.
DeVille, and David Lee Roth, and Eddie Van Halen, and
all these motherfuckers. Everyone just hung out and partied
and got fucking crazy.

But Stephen was the only guy from the band to show up
at the party. To me, that was kind of a sign, you know?

Robbin came back into town, looking sober-ish. The light was
back in his eyes for a while there. The label started talking promo.
They wanted us to make a half-hour video featuring some of our
best songs.

"We got a budget?"

"Sure, $250,000. You can make it happen for that, right?"

We spent that in preproduction just building ornate sets. A life-
size replica of a plane was built, with painstaking attention to detail
and craftsmanship; it seemed important at the time. Half-naked
women crawled all over the set, dressed in futuristic stripper costumes. We may have employed half the strippers in Los Angeles
County. Someone decided it would be a good idea to bring in Little
Richard to narrate and act as a host for us. He showed up all in
white, eyes gleaming, with a couple of bodyguards holding his suitcase for him.

"I been around for a long time, gentlemen. I'm your man. You
want to know something, just ask."

We gathered around him in the dressing room like kids around
Santa Claus.

"Tell us about the old days, Richard. . . ."

"So much to tell. A lot of heartbreak. A lot of triumph. Elvis Presley learned everything from me. He was my baby. Loved him, I cried when he passed. Jimi Hendrix, too. He slept on my floor for a time. Oo-wee. Such a loss, a crying shame."

"What else? Did Pat Boone really steal your song?"

"Pat Boone? I think about him every night before I go to sleep. Pat Boone stole from me, boys. He took my 'Tutti Frutti' and he turned it upside down. He made millions on a song I wrote and recorded. I got him back, though. The very next year I wrote 'Long Tall Sally.' It was too fast for the white boy to sing! Oo-WEE!"

Robbin didn't stay clean long. He'd disappear for lunch and come back four hours later. One day Phil and I discovered Robbin's dope stash and his used needles in a corner of the bathroom, on the floor. He'd covered them up with tissue paper.

The budget spiraled out of control, and the label threatened to stop paying the bills unless we reined it in. We only spent more. On the brink of some kind of collapse, we managed to convince the director to front us the rest of the cash. He wanted to finish this thing, and so did I. We were working with an intergalactic comical sci-fi Flash Gordon type of concept, and my clothes were somewhere along the lines of Clockwork Orange Gutter Space Boy.

Every day, Phil and I looked for Robbin's stash, thinking we could hide it from him temporarily and in the process get the video made. One day, during the second week, we found a big Clint Eastwood–size pistol in his bag, and that scared me.

"Someone's hiding my dope," Robbin confided to me.

"That's terrible," I said. "Who do you think it is?"

"I don't know," said Robbin. "Hey, Stephen?"

"Yeah?"

"You didn't take the dope, did you?"

"No," I said. "No way."

"What about my gun?"

"What gun?"

"I had a gun. Someone took it, man. Unless I'm just *really* losing it. . . . Fuck, man, I can't remember where I'm putting things. . . ."

We finished the video, spending nearly half a million bucks on it in the process. I took home the hottest chick on the set and made her kind of a girlfriend. Her name was Wendy, and she was tall, blond, beautiful, the standard deal. She and I commenced playing house. One day, a call came in from a casting agent at 20th Century Fox.

"We'd love for you to come in and audition for us," she told me. "We've got an Andrew Dice Clay movie in the works. *The Adventures of Ford Fairlane.* It's going to be a great, great film."

"Why me?" I said, suspicious. "I'm not really an actor."

"The role is for a rock singer," she said.

I went in, read for it, did a good job. I started planning for a second career. Then the bastards gave the role to Vince Neil. (In retrospect, I'm pretty glad I didn't get it, because the movie flopped.)

I was restless. At every opportunity, I sought distraction. Thank God I had drag racing, my first love. I sponsored a funny car for a couple of races with Dale Pulde, owner and driver. I could always count on the drag races to relieve me from this rock-and-roll headache nightmare success story. Every chance I got, I went racing.

I'd had the *Penthouse* girls, the Playmates, but when the porn star Savannah was making her rounds, I sat up and paid attention;

she'd been with Slash, Pauly Shore, and Gregg Allman. I guess she figured it was my turn.

JOE ANTHONY:

Stephen had this on-again, off-again thing with a chick named Wendy, but he never wanted to put all his eggs in one basket, so he would hang out with Savannah. They'd have a good time. And of course she was just crazy. Just out of her mind. Hot as fuck, but insane.

She'd take me and Stephen out to eat. We'd always go out for sushi. She'd recently done a spread for Hustler, *and brought a bunch of magazines. She'd sit at the table with you and open up the centerfold, and there's her fucking pussy, staring you right in the face.*

To my surprise, our relationship was basically asexual. Savannah was looking for someone to get fucked up with, not get pounded by. I considered for a moment, then decided I fit that bill, too. We'd drink all night and chow pills. At the time, Joe was seeing her hot friend, and we'd take over hotel bars, drink places out until they told us to leave. When it came time to go to bed, instead of getting it on, both of us would just pass out. I stuck around until she started to do heroin. Then I was gone. It was unfortunate what happened to her. Hollywood eats you up and spits you out.

DUKE VALENTI, SECURITY:

I went down to Miami with Ratt to warm up for the Detonator tour. The idea was to practice, get everybody in tune, give the engineer an idea of what to do. We go down

*there for three fucking days and all we did was argue.
Nobody showed up for sound check. Nobody wanted to do
anything. The tour manager was pulling his fucking hair
out.*

*The real problem with Ratt was Stephen and Bobby
Blotzer did not get along. At all. They hated each other, and
I never found out why. If I had to guess, I'd say it had to do
with money, because Bobby was not credited as a writer,
so he got a much smaller share of the publishing. And also,
you got to remember one thing: Who gets all the trim in
the band? Singer and lead guitar player, right? Fuck. Why
doesn't the drummer ever get the hot one?*

*Interviews were an issue, too. I'd take Stephen to do an
interview at a radio station. Not the band, mind you: Stephen. You know, the rest of the guys might like to be inter-
viewed sometimes, too. Everyone does. But they always
wanted Stephen. And that became a problem.*

The Detonator tour was our first taste of tour life on the
downhill slide. We were met with crowds that were increasingly
indifferent. Our agent had booked us our usual twelve-to-fifteen-
thousand–seat venues, but to our surprise, we were bringing in
only half that many.

"I hate fucking playing to empty seats," Bobby snapped, steamed,
after a show. "It's goddamn embarrassing."

We hit Europe and met with a little bit of relief there: smaller
venues and more enthusiastic crowds, folks who either hadn't figured out or didn't care that metal was dying. We bounced from Paris
to Bonn, Bremen to Hamburg, Karlsdorf to Munich, Frankfurt to

Nottingham, York to Newcastle, Manchester to Birmingham, and finally on to London, our pockets full of crumpled francs and marks, all of which we pushed across the bar.

Then we were on to Japan. They'd never let us down, and I hoped they weren't about to start now. But in Tokyo, things finally came to a head with Robbin. At one of our biggest shows of the tour, he played a couple of songs with a completely out-of-tune guitar. He sounded horrible, like a teenager in a garage band, but he paid no attention. Even if it could have been his guitar tech handing him an out-of-tune guitar. Still, he was so gone, he couldn't even hear the difference.

We finished the tour with him, one last blast in Osaka: sumo, sushi, noodles, pussy. But that was it. He was in another universe. He couldn't get smack out there, so he would drink all the mini-bars dry. Managers started booking him rooms without minibars, but he would just check out and book another room. When we came back to the States to finish our tour, Robbin went straight back into rehab. We hired Michael Schenker from Scorpions to fill his shoes. We also hired a keyboard player—so far off the Ratt sound. That was a sign something was really wrong. We were losing our sound, our image, and our desire. If we had only gotten off the road and taken breaks years before, who knows? But it was too late. So off we went.

DUKE VALENTI:

One time after a show, Pearcy had two girls in his room with him at the hotel. They were only about eighteen or so, and I got a call from Stephen. He says, Duke, we gotta talk. One of these girls' father is downstairs.

I said, Let me talk to the father—meanwhile, I want you to get them out of that fucking room. I don't even want them in that room.

The dad was livid. He was a huge guy, and he was really upset that his daughter went to this concert behind his back. Now they're in the fucking hotel room, with the lead singer? I said to him, Listen, girls are going to be girls. I have your daughter coming downstairs. More than that, I really don't know what to tell you. I said, Please, don't beat your daughter. Things like this are going to happen.

I finally got them out of there, but Stephen was shitting. Everywhere he went, he had to have girls. There's not a single place we ever went that he didn't get laid. Not one. It was every fucking night.

Another phone call came in: another pregnant chick. This time I felt kind of sad about it. But I did the exact same thing. I got my lawyer, Judith, to clean up the mess.

"Stephen," she said, "I'll take care of this. But you need to start being a little more careful."

DUKE VALENTI:

Pearcy fucked this girl before a show in his dressing room, and that night, during the show, he's onstage and he keeps trying to get my attention. I look over at him, and he's pointing at a guy in the audience. Keeps pointing at this one guy, over and over. Finally, I go to the other side of the stage so I can take a better look. And this guy is down there going, "FUCK YOU! YOU MOTHERFUCKER! YOU

FUCKED MY GIRLFRIEND! I'M GONNA FUCKING KILL YOU!"

I got the venue security to get rid of him right away. He was ready to slit someone's throat.

I got the message: Maybe cut back on the boning just a tad. I'd kind of had my fill of strange by this point, anyway. I was trying to keep a steady girlfriend. So to entertain myself, I talked many girls into letting me give them a shave. I got good with my Schick razor. Steady hand. I'd ask them, "What do you want, a landing strip, a design, a star?"

"Wow, that's *amazing.* . . . Now, how do you want me, baby?"

"I don't. But please enjoy the show."

As the tour progressed, Bobby kept adding to the mountain of monitors behind his drum set, so he could hear every rattle and smash perfectly.

"Do you need *that* big of a setup?" I asked him. "I've never seen a drummer with that many monitors, man." I think it was more of an ego trip than a hearing issue. The fucker was on a drum riser twenty feet high.

"Do your fucking job," was Bob's response. "And let me do mine."

It got so bad we were pushing and shoving in our changing booth, backstage, and beers were being thrown at each other. I was thinking to myself, *This is fucking insane.*

That very night, Bob launched into a rage, throwing sticks at the monitor guy, convinced his sound had been miscalibrated.

"Get it right!" he screamed. "I'm gonna fire your fucking ass if you don't."

It was terrible, really, how many monitor guys we lost that tour. One night one of our monitor guys snapped and charged at Bobby. He got close to killing him onstage, but was held back. We had no choice but to let him go.

We were trapped on autopilot, locked into a mode that we'd long since outgrown, and none of it was fun anymore. We were forced to deal with guys whom we not only didn't care for, but whom we were beginning to actively hate. I withdrew from the band as much as I could. While they rode the bus, me and Duke took a plane. Was that a prick move? Perhaps. Maybe I was turning into a prick. Just like the rest of them.

DUKE VALENTI:

I liked Stephen. Really, I did. Only once did me and him actually have a feud. We were in Atlanta. We got in at one o'clock and he wanted to go to last call somewhere. I took him down to the pier area, and we got a drink. And I don't know if he took a pain pill or something, but he started to get really fucking stupid. I said, Let's go. Time to go.

And as we're walking through the lobby of the hotel, what does he do? He punches a fucking picture. Rips his knuckle and he's bleeding profusely. I rush him to the bathroom, tell him to put some towels on it, and tell him I'll be right back.

Now, it's kinda breaking my fucking balls that he punched a framed fucking picture. I'm like, You gotta be fucking kidding me. I'm trying to help you? You can't be breaking shit.

Security comes down, all pissed at me, wanting to know what happened. So what do I do? I lie. I tell him my guy was drunk, and he slipped and pawed at the picture to stop his momentum. I said, I'm going back to the restroom, he's bleeding profusely, I gotta get him to a hospital.

He ended up getting seventy-five stitches in his hand. They had to cut one of his rings off to give him the stitches.

We were beat up, fried, hating life, hating the road, hating each other. After seven years, we weren't the flavor of the month any longer. My vocal cords began to feel irritated all the time. I'd done literally thousands of shows, screaming for hours on end, and now my body was starting to scream back at me. I'd get a cortisone shot before some shows, to relax the muscles in my throat, but I tried not to go overboard with it, as cortisone eventually thickens the cords. Luckily, I found a shitload of Jack Daniel's numbed me up just as well.

"We sounded like crap up there," Bob said, after one particularly lackadaisical effort. "And hey, here's a news flash for you, singer guy: We're not in New Orleans, okay? We're in fucking *Texas*."

"As if it mattered," I mumbled.

"Man, if that's how you feel, Stephen, you should just quit! I'm dead serious. Do us a favor and get the fuck out of here."

"I'd love to," I said. "I'll be honest with you, man. At this point, I'd *love* to."

"Fine," said Blotzer. "When this tour is over, man, you should. Go your own fucking way, Stephen, and let's just cut our losses."

"Why wait?" I shouted. "Why delay the inevitable? We suck anyway."

"*You* suck. Not us: you!"

"No one gives a shit! No one cares, Bob! I'm going home, man. And I'm going now."

"The hell you are. We have eight more shows to do, you imbecile!"

"No, we don't," I said, looking around for my shit. "I'm gone. I'm taking us off the road."

OUTTA SIGHT, OUTTA MIND

HAVING ABANDONED THE RATT ship, I came home and slept for a week. Every single nerve in my body was shot. My own bed had never felt so good to me. For the first time in years, I drew myself a bath, lit some candles, and settled my aching body inside. Smoking a joint and looking up at the ceiling, I tried to figure out where and when things had gone wrong.

"Mom?" I said on the phone. "Mom . . . I think I quit my own band."

"Really?" She sounded concerned. "Are you sure that this is the right thing for you, honey?"

"I was totally fried." I felt like a stepped-on potato chip.

"What about your friends? Aren't they upset with you?"

"I'm really not sure we're friends anymore, Mom," I admitted.

After another week of hibernation, I drove south and retreated to my house in San Diego. It was an enormous property in nearby La Costa that resembled a castle more than anything else.

"Do you really need all this space?" my mom had asked me when I first bought it. "This is a very vast home, honey."

"Probably not."

It was a ridiculous, overblown house. My mom was right: I didn't need half that space—after all, I was so used to living in tiny rooms and bouncing from hotel to hotel that I could have bought a 4,500-square-foot home with a kiddie pool and a microwave and been nearly as satisfied. But something inside me told me to go big. Go gaudy. Go dumb. I needed help to transition back into civilian life. After almost a decade on the road, I had a bad case of rock fever. I was suffering from ego-phobia—so surrounded by arrogant pricks at every turn that I could no longer be sure I wasn't one of them. The castle would be my solid foundation.

Of course, things never turn out like you want 'em to. The first week I was there, the quiet prickled the hairs on the back of my neck. My new home was eerie and uncanny: an immense nightmare with turrets and towers. I hated it. But then I heard someone across the street playing a Metallica song in his garage at full volume. Relieved, I leaped out of bed and ambled over to check out the sound. A teenage kid with long hair was bent double over his electric guitar, playing along with Kirk Hammett note for note.

"Sounds great!" I yelled. "All right, man! *Master of Puppets*! I'm a huge fan."

"Hey," he said, stopping the strumming immediately. "Who are you?"

"Stephen," I said. "What's up, man? Dig the music."

"Cool," said the kid, examining me. "Hey, wait. I know who you are. Aren't you that Ratt guy?"

"Used to be," I said. "Now I'm just Stephen."

He stuck out his hand. "Erik Ferintinos. I play guitar."

"Listen, Erik, I got a problem," I said. "I just moved in across the street, and I don't know *anyone* around here. I'm kind of losing my mind, to be completely honest with you."

Erik stared at me. "So?"

"Well, you know, man," I said, fixing him with a smile. "Got anything to smoke for a new neighbor?"

He promptly stuffed us a bongload, and we soon commenced getting high. Erik had big dreams of success, and as I listened to him I remembered fondly the days when I had that kind of idealism.

"I got a *band*," he declared, "and we're gonna make it, dude."

"Well, hey, as it just so happens," I said, "I got a brand-new recording studio built into my house. You should come by sometime. Maybe one of my friends could engineer some shit for you and your guys."

"Serious?" He looked surprised. "That would be . . . so cool."

"No problem," I said. "By the way, my lawn's gigantic. How would you feel about mowing it every once in a while?"

Erik had a pretty cool gig for a teenager. He'd come over, we'd get high, and then I'd gas up the lawn mower for him. He'd do the grass, tending to concentrate mostly on the patch of ground out by the pool, which just happened to be fifty feet away from where my girlfriend would sunbathe topless. You could see the longing on his face and had to assume he was pushing that mower with his chubster.

"Stephen, baby—who is that?" my girl asked me, covering up one of her tits with her hand.

"Be nice," I answered, pulling her hand back. "Give him something to dream about, okay?"

Some deep part of me was ready to retire from music altogether. I pictured myself trying to be a normal kind of guy, with normal friends. *Here's Stephen Pearcy, heading to the grocery store for a pint of vanilla ice cream and a bag of cherries, to eat in front of the TV.* Or maybe start my drag racing career, a little late. Maybe the best plan was to lie back in the cut, wait for the right moment, then reconcile with the band.

But my brain was corrupted by fifteen years in rock. I realized that I just was not cut out for the simple life. I needed fresh tits and new riffs and a stage under my feet. And since retiring wasn't in the cards for me, I had no choice but to look around for another kind of musical enjoyment. Fred Coury, the drummer from Cinderella, had just left his band. He and I began to talk about forming a group together.

"I'm only willing to do this if we can make something that rocks hard," I insisted. "No power ballads. No two-minute cock-rock guitar heroics. None of that hair-metal nonsense, seriously. Let's go lean, mean, and stripped down, or let's not go at all."

"Absolutely," Coury said. "I'm right there with you."

FRED COURY, DRUMMER, CINDERELLA AND ARCADE:

I met Stephen for the first time in Germany, at one of the Monsters of Rock shows. Cinderella was playing on the same bill as Ratt and Bon Jovi, and we kinda hit it off. He goes, "Let's go out and have some fun tonight." I was freaking out. This is the guy from Ratt! So I get this knock at my door, and I look through and I see it's him. Oh my gosh, I thought. It's the guy from Ratt!

I open the door, and I friggin' get hit with this fire extinguisher full in the face. He blew up my whole room. We looked like ghosts. He was laughing like a maniac. It cost us three grand in damages.

We pulled some chicks that night, though, some German honeys. Mine had really hairy legs. Hot.

I ended up getting canned from Cinderella in '91 or '92. I'd been with them since 1986. We'd sold six million records by then. It was a really scary moment for me. I called Stephen and told him, "Hey, dude. I just got fired."

And he goes, "Yeah, you and Vince Neil and C. C. DeVille and Jeff Cease." All of us got fired in the same week.

He goes, "Hold on, I'll call you back."

I'm like, Hey, dude, I want to cry to somebody! And he hangs up on me. Unbelievable.

But then he called back. "I just quit Ratt. Let's do this." And a month and a half later, we had a deal on Epic, for our new band, Arcade. It was unbelievable. Almost like dreamy, how it happened.

Arcade featured solid musicians Donny Syracuse, Frankie Wilsex, and Michael Andrews. Grunge was winning in the early '90s. Our hard-rock brothers were starting to panic. Maybe Arcade could save us all.

Or maybe it would just save me. I found it such a relief to be with guys who didn't hate me, I just wanted to sit back and soak up all the fun. From moment one, we were a hard-partying, hard-playing band—booze-oriented, strip-bar obsessed. Frankie Wilsex, in particular, shared my passion for the cheaper clubs.

"Frankie! Let's party, man! Should we head to the Tropicana?"

Frankie shook his head in the negative. "I'm in more of a Jumbo's mood."

Jumbo's was a destination where fat girls danced in jean shorts and vinyl bras. As legend had it, David Lynch used to write some of his best scripts there. It never really mattered where we began, though, because we were on a strip-club world tour and would take in up to ten clubs a day. Before the show, we'd head to a bar, toss back a drink or five, get nice and hammered, then head to the next. We'd repeat our formula ad infinitum, until ten minutes before showtime, when we'd haul ass to the club, play the show, yell at the crowd, sweat out the booze, and, as soon as we'd showered, head right back to the club. It was a joyous, repetitive, disgusting way to live, and it felt right for that particular moment in time.

When Arcade's first album came out, we charted two singles, "Nothing to Lose" and "Cry No More." I was pleased with our success.

FRED COURY:

When he was sober, he was the most incredible guy. When he was not, he was kind of a nightmare.

One night we were at the Troubadour and some chick was giving him shit from the front row. So what does he do? He engages her. "Hey! Before the show I butt-slammed your dad!" Me and Frankie looked at each other like, What? Did he just say that?

My wife at the time was standing next to Gene Simmons, and he just went, "No! No no no no!"

If I was a bit of a dickhead in the Arcade days, to my bandmates or to the strippers with whom we fraternized, then I must apologize. Increasingly, I was just pretty drunk a lot of the time. Sometimes my days would begin in pain, and I'd have to guzzle down a brew or two just to get my hands steady. When you're drinking beers in the shower, that's generally a bad sign.

Arcade toured constantly, and with the help of my beer and my dancing girls, I generally managed to stay one pace ahead of feeling much emotion. I had little to no contact with Warren, Bobby, or Juan. Robbin and I saw each other only intermittently. He was heavily into his abuse, and his marriage was falling apart. His wife tried to kick him out of his own house, and after a while he gave in and got a place of his own. None of it was pretty.

Like most guys going through a divorce, Robbin was bummed and cynical; making it worse, though, was the fact that he was so hopelessly addicted, a two-time failure at rehab. I went over to his apartment a couple of times just to visit him during the divorce time, and in every drawer that you opened, there was foil and tar.

"Hey, man," I said one day, after having a couple of drinks. "Is it cool if I try some of this?"

"Well, sure," Robbin said, sounding a little surprised. "You got a lighter?"

"Yeah, I'm equipped."

Smoking heroin is very simple. You start by placing a small piece of tar on some sort of flat surface with low heat capacity—aluminum foil is ideal because it gets hot right away and cools down almost instantly. Then you light a flame below the foil with a Zippo lighter or a candle. A Zippo works better because it won't leave soot. The heat from the flame vaporizes the heroin, and you just suck the smoke into your lungs, using either a straw, a tube, or just your mouth, with big, greedy gulps. Simple as that. It's more economical to use a tube—you waste less—but some rock stars just feel weird with a cardboard toilet paper tube around their lips.

I remember sitting there after having smoked, with Robbin in the next room puttering around, and feeling perfectly empty. Just like, a cool, ethereal zero. That's when I realized exactly what the attraction of heroin was. It was like, I got it: *Ohhhhhh. THAT'S why he does this shit.* For the first time in what seemed like fifteen or twenty years, I didn't want for anything. I had every single thing I needed and wanted right there inside me, all tied up in pure sweet calm and understanding.

Suddenly, I was struck with how much I loved Robbin, really cared for him. He was my brother. And yet I lacked the inclination to share that information with him. That would involve speaking. I felt far too perfect and far too peaceful to risk squandering my buzz on idle talk.

Tell him you care about him, a little voice inside of me spoke. *Now's the time, man. . . . Tell him you'll help him get sober, if he wants. . . .*

I stared up at the cheap ceiling of Robbin's apartment and found it somehow beautiful. I felt so physically blissed out that my spine felt nonexistent, my tongue feathery, and even my underarms were coolly perfect pits.

But his life is falling apart, I thought. *You're just a visitor in heroin land, but he fucking lives here. King's hands are all swelled up like balloons. . . . He's out of shape, out of mind, out of body, out of spirit.*

I readied myself to speak, but then I breathed in, as an experiment, and it was the longest, smoothest, slowest, most sensual inhale of my life. As I let the breath go, an unshakable sense of rightness and clarity flooded my central nervous system. My head tingled, the base of my skull filling with light, and I closed my eyes. If I concentrated, I could actually feel the lids on my eyeballs, sleek and heavy on the orbs.

We will talk later, I promised myself. *We'll figure this whole thing out.*

I settled deeper into the couch, in gentlemanly repose. I thought that would be my first and last trip on that shit. Little did I know.

■ ■ ■

ARCADE PUT OUT ANOTHER ALBUM, IN 1994, *A/2.* The follow-up effort didn't do quite as well. The Seattle sound was so prevalent around that time and so beloved, and metal and hard rock were pretty well played out. Not too many guys in our genre were finding much love. Even our hard-core fans were a bit bored after a solid decade of oversaturation. The critics had never really thought much of us even at the height of our popularity. Personally, I didn't give that much of a shit: If I was making music, then I was pretty happy. Anyway, I always found chemical ways to pass the time.

We toured with Arcade to promote the second album, hitting the smaller venues and continuing our strip-club world tour. I'd planned to be just as relentless as in our early days of Ratt: twenty shows in twenty days. But I knew it was time to adjust my expectations when we started to get booed by our own fans.

"Play 'Round and Round'!" they screamed. *"Play it!"*

"We're not Ratt," I laughed from the stage.

"'Round and *Round*'!"

I looked back to the guys in my band, shrugging. Fred launched into the opening beat, and we gave them the old hit.

"That was pretty fucking brutal," one of our roadies commiserated with me, postshow. "Sorry, dude."

"Nah," I said, cracking a beer. "Hey, they bought the tickets, right?"

I tried not to let any of it get me down. We were out, we were touring, we were making a little bit of money. So what if it was somewhat difficult to get out from underneath the shadow of my past? At least we were still in the game, right? I was firmly resolved to have a good time.

FRED COURY:

He was practically sober when we first did Arcade. What broke up that band was him leaping off the wagon. You can't run a business unless you're sober. Can't be done.

I used to watch his house sometimes: The back door was always loose, and the alarm would always go off, and the cops would show up. One time the cops came and split, and I went upstairs and found Stephen asleep in his bed. I pulled the sheets back and started to shake him. He looked dead. I gave him a full-on soccer field goal kick in the ribs! I'm surprised I didn't break his ribs. Over and over, I kept kicking him so freaking hard. . . .

Finally he woke up and kind of squinted at me. "What are you doing?"

He'd taken some sleeping pills. Lumina, I think. But for a long time there, I really thought he'd died.

A/2 soon disappeared from stores. For a moment, it may have bothered me, sure. But there's always freedom in failure, if you look at it right.

The kind of music that we'd made our living off of for so long was finally going out of style, and you just couldn't ignore it. Some of us metal guys got tired of licking our wounds, though, and we started to vary the formula. I soon found out that I actually *liked* playing in different styles. I was asked to be part of an industrial band called Vertex with a Japanese drummer named Hiro Kuretani. Al Pitrelli, who had played with Alice Cooper and Savatage, joined us on guitar, along with Robbie Crane, who eventually would end up playing bass for Ratt.

I went out and did my homework. I was kind of excited to explore a new, darker way of singing, expressing myself. I wouldn't say we were a total success, but it was very different from anything I'd done before, and interesting for that. It wasn't like I was look-ing for a hit or a top-ten single: Our band was about niche appeal, right from the very start, and we all knew it. Our self-titled *Vertex* was a thinking record, with songs like "Mother Mary" and "Fuck the World" weaving bleak, dystopian tales about society and life in general.

I was furious up onstage, some nights. Ratt had been all about sex and partying; this new music was about cynicism and rage and the energy you could tap into by admitting your own slow burn. It was the '90s, so I didn't have to look far for reasons to complain. We'd been kings for ten years. Now we were picking up the pieces, part of a bleaker landscape. The old family was split up. Each of us was just trying to get by.

JOE ANTHONY:

After Ratt broke up, I still had to make a living, you know? So I went out on the road with other bands. Around 1994, I was out with Chicago, and we came through Little Rock. And wouldn't you know it, Sweet, Sweet Connie came to my hotel room. Actually, she came to the tour manager's hotel room first. We had adjoining rooms. She did her deal, and he knocked on my adjoining door. "Hey. Sweet Connie's here. She wants to suck your dick." I was like, great. And of course I said, I'll get you backstage.

But later on that day, the band took me aside and said, "Hey. We don't want to see Sweet Connie backstage. Got it? We don't want to see her anywhere." They'd been through Little Rock a bunch of times before, and they knew the deal. None of the guys wanted anything to do with her.

So it's six o'clock, and I'm having dinner. Now, the people who do the catering are like family. They got their kids there helping. And off in the distance, I started to hear this fucking loud screaming, and shit getting thrown around.

If you've ever been to a backstage gig, they've got all these curtains set up. The screaming keeps getting louder and louder, and finally, Connie breaks through this curtain. She comes flying in and runs right over to my table. "YOU FUCKING ASSHOLE!" she yells. "You didn't leave me any tickets at the fucking window!"

I didn't know what to say.

"I SUCKED YOUR COCK TODAY!"

I'm looking around, all these old ladies and men, and these fucking kids are staring at me. It's one of those times you want to shrink into an ant.

Connie was something else, man. I mean, she used to walk into a venue and blow fifty or sixty guys without shedding a fucking sweat. It was fucking amazing.

Sometimes it was tough, getting older and looking in the mirror every morning. I'd stare into the glass and see a different guy, someone different from the kid who'd come to L.A. in search of the Sunset Strip in January 1980, determined to battle his way to the top. I'd made it. I'd drowned in oceans of trim and adulation. What was the next move?

I was boozing all the time, and it showed on my face, in the way that I moved. When I wasn't able to distract myself with constant touring or by blaming the members of my old band—and them blaming me—my own self-destruction was harder to ignore. I needed activity, movement, so, without pause, I formed yet another ensemble, an alternative rock band named Vicious Delite, and created an independent label to promote and distribute us: Top Fuel Records.

"Why bother?" a friend asked me, as we watched a boxy Puerto Rican chick work the pole at the Spearmint Rhino. "Why don't you just let someone else worry about the technical stuff?"

"I've been through so much shit with labels," I explained, breathing in the sleazy, smoke-filled air of the strip bar. "This way, I'll have artistic control and financial independence."

What I hadn't counted on was the fact that I also had more responsibility. Adding to my surprise was the fact that the guys in

Vicious Delite were even more into partying than I was. They were younger dudes, constantly on ten—getting fucked up, not sleeping for days, passing out in airports. We were out of control. (Most recently, Robby Karras died from his abuse. He was a great kid.) In attitude and sound, we were really a punk band. The bleak mood I'd been carrying around for some time seemed to fit the aesthetic perfectly. I didn't talk much onstage, and rarely interacted with the audience. I was just this gloomy character who wanted to yell, Fuck you, fuck this.

I was on a mission to escape from myself. I always had to be moving, making deals. My castle house in San Diego was beautiful, but too impractical to serve as my only residence, so I bought another property in Studio City. Often I had friends stay there when I was gone. One evening, I came back to my pad to find a pretty large shindig going on.

"What's going on here?" I asked some drunk, sipping from one of my cocktail glasses.

"The fucker who lives here is out of town!" he explained. "We're gonna empty his liquor cabinet."

I joined in and tried to help the mission along. A beautiful dark-haired woman was standing with some rocker guy in a corner. She and I made eye contact, and an hour later, she approached me. We began to talk intimately. After a little while, she ended up giving me her number and asking me to call her.

"What's up with the other guy?" I asked.

"That's ending," she assured me.

Her name was Melissa, and soon we started hanging out. I liked her vibe: laid-back and reserved. She preferred staying in for the night to going out and partying. By this point in my life, I found that to be a relief. As I started to develop feelings for Melissa, I couldn't help but realize how closed off I'd been for so many years, fucking any chick I felt like on the road, watching women bang double-headed dildos in the backs of tour buses. Suddenly all of that felt like nonsense.

Within a few weeks of meeting each other, Melissa and I were spending all of our free time together. She worked late, but after she'd finished, she'd come over to my house and we'd stay up all night together, laughing, making love. Soon, we'd made the rocker plunge: We went out and got tattoos together. She got my name on her toe. I put her on my arm.

Shit, I thought to myself. *Looks like I'm falling for this one. . . .*

Melissa was much the same as the other girlfriends I'd had: She liked my rock thing, but at the same time, she wanted to be the most important thing in my life. And as for me, I pretended I told her everything, but of course, there were a few things I kept to myself. My pain pill addiction was starting to really gear up, and that was my business and mine alone. I gobbled down a handful or two of hydrocodones every day, drinking and smoking right along with them.

The constant-snuggle thing went on for a few months between me and Melissa, then it cooled just a touch. I had two houses, so there was always room for me to hang out with other women; not to mention, I was in a band with a bunch of hard-partying younger guys. Temptation was always around. Even if I didn't have the inclination to throw down like I'd done as a kid on the Rolling Hilton, I succumbed from time to time. Melissa and I would probably just sort of fade away, I reasoned. After all, that was what had happened with the rest of them. But one evening, she came to me, looking serious.

"Hey," she confessed. "I'm . . . I'm pregnant."

I wasn't sure how to respond. "Is it mine?"

"Of *course* it's yours!"

I apologized, but still, we went to the hospital and took a test. Yes, the baby was mine, and immediately, I knew I had some thinking to do.

I called my mother and told her the deal—that I'd gotten my girlfriend pregnant.

"Well?" she said. "What are you going to do?"

"I don't know. . . . I don't know if I'm ready to be a dad."

My mom was silent for a while. "Do you love this woman?" My mother knew best.

"I think so," I said. "I'm not sure, but I think, yes, I love her."

"Then you might consider giving it a go," my mom said, after a moment. "You know, having a child is one of the most amazing things a human being can do."

I hung up the phone, realizing what I was about to tell Melissa, what I was about to commit to. I was nervous, but I was also almost forty years old. It was time to step up to the plate and, for once, be responsible.

Melissa and I came together for a conference. I poured myself a big drink, then told her, somewhat tensely, that I was in.

"I'm going to do this, okay?" I said. "I want to be a dad. I want to be with you."

"Oh my God!" Melissa cried. "That's so exciting. Are . . . I mean, are we going to get married?"

"Well, I don't know about that," I said. "Let's take this one step at a time. Look, I'm thinking you can move into the house in La Costa for a while. It's a huge place and very peaceful. It'll be the perfect spot for you to be pregnant."

Melissa frowned. "Will you live there with me?"

"Sometimes," I said evasively.

"Sometimes?" said Melissa. She placed both hands atop the tiny bump on her stomach.

"Melissa," I said, "I'll be there when I can."

I was rarely around, though. I shipped Melissa off to the castle and left her there well taken care of. Meanwhile, I stayed out on the road with Vicious Delite and drank through the days, working my way steadily through bottles of prescription pills, recording albums, writing endless lyrics and titles in spiral-bound notebooks with my Bic pen, sleeping the Lumina sleep of the dead.

Her belly grew bigger and bigger. In my absence, her eyes turned darker and more withdrawn. And the months did pass.

WELCOME

HALF AN HOUR BEFORE my only child came into this world, I swayed back and forth in the hallway of Beverly Hills Hospital, drunk beyond repair, my stomach filled with bitter liquids and my pockets stuffed with several miniature bottles of liquor that I'd brought with me. I leaned up against the hospital wall, mumbling to myself, waiting impatiently for the nurses and orderlies to pass me by so I could unscrew the lid of a vodka and tip back the shot into my mouth. Underneath a bank of fluorescent lights, I took in the familiar beeps and groans of hospital life.

I stared at the door of the room where they had Melissa, swallowing back a wave of nausea.

"Hey," I said, ducking my head into the room, unable to stand the suspense any longer. Melissa squirmed uncomfortably on a bed. "How are things going in here?"

"Sir, as we told you, *stay in the hall*," a nurse snapped at me. "We will *tell* you when you are needed."

"I have a right to see my child get born," I demanded. "I want to be here for this birth."

"Stephen, you are totally lit," Melissa said, sweating. "Leave us alone for now, okay?" Her face wrinkled in pain.

"Of course," I snapped. I tucked my shirt into my pants. "I want to help. . . ."

"Sir, the best way you can help us is by letting us do our *work*," the nurse said. "Outside, please. Now."

I retreated out to the hall. I rummaged through my pockets until I found a few oxycodones. Looking both directions first, I took a dose, dry-swallowed the pill. I looked back at the closed door of Melissa's room, nervous to meet my baby.

■　■　■

JEWEL PEARCY CAME BUSTING INTO MY world on July 25, 1996, a beautiful, black-haired blessing. From our first day together, she was aglow with soul and love and light.

"Aren't you the most lovely thing," I cooed to her, holding her in my arms. "Aren't you just the most *unbelievable* baby I've ever seen in my whole life. . . ."

Melissa and I tried our best to be a legitimate couple. Having moved in together several months before Jewel's birth, we were sharing the house in Studio City, changing diapers, warming bottles, getting up at night to be with our kid and make her happy. We were parents now. Adults. It was time to act like it.

"Hey, Melissa, look at Jewel—don't you think she looks like me a little bit? Like, around the eyes?"

"Wow, she really does. . . ."

Having a perfect little human around probably put me on my best behavior for at least a good two weeks. Then I was back to my old tricks, sucking on painkillers like they were Tic-Tacs, smoking powerful weed. It wasn't even that I didn't want to be sober at this point: It was more that getting high was so much a part of my everyday life that I didn't really see an alternative.

I considered myself a decent dad with a buzz on, anyway. Maybe you wouldn't want me to drive you to Orange County in the rain, but I *could* change a dirty diaper.

I loved my new daughter so much, the job just kind of came naturally. Gazing into her eyes, holding her tiny perfect hands in my hands and marveling at each tiny digit—those moments were more filled with joy than any I'd experienced on a stage or a bus.

I took Jewel everywhere with me, on trips to the mountains and to the beach, just the two of us, a bottle for baby and a cooler full of them for Daddy. I drove her down to San Diego to introduce her to my mom, and their meeting was joyful.

"I finally did something right, huh, Mom?" I said.

My mother gathered Jewel in her arms and closed her eyes in grandmotherly bliss. "I'll say."

Before we left her house, though, my mother beckoned to me.

"What's up, Mom?"

"Stephen, get it together," she said.

"What do you mean?" I said.

She looked at me pointedly. "You have someone to look out for now. So get it together."

It was easier said than done. The baton of booze and dope had been relayed hand to hand through the family history, right into my waiting grasp. I never got to know my old man, but I do know he liked to get a blur in his vision more often than not. As it turned out, so did I.

After I woke up and saw to Jewel's needs as best as I could, I generally felt justified in sneaking over to the bar around the corner for a drink or two before lunch. Sometimes the lunch part of it was optional; the beers never were. And man, once that buzz got some momentum under it, there was just no stopping it. I'd drive back to the house, leave the car running in the driveway, keys still in the ignition, motor on, door open. Sometimes I'd walk into the house and just fall on the floor. If the kid was sleeping, then I'd go to sleep, too, just exactly where I felt like it.

More than once I went to the bathroom to take a piss, took a look at myself in the mirror, and bashed it with my fist. And then I'd just pass out.

In 1997, when Jewel was one, the guys in Ratt started to make noise about getting back together. We hadn't really made the effort to mend any fences, but our catalog needed stimulation, which is to say, people weren't buying our albums anymore. So we started to see the wisdom in making a new record. The result was *Collage*, with Robbie Crane from Vertex coming in to help out as best he could. It was a strange album, not only because we didn't have anything new to say, but because Juan chose to no longer be part of our group. We said we were Ratt, yet without Juan and Robbin, we weren't, really, at all. Nevertheless, we filled up a record's worth of time with B sides and old Mickey Ratt material.

The Collage tour started off as well as could be expected. After our long hiatus, audiences were psyched to come out and see us, and we functioned as a band with a minimum of bickering. I even started to think that maybe we'd put some of our differences behind us. Then midway through the tour, I was out on the edge of the stage at an enormous festival when suddenly I lost my footing and I fell off the stage. It was a sheer drop of ten feet or so, and I landed directly on my knee, and the kneecap more or less imploded.

Oh, man, I thought, the old pain flaring inside me. *This is* so *not good. . . .*

Maybe I was just older. But the pain felt more intense than anything I'd ever experienced, and it just wouldn't go away. Being run over by a car truly had nothing on this. I went into shock immediately, and I ended up at the hospital. The tour was over that night. I was flown back to our house in Studio City, and on that flight, I actually thought about taking myself out. I really did. I was in so much pain.

The doctors patched me up. I've always been lucky like that. But the first few months of my recovery were living hell. If I'd been a little out of control with my opiates before, well, now I was literally eating pain pills by the dozen. Drinking shitloads of booze right along with them, too. And then trying to help care for the kid on top of all that.

I was in pretty terrible shape there for a bit. I was on crutches for six months, and I felt like an invalid, just like I had when I was in high school. Crutch my way out of bed. Crutch to the kitchen to get myself a beer. Crutch my way to the baby. Then to the bathroom. There was no escaping myself or the constant dull ache that spread from my leg through my whole body.

Take the easy way out, I kept thinking to myself. *You know how to do it. . . .*

Jewel was probably the only reason I got through it. I had a child to look after. So even if I was never going to be nominated for dad of the year, at least I knew that I had to keep myself in the game, for her sake.

Painkillers were central to my life. You name it, I had it. The worst part about pain pills is that the more you use them, the less they work. I'd been abusing opiates for my own cloudy-headed pleasure for decades. Now that I needed them for legitimate purposes, they weren't working according to plan. I moved up to heavier shit, like hospital-grade Demerol. Eventually I had to find a Dr. Feelgood. It wasn't right, but I felt like I had to have a bunch of those pills around constantly.

"Stephen, Jewel's crying. Can you change her diaper?"

"Really? My knee is killing me, and I'm supposed to change the fucking *diaper*?"

The healing process was probably tougher on me mentally than it was physically. I'd gotten through this whole thing once when I was a teenager, and I just wasn't sure if I could do it again. Some mornings I'd wake up, look around at the walls, the woman sleeping next to me, and my ruined leg, and just think to myself, *How the fuck did I get here?* Wasn't I, like, playing Madison Square Garden just a little while ago?

My ego was bruised. I wanted to be the Stephen who was on top of the world, not the Stephen dragging around a busted leg—a guy on stages, not crutches. It would take a river of booze to turn my head around. As soon as I felt comfortable getting behind the wheel of a car, I reclaimed my bar stool at Mexicali. It was there that I met a guy who revealed to me, after a couple of drinks, that he had a good heroin connection.

"Ever try it?"

"I've smoked it," I admitted. "Pretty fun. But that stuff'll get under your skin. My buddy's off God knows where because of it."

The dude shrugged. "I'm just saying, if you ever need some, I can hook you up."

Of course it wasn't too long before I decided to take him up on it. I never got a stash for myself at first: Just on the way to the bar, I'd go over to his studio and smoke. Then I'd pop over to Mexicali, dig into some brews, have lunch, waste away most of the day. Then, on the way home, I'd have another little smoke, just to level me out, help me deal with the wife. . . .

Heroin did a number on the knee pain, I will say that. It got my mind off the physical agony inside me. It got my mind off everything, really. I grew to love and depend upon that blankness—the peace, that utter lack of worry. Soon I was buying a little stash to take home with me, and holing up inside my studio for hours at a time.

"Stephen?" Melissa said, banging on my door. "Want some dinner, honey?"

"No, I'm writing. Please don't bother me."

Smoking heroin will keep you high for a couple of hours, unless you're constantly smoking it and have to keep chasing that dragon all the time. I wasn't there yet. I'd sit back, relax, watch the tar evaporate, and suck the sweet smoke into my lungs. I don't believe Melissa ever had a clue.

"What's that smell?" she said, wrinkling her nose, when I opened up the door of my studio after a long afternoon spent in the pleasure of my own body.

"Hash," I said, brushing past her. "I've been smoking some really good hash. So, try to be mellow, okay?"

Still, even as my substance abuse issues steadily grew harder for me to ignore, I never lost sight of the fact that I had a little kid. *This is special,* I told myself, on an almost daily basis. *She'll only grow up once, so don't fuck it up. Don't miss it.* I would always play with her, spend time with her, laugh and stare into her eyes. She was growing up to be a playful, gorgeous little toddler, always smiling.

"Your dad loves you," I told her, every day. "Hey, can I tell you a secret, kid? Huh? Can I tell you Daddy loves you so much?"

We horsed around together and drew with crayons. When I felt like I needed space from the house and my domestic situation, I'd pop Jewel in her stroller and we'd go out on long, slow walks together, as I tried to get that knee back into something resembling working order. I had no trouble communicating with my daughter, even when her vocabulary consisted of about five or six words. We had a heart connection.

Getting along with her mother was much more of a challenge. We bickered and fought a lot. Rarely did I feel carefree in our relationship. But when Melissa started to talk about getting married, when Jewel was three or four, I listened to her. Maybe marriage would provide some perspective for us—shift things a bit, make us more like other couples we knew, couples who got along.

"I think it would help us," she said. "But it would also be good for Jewel."

"I guess it would be good for her," I admitted. "Most parents are married."

"So, you're okay with it?" Melissa asked. "Are you serious?"

"Sure," I said. "I guess so. We'll be together, you and me."

"Man and wife," Melissa said, giggling. "And baby makes three."

We were married in the summer of 2000, out on Catalina Island. Chris was there, and Melissa's dad, and of course my mom and some of my family. Jewel was along for the ride, our perfect little flower girl. Melissa looked incredible, dressed all in white. Yet of course, I wouldn't have been satisfied if I didn't get smashed for my own wedding. I was so high on pills and smoke and booze that I could barely stand up straight.

"Stephen?" the minister asked me, sternly. "Do you take this woman to be your lawfully wedded wife?"

I squinted my eyes a little, felt a sweet little opiate rush. Through my haze of Percodan and Valium, we all looked so beautiful.

"I do," I mumbled.

We were official now. But nothing had changed. If anything, it was worse—now we felt obligated to each other. We were still getting on each other's nerves, constantly at each other's throats. Taking part in a legal ceremony had fixed none of that.

I started not coming home. If a fight developed, I always had a set answer: "I'm out of here."

"Where are you going?"

"I'm going to go cool off, and wait for you to change your attitude. I'll be at a hotel. See you in a day or so."

Hotel rooms were my portable party spots. They reminded me of all the years I'd spent on the road, although this time, I was partying by myself. It was so much calmer, so much less stressful than back in the Ratt days. Now, all I needed was a balloon of heroin and a couple of grams of good weed, and I'd just celebrate my independence for six or eight hours. I'd sit back, break out the notebook and the pen, and write song lyrics. That was living life. . . .

"Hey," I'd say nonchalantly when I returned. "How's it going?"

"Oh, great. Have a good time?" Melissa spat.

"Still stuck on bitch, huh?" I turned on my heel. "Guess I came back too quick. See you in a couple of days."

I realized pretty quickly I wasn't cut out to be anyone's husband. I tried to be a good dad, at the very least, but it was the strangest period. By the early 2000s, I hadn't been on top of the music world for a good long while, yet I was still selling records and still getting checks in the mail, royalties flying in. Not bad—and yet somehow, not so good. Since I was never completely clueless, I knew that things weren't exactly going to turn around right away. I had to reevaluate who I was, and what I could give to the world. But I had the baggage of an entire life of partying to deal with and the bad habits that came with it.

Life was gradually starting to spiral out of control for me. Then, in June of 2002, I got the news that I'd been waiting to hear for a long time. My brother—my partner in crime, my right-hand man, our Ratt leader, the King—was gone. Robbin had died.

He'd been HIV-positive since 1994, on and off drugs and in and out of rehab. Losers had surrounded him. He'd never locked the door to his place, and nearly all of his treasured goods, his gold records and his guitars, had been looted. His weight had ballooned to epic proportions, and his music career had almost completely petered out. But the news still shocked me. He had been my best friend and my closest musical collaborator. Now he was gone forever.

The grief over Robbin dying combined with my own feelings of helplessness, and together they created a psychic sludge that surrounded me on all sides. I was trapped in a marriage that wasn't turning out right. I felt myself sinking downward.

I received a phone call from the director of an independent film called *Camp Utopia*. Some months prior, I had agreed to score the film for him.

"Stephen, hey, man, I need a favor."

"Huh?" I was in a haze of confusion and grief. I was searching my pockets to see if I had any bits of heroin to smoke.

"Our main actor, he just backed out—listen, do you think you could come out for filming this weekend?"

"For what reason?" I turned my pockets inside out. There was nothing there.

"We were all talking about it—we'd like you to play the role of Timothy Bach, the cult leader who happens to slaughter his whole following!"

It was just insane enough to attract me. *Why the fuck not?*

I drove about an hour outside of Los Angeles to the site where they'd be filming, in some national forest at the foothills of a clutch of mountains. All the actors looked young and bright and ambitious, so excited to be on the set of an indie horror film.

"Hey, aren't you that guy—?" one of them began.

"Yes," I said shortly. "I'm that guy."

I was looking around for anything to get fucked up on. I didn't have any smack with me, but I had a few pills, which I swallowed in the first few minutes of being on set. I had never really acted before. Sick with grief, I wondered why I was beginning my career as a thespian at this particular moment.

"Stephen, Dr. Timothy Bach is a madman—a serial murderer," the director explained to me. "He's a real creep. Think you can go there for us?" I couldn't stop thinking of Robbin. Not for a single moment.

"Watch me," I said.

The film had a couple of sexy scenes: A young, dark-haired female costar got naked and lay on top of me. The set was cleared. It was just me, the director, and her. She writhed on top of me, pantomiming sex. I could feel her hot breath on my cheek.

"SAY MY NAME," I ordered her, reading off a cue card.

"Timothy Bach, *Timothy Bach*," she cried, bouncing up and down. "You're my hero. . . ."

We pretend-had-sex for a while. Then I took a sword and chopped her head off and carried it around with me. I proceeded to slaughter the entire cult after that, chopping off limbs, heads— anything I could get Timothy's hands on.

Home wasn't good. I found myself out on the East Coast for a while, in Philadelphia, shacking up with some funky little pop tart who had dated some professional hockey player. He was out of the picture, I was in for that moment.

It was the strangest thing. She was a good-looking chick in her early twenties with a septum ring whom I'd met in some bar when we were out on the road. We didn't have a sexual relationship. She didn't give a shit about Ratt. She just liked to drink. So that's what we did.

"Hey, let me buy this one. . . ."

"It's on me," I said, laying my wallet down on the bar. "You're the one putting me up. Drinks are on me."

"You're too generous."

"No," I said, smiling sadly. "I'm not that."

Every night for weeks, we hit the bars and sucked back Jack or gin and tonics or vodkas on the rocks. Come closing time, we'd stumble home to her little brick apartment in South Philly and crawl into her bed, fully clothed.

I was running away from everything that mattered. *You got a little girl at home, Stephen,* I told myself every time I looked in the mirror. *What are you doing here, man?*

I tried to silence the voice. I ate, I drank, went to clubs, stayed out all night. I found her stash of painkillers and dove in.

■ ■ ■

IT WAS FALL IN PHILADELPHIA. MY heart was turning brown, dying.

November came, then December. Snow began to fall. I walked out into the cold with my leather jacket on, shivering. Flakes flew into my eyes and mouth. I breathed in the cold winter air, sensing something awakening in me. Was I going to die one of these nights? I welcomed the thought of it, some days. I wondered who would miss me, exactly.

I'd like to say it was thoughts of Jewel that brought me home, and that's partially true. But I was also having way too much trouble getting heroin. I knew my connections back in L.A. They were reliable. I said good-bye to my dark-haired septum-ring chick and got onto a plane, heading for the place where it would never snow.

My wife met me at the airport.

"Hey there," she said. We shared a long silence.

"You didn't have to pick me up," I said, finally. "I could have taken a taxi."

"I didn't want you to get lost."

Reconciliation was always on my mind. Jewel had grown up in the few months I'd been gone. When I looked at my kid in the face, noting her longer hair, the shape of her head, her clearer eyes, I couldn't believe I'd gone out on the road at all. But heroin really helps you not experience any of the tough emotions. Remorse and shame, they're not really part of the heroin equation. Booze isn't too bad in that department either, now that I think about it.

If me and smack had been flirting before Robbin's death, we were fucking now. I'd started out real slowly, rationalizing my behavior by telling myself that I was smoking, not banging, but it had caught up with me. I might have been back home, but I was a slave to something that had nothing to do with family.

Melissa and I labored painfully to improve our relationship, but when we fought, we fought loudly. Once you get past a certain point in your relationship, the littlest thing can set you off, and for me and Melissa, it could be anything.

"Why do you and Mom always *yell* at each other?" Jewel asked me once, with such confusion that I started tearing up immediately.

"Kiddo," I sobbed. "I'm really sorry. . . . I don't mean to put you through this stuff. . . ."

"Dad, why are you crying? What's wrong? Don't worry, okay? Everything is going to be all right."

Heroin was my problem. And yet, it was also my greatest comfort. Heroin was my lover, my friend, and my enemy. It was my everything. Subtly, my life turned into a twenty-four-hour maintenance program. Making sure that the levels of opiate in my bloodstream were properly attuned became priority number one. If I didn't have my smack, the day was simply fucking ruined.

My connection lived right around the corner. He was dependable, close-lipped, prompt, and best of all, he never passed judgment.

A balloon costs from sixty to a hundred dollars and lasts you a day or so, depending on your addiction. You can sit there and smoke it every ten minutes. Some people will smoke every half hour, or every hour. Beginners can get off once and stay good for half a day. It depends on your metabolism. It depends on what you're going for.

I always felt better if I had some tar in reserve. I kept a little bit in my car, a little bit in my studio. Something like a security blanket.

I would hole up in my studio with my guitar, a good hunk of tar, aluminum foil, my Zippo, and think about better times. My happy times . . .

On New Year's Eve, just a couple of months after we'd gotten signed, we had a huge gig scheduled at the Santa Monica Civic. The mood backstage before the show was festive. My mother showed up early with my uncle Sal, and she walked around, a drink in her hand, smiling from ear to ear, inspecting things.

"So this is what a backstage looks like!" she said. "I've always wondered."

"Mom, what do you think, you like it?"

"I'm having the best time!" she laughed.

I folded my piece of foil in half, flattened it slowly with my hand, then folded it over again, flattened it again.

We waved good-bye to our friends and family, told them we'd see them after the show. We strutted out, nodding our heads to the beat that rocked us, the baddest motherfuckers in the building. Album coming out in the spring. The lights went down. The smoke machine kicked in. We stepped onstage.

I placed a chunk of heroin on top of the foil and flicked my lighter, watching the blue flame intently for a moment, mesmerized.

Halfway through our first song, I noticed a small woman come walking out onstage, right in the middle of our act. She was smiling the widest, most beautiful smile I'd ever seen. My jaw dropped, and I broke out in laughter when I realized it was . . . my own mother.

I applied heat to the foil, making sure there were a few inches of space between the flame and the foil, and slowly the heroin began to vaporize. I pulled the flame back, being careful not to produce any smoke on the first attempt. Then I reapplied the heat, and the tar gave off vapors this time, and I sucked them through the tube of an emptied ballpoint pen, holding the smoke in my lungs for as long as possible.

My mother shuffled toward me slowly, without hurry, a drink in her hand. When finally she reached me at center stage, she threw her arms around me and gave me the warmest hug.

"You DID it!"

Then she turned, saluted the audience, and walked back toward the wings. I burst out laughing.

"Ladies and gentlemen, the woman who gave me life!"

The audience roared.

Exhale.

■　■　■

SURPRISINGLY, THROUGHOUT ALL THIS, I MANAGED to remain mostly functional. I formed a solo band and toured with them occasionally.

My guitarist was Erik Ferintinos, the next-door neighbor I'd met years before, coming off the Detonator tour—and I tour with him to this day. He'd evolved into a great guitarist. I helped sponsor a Top Fuel dragster with my friend Dan Prakowski. We had two semis with the Ratt logo, crisscrossing the whole circuit, and found a sensational driver, Clay Millican, to race for us for a full season—one of the biggest deals we've accomplished with our company. We sponsored a Top Fuel funny car for a race with James Day. I still had that intense love for racing, and I made as many races as I could. That is the love of my life. I feel more at home at the races than anywhere else—smelling the nitro, feeling the thunder, the power, the color, the excitement.

I was getting kind of reckless. I snuck tar with me on the plane every time we flew, hiding the smack in my clothes. The moment we'd land, I'd take a piece out and put it on the tip of my cigarette, which I called a bullet. I'd smoke it as soon as I touched down.

"Hey, what's that smell?" one woman asked me, looking curious.

"A good thing," I told her.

I was white and skinny, the typical junkie look. When you're smoking all the time, you just don't have that much interest in eating. I was busy, anyway, banging out my solo records. They were beautifully imperfect, and to me, they were a welcome departure from our days when award-winning producers came in and picked through every note with a fine-toothed comb. I didn't care what people thought of them. I deliver. I don't waste time. I go into the studio, and it's a go.

And as always, there were many ups and downs with the members of Ratt. We went through several lawsuits, putting one another through hell, doing much name-calling and finger-pointing. And yet, somehow, every few years, we tried to put the differences behind us and come together around the one thing we all still loved: our music.

Ratt put out a best-of CD in 2007; we did a European tour in 2008; and in 2009 we came together in Virginia Beach to try to record our first real album in a decade.

The album was called *Infestation*. We wrote some great songs, but I had to endure some pretty tedious writing sessions with Warren.

"Okay, great, man," I said. "I like what you just played there. Let's take that and run with it."

"Hold on, hold on," he said. "I want to work on this some more."

It got harder and more complex to write with him. I used to just hear a riff coming out of Warren, and I'd go "What is *that*?" And there was our new hit tune. But it got to be like pulling teeth with him. He had a methodical, mathematical sense of writing, which I felt was anything but Ratt.

"Dude, the best work we ever did was spontaneous. Fast and raw and blunt, that's how we work best," I said.

"You're the one who stepped away, Stephen," Warren said. "So I think it'd be better if you learned to roll with the punches."

So we wrote some songs in the slowest, most agonizing way possible. I stewed, feeling like I could have written the whole thing myself in a month. And of course, every day, in the back of my mind, I was just waiting for our recording session to finish, so I could go back to the hotel room to get high.

Some mornings I'd come in with tar in my pocket. I thought I was doing a pretty good job of hiding it from my bandmates. But then again, there were those days when I'd go into a long nod in the studio, and they'd have to nudge makeup mirrors underneath my nostrils to make sure I was alive. They weren't always the nicest guys, but none of them were dumb. They knew something was going on.

But I had that fucking demon on my shoulders, whispering to me. I mean, I was in deep. I was getting smack sent to me through the mail as much as I could. When that started to fall through, I tried to get pills sent to me. I needed some sort of opiate to level out the smack need.

"You doing all right there, buddy?" Blotzer asked me, noticing me looking sickly in the studio.

"Oh yeah," I mumbled. "Getting by, Bob."

But when I came to a place where I could get neither smack nor pills, I began, horribly, to withdraw. I was feeling dope sick. It wasn't good. *This is what Robbin went through,* I thought. So I'd have to find a bunch of cheap pills, anything to kind of get me through the day. I couldn't wait to get that record done.

I made it home and celebrated with a junk blowout. Just smoking all day, every day. I had my connection coming and going. He was the main person in my life. Finally one day, I exhaled a mouthful of smoke and just realized that the situation had come to a head.

I stumbled out of my studio and came into the house, where I found Melissa.

"I need to go to rehab," I said, my hands trembling. "I need to go *now*, okay?"

"All right . . ." she said, looking frightened.

"You're not getting it," I hissed. "Drive me somewhere right fucking now, before I change my mind. Not in an hour, not in half an hour. NOW."

We tore down the highway, Melissa driving me in my car. It was an impulsive decision, so we literally just picked a place from the phone book, a clinic in Van Nuys. It was straight out of *One Flew Over the Cuckoo's Nest*.

"You'll get your methadone starting tonight, Mr. Pearcy. . . ."

I wasn't supposed to get methadone, though. I wasn't injecting—supposedly, diacetylmorphine was the thing that would help me stop smoking, without crazy withdrawals. But this clinic was caught back in the previous century. They wanted to see me sweat it out. And that's exactly what I did.

I kissed my wife good-bye and for an hour or so I felt good, virtuous, upstanding, sure I had made the right decision. Then the cold sweats started. It was night and I was shown to my room. I curled up in my bed, clammy white sheets tangled around me in a dank white room, some other bearded guy snoozing away happily in a bed about six feet away from me.

I can do this, I told myself. *I can kick this. I have the power to rid this shit from my body.*

My head began to thud with pain, and chills ran up and down my body. I felt panicked suddenly, like I needed to leave the room. My stomach filled with acid and I didn't know whether I needed to shit or jump out of my skin.

"Let me get through this," I prayed out loud, gathering the sheets around me weakly. *Let me rid myself of this poison.*

I bit my lip, willing myself not to puke my fucking guts out and shit on myself. Everything felt cold. I wanted to take a pill so badly I could almost taste it in my mouth. *Just one,* I thought. *Just one oxy . . .*

I gritted my teeth, begging the time to pass. I looked at my skin, hallucinating with sickness, and saw the sweat rising on parts of me that never sweated, like my forearms, even the backs of my wrists. I found myself searching my memory for distractions, for anything that had happened to me when I was younger, anything to get my mind off the present moment, this Van Nuys hell.

When I was fourteen, Walt Rhoades took me to Indy, and on the whole trip there, I never slept in a motel room. Never slept in a bed. Each night, I crashed out underneath the trailer, lying on top of a pile of army blankets, a couple of feet over from the wheel well. Gazing up, instead of stars, I saw the soot-soaked piping of the undercarriage of the trailer, and I had never felt more happiness or excitement.

My mouth felt thick with my own spit. I gagged on my tongue, a disgusting feeling. I wrapped my sheets around my midsection, writhing against the mattress.

"Is there anyone fucking out there?" I called out into the hall. "Goddammit, can someone get me some new sheets? Or a blanket?"

There was no answer. A wave of pain throbbed through my stomach, and I bolted to the bathroom.

The moment before the races started was the most exciting moment of all: the Christmas tree counting down . . . . four amber-colored lights . . . every cell in your body electric . . . sweat circles spreading out from your armpits, teeth biting down . . . and with the last light a green, the dragsters exploded out of the gate. Seven seconds later, the parachutes pulled. . . .

I sat naked on the toilet, my leg drumming up and down nonstop, rivulets of sweat rolling down my forehead, my stomach clenching convulsively, as I discharged the contents of my stomach through my sphincter. Humiliated and helpless, I sat there, smelling my own stench, nowhere to go.

We took the long way back from Indy. Walt drove us through mountain ranges and the twisting highways that cut through them. On the third day, we passed through Vegas. The pit crew voted to stop at Circus Circus for lunch. We hadn't showered for a week. We strutted through the low-end casino like a team of proud war-torn veterans, past the slot machines and the hard-eyed girls, where we ate steak and biscuits and coffee. . . .

I stood up in the bathroom, eyeing the shower. I lacked the strength to step in there, though. I turned on the faucet of the sink and splashed cold water on my face. It made no difference. None of it did. Every molecule of my body was in pain and every mote of me wanted one thing: smack.

"Hey," I whispered, going back into my room. "Hey, dude."

My roommate continued to sleep soundly.

"Dude," I whispered.

He stirred. "Huh? What do you want?"

"Hey, listen, could you go sleep somewhere else tonight?" I said. "I'm in hell over here. I need to be by myself, man."

He just rolled over and fell back to sleep.

My head was feverish. I felt like crying. I did cry. I cried for myself and the pain I was in, for the marriage I'd got myself into. I cried for my brother King, who'd died. I cried because I'd been half a dad, half a man. I cried for the group I'd once formed that had dissolved, bickering. I cried for the simple beauty of life and my refusal to accept it on its own terms.

Robbin came to visit me right at the end, a couple of years before he died, when he needed some money. His weight was out of control, and all he wanted to do was play some music with me. "I've been writing," he said. I brought him back to the studio to play, but first I had him shower. He had track marks in his feet and open sores. The only place he could shoot up was between his toes.

We played music together. I gave him clothes and he ate at our table. He met my baby. And then he had to go.

I cried until the pain felt good, until there were no tears left inside me and the only thing I wanted to do was vomit. I crawled to the bathroom that smelled like my own shit and felt my gorge rise, and there I was, heaving chunks into the toilet, bile, the dizziness unbearable, my heart sick with disappointment and shame and, finally, relief.

■ ■ ■

I DIDN'T SLEEP FOR FOUR DAYS, and it got worse before it started to get better. After a few days of hell in the cuckoo's nest, I moved from the clinic in Van Nuys to a nicer one in Pasadena, where that Dr. Drew guy was, and I continued my drying-out process there. Slowly, I kind of started to function again.

I met therapists in Pasadena like Dr. Roberts, who took me and forced me to ask myself questions about who I was. Under all that bravado and all those addictions, I found there was a Stephen who could exist on his own terms, stand up without a buzz on, and dig into his own life.

My mother died after a long bout with cancer two years ago. I tell myself that at least she saw me get sober and really try. She saw me go through rehab.

Ratt is always up in the air. *Infestation* was released in 2010 and it garnered us the best reviews we'd had in years. We reunite onstage from time to time, and always seem on the verge of forgiving one another for our past. Yet we'll probably always be dysfunctional, bitter. There's a lot of water under the bridge, and now that King's gone, it's that much harder to envision a true reunion. More than likely, there will never be one. I've accepted that. For whatever reasons, some others haven't.

But music for me isn't just about Ratt. The beauty of music is that it's not in the past: It's right now. That's why I love my solo band so much. Ratt used to do 225 shows a year, and in a decade of touring, I don't think we ever once went to a museum. We went to the ends of the earth—but where did it get us?

Now when I tour, I enjoy the country. We make stops. We get out. We touch the dirt. Check in: How's your strip bar over here? Some toothless hags dancing around? Hey, it's a beautiful thing.

The years have been tough on me physically. I'm walking around in an older body, with a destroyed kneecap, a heart broken a few times. I didn't preserve my vocal cords: It was always about drinking a beer and having a smoke. I could have gone out there and shoved a towel in my mouth and done vocal exercises, but that never quite fit my vibe. I tell myself I've never sounded better. Hopefully others agree.

We had a solo show last week, in Vegas. One dude in my solo band has this chick who comes to a lot of our shows to watch him, sort of a groupie type. She was there last week. She brought her husband to the show, and the husband came backstage, did a bunch of blow, and watched his wife get fucked by a rock star. And when that shit goes down, you just go, *What?* Why are we allowed to do this?

It kinda got to me, for a second. Not like it disturbed me; it just kind of confused me. This kind of thing has been happening since the beginning of rock, of course. Been there, done that, thousands of times. But it was like I was seeing it with new eyes, having gone through rehab and all that. So I thought about it for a while, and it came to me: It's because we have our gold debauchery cards. Those cards aren't given. They're earned. I used to have a platinum debauchery card. Had to get rid of that one. It got me into too much trouble.

I have a motto: A hundred people, a thousand people, ten thousand people. It's all the same to me. It's a fucking party.

My kid is the most important person in my life now. She's sixteen, a true teenager. We have the best time together, taking trips down to San Diego, trucking over to the beach. I do any show, she's always there. She's jaded already. She knows her old man. Now I take her to concerts of her choosing and have to sit through watching the bands she's listening to, thinking, *If she only knew what was going on backstage.* I think she already does. She hasn't been blind all this time. She's too smart for that. That's why she's my Jewel.

When my solo band had a gig at the Whisky this summer, she came backstage with me, looking around curiously.

"So this is where it all went down, Jewel. Your dad was sitting right over there with David Lee Roth. Isn't that cool?"

"Who's David *Roth*?" she said, wrinkling her nose.

"Some old guy," I explained, laughing. "A singer."

We went out there that night, with my kid in the audience, and just had the best time. Slayed the Whisky crowd like it was 1982, screaming and yelling and fucking with the audience. We even blasted out "Round and Round." Gave the crowd something to take home.

ACKNOWLEDGMENTS

SPECIAL THANX:

God for giving me this life; my mother, Joanne Ruaben (RIP), I miss u dearly; John Ruaben; my beautiful Jewel Pearcy; Melissa—NFLW; Robbin "King" Crosby (RIP), it's never been the same again; Warren DeMartini, Juan Croucier, and Bobby Blotzer; Phillip Schwartz; Walt Rhoades; Dale Pulde; James Day; Clay Millican; Johnny "Road Ratt" Gehring; Duke Valenti; Tina; Wendy; Britta Wilson; Sam Benjamin (strange trip thru heaven and hell); Marshall Berle; Mark Leonard; Bobby Collin; Jim Kuzmich; Adam Chromy; Jeremie Ruby-Strauss; Heather Hunt; Big Bruce; Chris Hager (my brother); Big Joe Anthony; Victor Mamanna; Mike Hartigan; Bill Gazzarri; the Rainbow; Mrs. O' (RIP); Thomas Asakawa; Wade Smith; Erik Ferintinos, my Rat Bastard partner in grime; Tim Garcia (RIP), brutha; Bob Eisenberg; Dave Thum; Dr. Rock Raskind; Steff, my twin; Debbie and Will; every road manager, crew, and tour manager thru the years; Evan Cohen; Robert Crane; Matt Thorn;

ACKNOWLEDGMENTS

Fred Coury; Donny Syracuse; Mike Andrews; Johnny Angel Sca-
glione; Neil Zlozower; my Rat Bastards thru the years; Troy Johnson; Frankie Wilsey; Todd Roberson; Mike Duda; Greg D'Angelo;
Scott Coogan; the Gladiators. To all those friends I might have forgotten, and foes. A long, strange trip it's been, and it's not over yet!

PHOTO CREDITS